THE
WILDFOODS
COOKBOOK

Flowers for the table: a, Dog rose (*Rosa canina*); b, Honeysuckle (*Lonicera periclymenum*); c, Meadowsweet (*Spiraea ulmaria*); d, Hawthorn or may (*Crataegus monogyna*)

THE
WILDFOODS
COOKBOOK

JOY O. I. SPOCZYNSKA

Illustrated by Kenneth H. Poole

ROBERT HALE
LONDON

© *Joy O. I. Spoczynska 1985*
First published in Great Britain 1985

ISBN 0 7090 1748 0 (*cased*)

Robert Hale Limited
Clerkenwell House
Clerkenwell Green
London EC1R OHT

British Library Cataloguing in Publication Data
Spoczynska, Joy O. I.
  The wildfoods cookbook.
    1. Cookery (Vegetables)   2. Cookery (Fruit)
  I. Title
  641.6'6   TX801

  ISBN 0-7090-1748-0

Typeset by Rowland Phototypesetting Ltd
Printed in Great Britain by
St Edmundsbury Press, Bury St Edmunds, Suffolk and
bound by Woolnough Ltd

This book is dedicated to
MANUBHAI R. DESAI
in appreciation of his help
and friendship

Inexpensive Pets
Pets for Pennies
The Aquarium
The Vivarium and the Terrarium
Practical Fieldwork for the Young Naturalist
A Zoo on Your Window-Ledge
Fossils: A Study in Evolution
Nature Close to Home
The World of the Wasp
An Age of Fishes
Self-Sufficiency in a Flat
Look After the Pennies

CONTENTS

LIST OF ILLUSTRATIONS

AUTHOR'S ACKNOWLEDGEMENTS

It is always difficult to avoid inadvertently omitting names in cases where one's debt of gratitude extends to many persons, all of whom have played some part in the conception, growth and ultimate birth of a book, especially when the gathering of material has taken place over many years. I trust, therefore, that I may be forgiven if one of these sins of omission may, possibly, be laid at my door.

I should, however, like to take this opportunity of expressing my thanks individually to Sister Jadwiga of the Holy Family Convent 'somewhere in the Midlands'; Dorothy Cierpiala of New York City; Lotte Heidemann of Düsseldorf; Maria van Booys, Neltje Kaufman and Laura Kroy, members of the Mennonite Community in Akron, Ohio; and Deborah Turner, of the Wooden Shoe Commune, also in Ohio.

Finally, my thanks are also due to my illustrator, Kenneth H. Poole, who kindly provided all the line drawings – a task not to be undertaken lightly!

J.O.I.S.

1985

I

A NEW LOOK AT WEEDS

'Weed, n. A wild herb springing where it is not wanted.' So the word is defined by the *Oxford English Dictionary*, which goes on to say that it derives from the Old English *weod*, a herb. No mention here, you will note, of the notion that it is not wanted. And, since it does not mention that an Old English *weod* was necessarily wild, we must assume, in the absence of any evidence to the contrary, that it was just a herb pure and simple.

Our ancestors did not have the benefit of the horticulturist's art. They knew nothing of cross-pollination, grafting, insecticides or fertilizers. They cared not a jot whether their vegetables were all the same size or all the same shape. A wild root was a wild root whether it was straight, bifurcated or twisted. It tasted good and kept them going while they went out hunting for more substantial fare in the shape of woolly mammoth, sabre-toothed tiger or whatever.

Every cultivated vegetable and fruit, whether growing in Britain or abroad, was once a wild herb. First experiment, then decades of breeding in artificial conditions, have produced the cultivars that we buy from supermarket shelves, from street market stalls or at the greengrocer's these days. Most of these 'improvements' have been aimed at producing bigger plants and more prolific crops; a few have been aimed at improving flavour and texture. Colour and shape, too, have come in for their share of 'improvement' with a view to capturing the gullible consumer's fancy, especially where fruits are concerned. Many contain artificial dyes intended to make their colour more appealing. But obviously it is not possible to stamp an orange with a notice that artificial food dyes have been used, in the way that a notice can be put on a can of beans that it contains monosodium glutamate and God-knows-what besides.

It has come now to the point where appearance, from the advertiser's point of view, means more than anything else, and to this end the robust flavours of the original natural fruits and vegetables have in a good many cases been sacrificed, leaving in their stead the bland taste of an artificial product – artificial because the plants have been grown in artificial conditions with chemical fertilizers and other stimulants, frequently in vast glasshouses, heavy with the odours of toxic insecticides, where the rays of the sun, fresh air and rain never reach them.

But is the difference between the horticulturist's carefully nurtured varieties and the original herbs from which they have derived so great, after all? I am speaking now of their nutritional value, which surely should be the first consideration with any food. According to scientists, it appears that some garden vegetables are actually inferior in mineral and vitamin content to some of the common 'weeds' that grow alongside them. To give but one example, the abundant weed called 'fat hen' (*Chenopodium album*) has more iron, calcium, protein and vitamins B_1 and B_2 than either spinach or cabbage. Small wonder that its popular local name is 'allgood' in Hampshire and some other parts of southern England.

I think the time has come for us to take a new look at the 'weeds' in our gardens, in the hedgerows and fields, on wasteland and by the roadside, in woods and by streams, even at the seaside. More than three hundred edible wild plants can be found in Britain more or less commonly, which can be used in diverse ways to make soups, stews, casseroles, stuffings, flavourings, dressings, sauces, salads, green vegetables to accompany meat and fish dishes, desserts, sweetmeats, jams, jellies, syrups, soft drinks, beers and wines. This book will introduce you to some delicious recipes which you can make from wild plants. Almost all of them are for dishes that I have actually made or tried myself and thus can recommend from personal experience. I shall confine myself as far as possible to plants which are common in most parts of Britain, omitting any rare ones which should never be picked at all.

The wildfood cook should make an effort to remember the botanical names of the plants used. This is because these are the same wherever you may live, from London to Lyons or from Florida to Fujiyama. The common or vernacular names vary from country to country, even in those where the same language is spoken. Thus, if I spoke to an American of reedmace, he would not know to which plant I was referring; similarly, his mention of cattails would fox me. But if we both say we've used *Typha latifolia*, then we know what each is talking about.

Many of the botanical names are more descriptive than some of the local names. The truffle, for instance, is *Tuber aestivum*, which means firstly that it is an underground tuber, and secondly that it is a summer plant. Thus, one digs for it in summer. What the name does not convey is that you find it only if you are very lucky. Then, again, 'heg-peg' would mean little to most people (unless natives of Gloucestershire), but *Prunus spinosa* tells you firstly that the tree or shrub is one of the plum family and secondly that it is thorny – a blackthorn or sloe, in fact.

Finally, all the wild plants described in this book are free for the gathering, which makes them a great contribution to the budget-conscious self-sufficiency enthusiast's kitchen. Many of the equivalent supermarket products are grossly overpriced, providing fat profits for the middlemen who sort, grade, pack and distribute the goods and for the retailers who sell them, while the grower who has had all the hard work of raising the plants reaps the lowest percentage for his labours. If we can find substitutes which are as good as, or even better than, these products, free for the picking and at the cost only of our own time and effort in gathering them, we not only save considerably in these inflationary days but enjoy the satisfaction of discovering our own sources of fresh food and, like the gardener, knowing what has gone into it, because naturally we shall avoid gathering our wild harvest anywhere near areas where crop-spraying has taken place or where roadside verges have been contaminated with toxic sprays or traffic exhaust fumes.

I hope you will enjoy using the recipes in this book as much as I have enjoyed compiling them from the notebooks I have kept over the years I have been a wildfood enthusiast. And if you have lately become more than a little bored with food that has had all its natural flavour cultivated, mass-produced, processed, adulterated, canned, bottled and frozen out of it, join me in my wildfood kitchen and be prepared for some taste treats of a lifetime!

All the recipes in this book, unless otherwise stated, serve 4. Choose either metric or imperial measures when calculating amounts of ingredients required, but never attempt to combine the two.

2

SALADS WITH A DIFFERENCE

The word 'salad' conjures up to many people a bowl of lettuce, arranged in various ways with slices of cucumber, sliced or quartered tomatoes, sprigs of watercress, spring onions, halved hard-boiled eggs, maybe the odd prawn or two, or perhaps a few dabs of cottage cheese. These are all very nice, but they can become wearisomely repetitive even with the more obvious variations.

First of all, the lettuce need not be any of the cultivated kinds. Why not try the various wild equivalents? The commonest of these wild 'lettuces' is not a member of the lettuce family at all but is a member of the valerian family. Its botanical name is *Valerianella locusta*. It has various English names, according to which part of the country one is in, but the commonest ones are 'lamb's lettuce' and 'corn salad'. It looks nothing like a lettuce, and I advise you to identify it from a colour photograph in a good botanical reference book (see Appendix I). It is common in midland and southern Britain, less so in the north. Hedge banks, waysides and the edges of farmland (hence the name 'corn salad') are the most likely places to find it. You can eat the whole plant – leaves, stems, flowers and all. The taste is mild and barely distinguishable from lettuce proper. All you have to do is to wash it to remove any creepy-crawlies. Do not gather it (or any other plants) from roadsides which may have been sprayed with toxic chemicals or contaminated with exhaust fumes from passing traffic.

The other wild 'lettuce' you can use is a plant called 'wall lettuce' (*Mycelis muralis*) which belongs to the daisy family. *Mycelis* refers to the spreading slender flower stems which are reminiscent of the way the *mycelium*, 'rooting' system of fungi, spreads out, but don't let that put you off. Botanists do usually try to be descriptive and sometimes have to stretch their imaginative powers a bit to do so! *Muralis* simply means 'of the wall', which is a good description, because the plant is most often found growing in the crevices of old stone walls and rocks. On chalk soils it is also sometimes found in woodland.

The plant is common throughout England and Wales, and grows

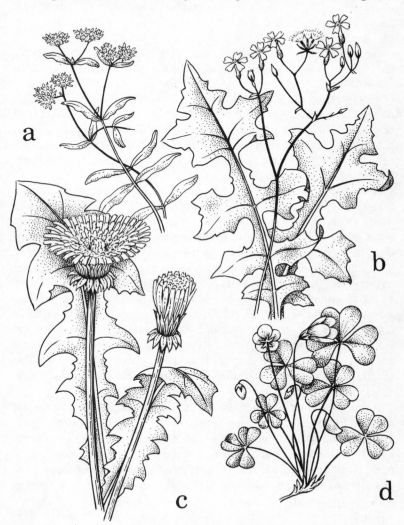

Some salad plants: a, Corn salad (*Valerianella locusta*); b, Wall lettuce (*Mycelis muralis*); c, Dandelion (*Taraxacum officinale*); d, Wood sorrel (*Oxalis acetosella*)

up to about 3 feet (90 cm). The leaves are shaped something like those of the dandelion, but the flowers, which bloom from July to September, are completely different in appearance, being very small and set at the ends of a tracery of slender stalks (just like a *mycelium*, in fact!). Check the identification in a book and then pick the leaves only. They taste bland and lettuce-like (hence the common name) and need only washing before use.

Among other common green 'weeds' which make tasty additions to a salad, the most abundant and best-known is 'fat hen' (*Chenopodium album*) which with its close relative 'Good King Henry' (*Chenopodium bonus-henricus*), gives you an all-round dual-purpose plant source, because both can be used either raw in salads or cooked in different ways as a green vegetable (see Chapter 4). Just the washed leaves are used in salads. They have a slightly stronger taste – rather like raw spinach – than the two plants previously-described; cooked, they are indistinguishable from spinach.

'Fat hen' has a number of other local names, such as 'lamb's quarters' in my native North Midlands, 'allgood' in Hampshire and 'bacon weed' in Dorset, to name but a few. It is common everywhere throughout Britain except in mountainous areas and is often abundant in waste places, even in big cities, as well as by hedgerow and wayside. It flowers from July to October, growing to a height of about 3 feet (90 cm), and can be distinguished from its near relative by having much smaller leaves and its flowers being more branched, whereas the flowers of 'Good King Henry', which appear earlier – usually from May to July – are normally confined to a single central spike, although there may be a few very small branches lower down the stem. 'Good King Henry' is also taller, growing to about 5 feet (1.5 m), and is found in similar situations to 'fat hen' but is rare in Scotland and Ireland.

A few dandelion leaves make an interesting addition to a salad, but they should be used sparingly as they have a diuretic effect. Only the young leaves should be used: the older leaves are bitter. The young leaves, which have a sharp tang, should be carefully washed. One good point about dandelion leaves is that they can be found at almost any time of the year in various stages of growth. I have even found fresh young shoots when there was snow on the ground.

Chickweed (see Chapter 3) makes an excellent substitute for cress and is terrific in salads. It has less of a 'bite' than cress and blends better with other green ingredients. The taste is rather like that of fresh young pea-pods, but milder. The whole plant is used, washed and gently patted dry with a kitchen paper towel. It is one of the earliest wild plants to bloom, and continues to flower for most of the year.

What shall we add to our wild green salad bowl to brighten it and provide contrasting colour, texture and flavour? Unfortunately we have no wild tomato or cucumber, so if we wish to include these, we shall have to use the real thing – and why not? Radishes, too, have no wild equivalent, but ordinary radishes look most decorative in a wild green salad. I see no valid reason why one should avoid any cultivated additions to a basic wild green salad; after all, radishes, spring onions, tomatoes and so on are all healthy raw fresh foods.

While you will have to use spring onions, in the absence of any wild onion species, if you like a touch of garlic in your salads you can use any of our native wild garlics. The commonest one is crow garlic (*Allium vineale*), which is much more pungent than the cultivated kind. Even after I had sealed one plant in a plastic bag after gathering, I almost emptied a bus on one occasion when carrying it home. Those who did not alight from the bus to catch the next one gave me some distinctly odd looks! On another occasion, when I gave a plant to my daughter-in-law, she rushed out of the kitchen with it and planted it at the very bottom of the garden!

You can use any part of the plant – bulb, stem or leaf. All parts are equally strong-smelling and pungent in flavour, and only a *very* little should be used in a salad, or in any other dish where it is used raw. Curiously, when cooked it loses much of its pungency and can therefore in such dishes be used in the normal proportions one would use for its domesticated counterpart.

A number of wild *flowers* make colourful and tasty additions to a salad – even to one made with garden lettuce! Some of these include wild violets, wood sorrel, may blossom (either white or the pink variety), blackthorn blossom, crab-apple blossom, wild rose, broom and mallow. Be sure to remove all green parts such as calyces and stems from the flowers before use, and pick them over carefully for insects.

Very young 'fiddlehead' bracken fronds may also be used, if no flowers are available. Do not use the more well-developed fronds, only the ones just peeping out of the earth 3 or 4 inches (8–10 cm) high. Scrape off the 'fuzz' which covers them with the back of a knife and then wash thoroughly in lightly-salted water and leave just slightly moist. Definitely an acquired taste, these.

I hope that I have given you enough ideas to help you devise your own individual basic wildfood salads. Salad 'recipes' as given in some books are, after all, basically just different ways of arranging the ingredients, which are endlessly variable; if one green wildfood is not available, another kind will do. If you have only a few wild greens, you can mix these with ordinary lettuce or watercress. The composition of your salad is a matter of individual choice, depending on the size and shape of the bowl or dish and what ingredients you have available. So I will not give you such 'recipes' but will leave the arrangements to you, and give you instead some recipes for various interesting dressings to go with them.

Instructions for preparing dried herbs for kitchen use made from our native wild herbs are given in Chapter 5. If the wild plants are not available, the cultivated varieties may be substituted.

Wild Herb Mayonnaise

2 egg yolks
¼ pint/150 ml. olive oil
1 teaspoon wine vinegar
1 teaspoon lemon juice
Large pinch salt

Large pinch white pepper
1 tablespoon wild chervil
1 tablespoon wild thyme
½ tablespoon wood sage

Whisk the egg yolks and add the oil a drop or two at a time, whisking all the time (a hand-held electrically operated whisk makes this operation much easier). Add the remainder of the ingredients and continue to whisk until the right consistency is reached. Chill in the fridge until required.

Chickweed Mayonnaise

2 egg yolks
¼ pint/150 ml. olive oil
2 tablespoons lemon juice
4 tablespoons chickweed, finely
  chopped

Large pinch salt
Large pinch white pepper
Large pinch dry mustard
  powder

The same method is used as that given for the previous recipe; in other words, you first make the basic mayonnaise by whisking egg yolks and olive oil, then you add all the other ingredients. If you can't find any chickweed, you can use very finely chopped cress, either watercress or the mustard-and-cress kind. It is just as good, though a little stronger tasting. You can include a small proportion of the 'mustard' with the cress if you like, but if you do, omit the dry mustard powder.

Chive Mayonnaise

1 egg yolk
¼ pint/150 ml. olive oil
2 tablespoons white wine
  vinegar
2 tablespoons very finely
  chopped chives (or green
  spring onion tops)

1 teaspoon dry mustard powder
Pinch salt
Pinch white pepper
Small portion wild garlic,
  minced (optional)

This recipe uses a different method from the basic method already described. An electric blender is best for this one.

Put about half the oil into the blender with all the other ingredients and blend at the lowest speed until absolutely smooth. Then add the remaining oil a very little at a time, blending for one minute, still at low speed, before adding more. Keep the mixture going until you have blended in the lot. Now you will appreciate why an electric blender is recommended.

Vinaigrette Dressing

2 tablespoons white wine
  vinegar
6 tablespoons olive oil
½ teaspoon sea salt

Large pinch coarsely ground
  black pepper
Large pinch paprika

Whisk the ingredients together until well blended, and store in the fridge until required. Shake well before use. Salads may be tossed wholesale in the mixture, or it may be served in a separate dish.

There are many different salad dressings which can be made with a yoghourt base. They are equally good used with wildfood or conventional salads.

Piquant Yoghourt Dressing

1 5 oz./150 g. tub plain
  yoghourt
1 tablespoon single cream
1 tablespoon castor sugar
1 teaspoon white wine vinegar

2 teaspoons dry mustard
  powder
1 teaspoon salt
1 teaspoon white pepper

Whisk the yoghourt, cream and sugar until thoroughly blended. Stir in the remaining ingredients, then whisk again until the mixture is absolutely smooth. Chill in fridge before use.

Mild Yoghourt Dressing

While the preceding dressing is more suitable for bland salads, this one is better suited to those which contain some ingredients with 'bite'.

1 5 oz./150 g. tub plain
  yoghourt
1 tablespoon single cream
2 tablespoons castor sugar
1 teaspoon white wine vinegar

Pinch dry mustard powder
Pinch salt
Pinch white pepper

Whisk the yoghourt, cream and sugar until thoroughly blended, as before. Then add remaining ingredients and whisk until smooth. Chill in fridge before use.

Variations on these can be made by adding finely chopped chives, green spring onion tops, fresh parsley, herbs (either wild or cultivated), chopped cress, chickweed etc. What you add really depends on what ingredients you have in your salad; obviously there is little point in duplicating them. Let common sense be your guide here.

3

CHICKWEED'S NOT JUST FOR CHICKS!

Chickweed is one of the commonest of all our native wild plants. There is scarcely anywhere you can go without finding it, even in the middle of big cities, where it may frequently be found growing between the cracks in the pavements. Such a situation would not, of course, be the best place to gather it, owing to big-city pollution; but it is unlikely that you need go very far before finding it in a comparatively uncontaminated environment. Along the base of a country wall, or in the hedge bottom; straggling in ditches, or rampant in damp woods: look where you will, and you are pretty sure to find this delicious plant.

For delicious it is — so much so, in fact, that less than a hundred years ago it was sold in bunches like watercress on market stalls throughout Britain, often called by its local names, such as 'skirt buttons' in Dorset or 'white bird's-eye' in Buckinghamshire. It was used raw in salads or cooked as a green vegetable. It is rich in iron and copper and full of vitamins. It grows almost all over the world in the temperate zone, being as ubiquitous in America as it is here.

Not only will you be able to find it practically wherever you may look, but almost any time of the year will see it growing apace, and it flowers for at least ten months of the year. I have found it in flower as early as January. It is not really difficult to identify, as there are only two plants with which it could, possibly, be confused by the uninitiated — though even this is unlikely. The true chickweed (*Stellaria media*) is smooth and translucent-looking, its delicate stems being easily broken, unlike the much darker green, tough and hairy mouse-ear chickweed (*Cerastium fontanum*) which usually grows rather taller and flowers only from late April to September. The other plant to which it bears a superficial resemblance is the petty spurge (*Euphorbia peplus*), a poisonous plant which always has *red* stems;

there is never any trace of red coloration on the stems of chickweed.

The generic name *Stellaria* refers to the tiny, star-shaped white flowers of the chickweed, which are just as edible as the leaves and stems and look fascinating dotting a green salad. The specific name *media* signifies the plant's position in the middle of its genus, in relation to other *Stellaria* species which are larger or smaller (though not much!) One of the larger species, *Stellaria holostea*, which can grow up to 18 inches (45 cm) high and is very common in damp woodland throughout Britain (except Ireland), is also edible but is better cooked than raw.

I've already recommended chickweed for use in salads in Chapter 2. We come now to some of its other uses. What about substituting it for cress in sandwiches? You can just use it by itself sandwiched between slices of bread and butter, seasoned with salt and pepper, adding a few drops of lemon juice or a dab or two of Worcester sauce if liked. This is particularly tasty if the slices of bread are the genteel, wafer-thin kind. With the more robust doorstep variety, using good chunky wholemeal bread, other ingredients may be added such as slices of ham, hard-boiled egg etc, just as you would use in any other sandwich, with the chickweed (well washed and dried, of course) on top. Don't be sparing – use exactly like cress, as much as you like, with salt and pepper to taste.

SOUPS

Cream of Chickweed Soup

About ½ lb./225 g. chickweed	3 tablespoons cream
1½ pints/850 ml. chicken stock	2 level tablespoons cornflour
½ oz./12½ g. butter	Salt and pepper to taste
¼ pint/150 ml. milk	

Wash the chickweed, reserving a few of the flowering sprigs for garnish. Put the butter into the soup pan and lightly cook the chickweed over a very low heat for 2 or 3 minutes. Add stock, salt and pepper, cover and simmer gently for about 20 minutes. Now press through a sieve (or put it into an electric blender) and return it to the pan. Blend the cornflour with the milk, making a smooth cream. Stir a couple of tablespoons of the hot soup mixture into this and then return the whole to the pan and bring to the boil, stirring until the mixture thickens, then reduce the heat and cook for a further 2 or 3 minutes. Test for adjustment of seasoning if necessary. Just before serving, stir in the cream, and garnish with flowering sprigs of chickweed.

Chilled Chickweed Soup with Yoghourt

About ½ lb. /225 g. chickweed
1½ pints/850 ml. chicken stock
1 small onion
1 level tablespoon cornflour

3 tablespoons cream
Salt and pepper to taste
Pinch paprika pepper
2 tablespoons plain yoghourt

Simmer the stock for 15 minutes with the onion, peeled and sliced. Add the washed chickweed, saving a few flowering sprigs for garnish, and simmer for a further 20 minutes. Sieve or put into an electric blender, and return to pan. Blend the cornflour with a little cold water to a smooth cream, stir in two tablespoons of the hot soup and return to pan. Add salt and pepper and bring to the boil, stirring until the mixture thickens, then reduce heat and cook for a further 2 or 3 minutes. Stir in the cream and test for adjustment of seasoning if necessary. Pour into a large bowl and chill in the fridge. Before serving, stir in the yoghourt and sprinkle with paprika, and finally add the flowering sprigs of chickweed.

Chickweed and Sour Cream Soup

About ½ lb./225 g. chickweed
1 pint/575 ml. buttermilk
½ pint/275 ml commercial sour
  cream

3 drops tabasco
Salt and pepper to taste

This soup is best made in an electric blender and, in my opinion, tastes best chilled. Blend the buttermilk and the chickweed (which you can chop first, if you like, after washing) at low speed for 3 minutes. Then add salt, pepper, tabasco and sour cream, and blend again at medium speed until smooth. It can be served hot or, as previously mentioned, chilled. You can ring the changes on the garnish for this one by using croûtons, grated Parmesan cheese etc.

Chickweed Dumplings

These can be used in other kinds of soup such as beef, chicken, oxtail etc, making a welcome change from the usual parsley and other herb dumplings.

4 oz./100 g. self-raising flour	1 heaped tablespoon chickweed,
2 oz./50 g. shredded suet	finely chopped
1 small onion, grated	Salt and pepper to taste
	Cold water to mix

Mix all the ingredients together with the water to make a springy dough. Divide into 16 portions and roll each into a small ball, using a little flour to stop them sticking together and to the utensils. When required to cook, drop them into the soup from 15 to 20 minutes before the estimated time that the soup will be ready to serve. Makes 16 dumplings.

CHICKWEED IN MAIN DISHES

Chickweed would form a very slight and insubstantial dish served by itself, but it can be used in main dishes as one of a number of ingredients. Here are some ideas.

Chickweed Omelet

½ lb./225 g. chickweed	2 tablespoons grated Parmesan
2 tablespoons olive oil	cheese
½ teaspoon salt	8 eggs
¼ teaspoon black pepper	4 tablespoons butter

Chop the washed chickweed and sauté in the olive oil over a low heat until soft. Add seasoning, stir and simmer on a very low heat for 10 minutes. Stir in the Parmesan cheese and simmer for a further 5 minutes.

Crack 8 eggs into a basin, adding a tablespoon of cold water and beat with a fork until well mixed. Some people like to season the omelet at this stage with salt and pepper before cooking; others prefer to season it to their own liking at table.

Make the omelet in the usual way (a non-stick, small-size pan is best), using one tablespoon of butter for each. As soon as the eggs no longer flow freely but the top still looks moist and creamy, spread one quarter of the hot chickweed mixture over one half of each omelet and quickly fold the other half over. As soon as it is cooked lift the omelet carefully out of the pan with a plastic or wooden spatula and slide on to the plate, garnishing as liked – a few flowering sprigs of chickweed if you have any, or watercress, perhaps, if you haven't. One final point: *never* overcook an omelet! It should still be deliciously moist and creamy inside and soft on the outside. Do not leave it in the pan until the outside is brown!

Chickweed Turnovers

These are made with cream cheese pastry, for which a separate list of ingredients follows to avoid confusion. For the garnish you will need one lemon sliced into thin rings and any pips removed.

For cream cheese pastry:

½ lb./225 g. cream cheese	½ teaspoon salt
2 oz./50 g. butter	¼ teaspoon white pepper
4 oz./100 g. plain flour	4 tablespoons water

For filling:

½ lb./225 g. chickweed	1 teaspoon basil (wild or
3 tablespoons butter	cultivated)
1 small onion	2 oz./50 g. breadcrumbs
	Salt and pepper to taste

To make the pastry, cream together the butter and the cream cheese and sift together the flour, pepper and salt. Blend the two mixtures, either with a fork or with the pastrymaking attachment of an electric blender. Then add the water gradually and mix the dough until it just holds together in a ball. Place in a plastic bag and chill for at least an hour in the fridge.

To make the filling, melt the butter in a pan over a very low heat and cook the washed and chopped chickweed together with the onion, peeled and finely grated, until tender but not browned. Mix in the breadcrumbs, salt, pepper and basil, stir until all ingredients are well mixed and remove from heat.

Roll out the pastry ⅛ inch thick and cut into 20 4-inch rounds.

Place about 2 tablespoons of the filling in the middle of each round and fold in half. Seal the curved edges with the tines of a fork and place the turnovers on a baking-sheet, being careful to avoid letting them touch or overlap. Bake for 15 minutes at Regulo 4 (350°F./180°C.), until golden brown.

Serve hot, garnished with lemon slices. Makes 20 turnovers.

Bacon and Chickweed Pie

1 lb./450 g. potatoes
½ lb./225 g. bacon pieces,
  chopped
½ lb./225 g. chickweed
1 onion
2 tablespoons milk

1 oz./25 g. butter
Salt and pepper to taste
Pinch mixed herbs
2 tablespoons stock

Boil the potatoes, drain and mash together with the milk, butter and seasoning of salt and pepper. Fry the bacon pieces together with the onion, peeled and finely chopped, in the bacon fat (no additional fat is required, but keep the heat low). When cooked, add the chickweed, washed and chopped, together with the mixed herbs, and moisten with the stock. Cook a little longer until all ingredients are well blended, then transfer to an oven dish and cover the top with a layer of mashed potato. Mark the top attractively in a pattern with a fork, and bake for 25 to 30 minutes at Regulo 5 (375°F./190°C.) on the top shelf of the oven, until the surface is crisp and brown.

Aubergines stuffed with Chickweed and Mushrooms

Four medium-sized aubergines should be looked for, to serve four; it is not a good plan to use two big ones and cut them in half, or the stuffing will fall out and make your gourmet dish look very untidy!

4 medium-size aubergines
4 tablespoons chopped
  chickweed
2 tomatoes, skinned and
  chopped
4 oz./100 g. breadcrumbs
1 onion, peeled and grated

4 oz./100 g. Cheddar cheese,
  grated
2 medium-size ceps
Salt and pepper to taste
1 egg

Cut the aubergines in half lengthways and scoop out the flesh, leaving a 'shell' about ¼ inch thick. Make the stuffing by combining the chopped chickweed, chopped tomatoes, breadcrumbs, grated onion, chopped ceps, seasoning and grated cheese, adding to the mixture the finely-chopped flesh scooped from the aubergines. Beat the egg thoroughly and use this to bind the mixture well together. Fill the aubergine 'shells' with the mixture, closing the two halves of each aubergine, and wrap in kitchen foil to avoid the two halves coming apart. The heat of cooking will in any case cause the stuffing to swell, but it will be more or less contained in the foil 'cases' and thus enable you to lift them out on to the serving-dish without mishap. Bake in the middle of the oven for 15 to 20 minutes at Regulo 6 (400°F./ 200°C.) until cooked through. Uncover the top part of the foil case carefully to allow the tops to become crisp – a further 5 to 10 minutes should suffice. Serve hot with one of the herb sauces described in Chapter 5.

If you are unable to find 'cep' mushrooms (described in Chapter 13) growing wild, you can sometimes buy the dried ones, imported from Germany or France, in the better-class delicatessen shops. If you cannot obtain ceps at all, you can use ordinary 'button' mushrooms, but ceps are far superior in this particular recipe.

We come now to the various ways in which chickweed can be used as a green vegetable. It cooks down just like spinach, so you need to gather twice as much as you think you will need in recipes involving boiling, such as, for example, using it as a straight substitute for spinach. For this all you have to do is to boil it in the water which clings to it after washing – no additional water is required – turning down the heat as soon as it boils so that it simmers in its own vitamin-rich juice. After about 5 minutes it is ready; drain and serve with a knob of butter and seasoning. But there are, of course, other ways of cooking it as a vegetable accompaniment to a main dish.

Piquant Chickweed

This is just a variation of the above, in which you add salt and pepper to taste, a dash of nutmeg (don't overdo this or you will ruin it) and a few chopped chives (or green spring onion tops). Simmer for about five minutes – no longer or it will become mushy – then drain and serve hot. Just before serving sprinkle with lemon juice for added piquancy.

Creamed Chickweed

½ lb./225 g. chickweed
¼ pint/150 ml. double cream
¼ pint/150 ml. chicken stock
2 tablespoons plain flour

1 teaspoon salt
¼ teaspoon black pepper
2 tablespoons butter

Cook the chickweed lightly over a very low heat in just the water left clinging to it after washing. Sprinkle the flour over it and mix thoroughly. Pour in the stock and the cream, stirring until the mixture is well blended. Season with salt and pepper, cover and bring to the boil; then lower the heat and simmer for 10 to 15 minutes, stirring occasionally. When it has reached a nice semi-firm consistency, pour into the serving-dish and dot the top with dabs of butter. Serve piping hot.

Herbed Chickweed with Bacon

½ lb./225 g. chickweed
4 rashers bacon
2 tablespoons chopped chives
  (or green spring onion tops)
1 tablespoon chopped parsley
1 teaspoon rosemary (wild or
  cultivated)

½ teaspoon wild garlic (finely
  chopped)
½ teaspoon salt
¼ teaspoon black pepper
2 tablespoons lemon juice

Chop the bacon into small pieces and fry over a low heat in a non-stick frying-pan to extract the fat. Remove the bacon pieces and put on one side. Pour the bacon fat into a saucepan and add the chickweed, washed and chopped, the wild garlic (see Chapter 5 for how to identify this plant), parsley, rosemary, chives or spring onion tops, salt and pepper. Cook over a very low heat for about 10 to 15 minutes, stirring from time to time. When tender, stir in the lemon juice. Turn out into the serving-dish and sprinkle the bacon pieces on the top. Serve hot.

Chickweed in Sour Cream

½ lb./225 g. chickweed
½ pint/275 ml. commercial
  sour cream
1 tablespoon lemon juice

½ teaspoon salt
¼ teaspoon white pepper

Cook the chickweed lightly over a very low heat in just the water left clinging to it after washing. When tender – which should take about 5 minutes or so – stir in the cream and heat the mixture through, adding the salt and pepper, without letting it come to the boil (this is important as if it boils the cream will curdle). Remove from heat, sprinkle with lemon juice and serve hot.

4

GOOD KING HENRY LIVES!

Although chickweed is good as a cooked green vegetable, it is not a very substantial plant and you need vast quantities of it if you are going to cook it as you would spinach. The two more robust plants described in Chapter 2 – Good King Henry (*Chenopodium bonus-henricus*) and its close relative fat hen (*C. album*) – are a better choice as a spinach substitute. You need to gather only the same quantity as you would need of spinach, and for another thing they taste more like spinach than chickweed does – the flavour is indistinguishable from spinach. Cooked chickweed is better used as a substitute for peas – it has a distinct 'new pea pod' tang.

Boiling in the same way as spinach, however, is not the only method of cooking these two delicious, vitamin- and mineral-rich 'weeds'. There are many other ways of using them in tasty and nutritious recipes. Before going on to these, however, I would just mention that if you are boiling them like spinach (i.e., 'plain'), they should not be overcooked – 10 minutes on a low to medium heat is more than adequate. As with spinach, just cook them in enough water to cover the bottom of the pot so that they do not burn. The water that clings to them after they have been well washed is usually sufficient for this purpose. And well washed they must be – like spinach, they can harbour a surprising amount of dust and grit, especially when gathered in urban areas.

Here is a variation on plain boiled fat hen or Good King Henry which makes a welcome change. Either plant may be used.

a   b

Fat hen   Good King Henry

Buttered Fat Hen with Nutmeg

Enough leaves for quantity required   Grated nutmeg
Water to cook as mentioned above   Salt and black pepper to taste
Knob of butter

Boil the leaves in the water and when tender put them in a sieve and press the water out. Chop finely when cool enough, then re-heat them over a very low heat, stirring in the salt, pepper and grated nutmeg. Serve piping hot.

Good King Henry and fat hen also combine very nicely with other ingredients to make interesting side-dish vegetables or main dishes.

Lambs' Quarters in Sour Cream

'Lambs' quarters' is a local North Midlands name for fat hen. You may substitute either of the two plants for the other in any of these dishes.

Enough leaves for quantity required	Few drops lemon juice
Water to cook	Salt and black pepper to taste
1 small tub commercial sour cream	

Cook the lambs' quarters in the water and when tender press through a sieve. Chop coarsely when cool enough, then re-heat over a very low heat. Stir in the sour cream and continue to heat, but be very careful not to let the mixture boil. Season with salt and pepper. Remove from heat, and just before serving sprinkle with a few drops of lemon juice.

Lambs' Quarters with Garlic

The garlic should be one of the wild garlics if you can find it, but if not ordinary garlic may be used.

Enough leaves for quantity required	Salt to taste
3 wild garlic plants (whole)	Pepper (optional)
3 tablespoons olive oil	Lemon juice to taste

Heat oil in a large frying-pan (or a wok) over a medium heat but do not allow it to heat to the point when a haze rises. Chop the garlic, using bulbs, leaves and stems, very finely (use two cloves if ordinary garlic is being substituted). Cook in the oil for a short time, then remove the pan from the heat and toss in the leaves until just beginning to soften. Add salt and lemon juice (and pepper if used) and toss briefly. Serve immediately.

Fat Hen with Bacon and Chives

Enough leaves to serve 4
8 rashers streaky bacon
4 tablespoons chives, minced
2 tablespoons plain flour
2 tablespoons white wine
  vinegar

2 teaspoons sugar
1 teaspoon salt
½ teaspoon freshly ground
  black pepper

Cook the fat hen as described in the first two recipes, reserving the liquid produced by pressing through the sieve. Fry the bacon until crisp but without burning. Remove from pan, leaving the fat in the pan. Crumble the bacon into small pieces, and set aside.

Cook the minced chives in the bacon fat over a medium heat for about 5 minutes, stirring all the time. Stir in the flour until the mixture is smooth. Set aside.

In another pan, over medium heat, combine the liquid pressed out of the cooked leaves with the wine vinegar, sugar, salt and pepper, then stir in the mixture containing the chives. Now add the cooked leaves and stir until the mixture thickens. Continue cooking for a further couple of minutes, adjusting the heat to avoid any possibility of burning. Remove to serving-dish and sprinkle the crumbled bacon on top. Serve piping hot.

Lambs' Quarters with Wild Rice

Wild rice does not, of course, grow in Britain but can be obtained in some wholefood shops. If you cannot find it use brown rice instead, obtainable from wholefood stores and also from ethnic food shops.

Enough leaves to serve 4
Water to cook
Salt and pepper to taste
2 oz./50 g. butter
4 eggs
4 tablespoons wild rice, cooked

5 fl. oz./150 ml. milk
6 leeks
4 oz./100 g. grated Cheddar
  cheese
1½ teaspoons chopped fresh
  thyme (½ teaspoon if dried)

1 ½ teaspoons chopped fresh
marjoram (½ teaspoon if
dried)

1 ½ teaspoons chopped fresh
rosemary (½ teaspoon if dried)
Few drops Worcester sauce

Cook the leaves as described in the first two recipes, adding salt and
pepper to taste, and press through a sieve. Melt the butter over a low
heat, ensuring that it does not burn. Beat the eggs until light and
frothy. Chop the leeks, including the green tops. Now combine all
the ingredients thoroughly, and pour the mixture into a greased 2-
quart casserole dish. No lid is required. Cook at Regulo 4 (350°F./
180°C.) for about 35 minutes, until firm. Serve hot.

Good King Henry with Herbs

Enough leaves to serve 4
4 rashers streaky bacon
2 onions
4 tablespoons chopped fresh
parsley

1 ½ teaspoons chopped fresh
rosemary (½ teaspoon if dried)
Salt and pepper to taste
2 tablespoons lemon juice

Fry the bacon until crisp but without burning. Remove from pan,
leaving the fat in the pan. Crumble the bacon into small pieces, and
set aside.

Slice the onions and fry in the bacon fat until just golden. Then
pour the fat, with the onions, into a saucepan and add the parsley and
rosemary. Leave on a very low heat, giving an occasional stir from
time to time to prevent burning. While this is proceeding, cook the
leaves in a little water with salt and pepper to taste, removing from
the pan when tender and pressing through a sieve. Now add the
cooked leaves to the mixture simmering in the other pan, add the
lemon juice and continue cooking for about 5 minutes, stirring all
the time. (A wok is useful for this part of the operation.) When
ready, turn into a serving-dish and sprinkle the crumbled bacon
pieces over the top. Serve hot.

Now for a soup recipe which takes its name from the local Hampshire name for fat hen. You can, of course, use Good King Henry if it
is more readily available.

Allgood Soup

A good handful young leaves
1 pint/575 ml. water
½ pint/275 ml. milk
1 tablespoon ground rice
Yolk of one egg

4 tablespoons single cream
Knob of butter
Pepper and salt to taste
Dash of nutmeg

Wash the leaves and put them in a pan with the water, ground rice, pepper and salt. Cook until tender, then press the leaves through a sieve in such a way that the liquid pressed out goes back into the pan. Add the milk and butter and the nutmeg, and re-heat, being careful not to let it boil. Beat the egg yolk until light and frothy, then remove the pan from the heat and blend the beaten egg yolk into the mixture. Finally, before serving add the cream, stirring thoroughly. Do not be tempted to re-heat after adding the cream, or the soup will curdle. The surface may be decorated by sprinkling with chopped fresh parsley, grated Cheddar cheese or croûtons.

Finally, here is a little-known recipe in which the seeds of these two plants are used as a kind of cereal. It is said to be a useful substitute for porridge.

Gather the seeding flowerheads and hang them up in a well-ventilated warm place to dry, when the seeds can be rubbed out between the hands. You will need quite a lot of the seeding flower-heads, as the seeds are very small – much smaller than the proverbial grain of mustard seed.

The seeds should now be roasted for about an hour in a preheated oven at Regulo 2 (300°F./150°C.), after which you can run them through a grain mill, if you have one, or pound them with a pestle and mortar.

This pounded seed is now used like oatmeal to make porridge, boiling it for not less than 20 minutes. When boiling, add the seed gradually, stirring vigorously, and if you wish to season with salt, add this while boiling. When you have boiled all the seed, lower the heat and simmer on a very low heat for a further 20 minutes or so, by which time you should have a thick 'porridge' of gruel-like consistency. Serve this as you would any other kind of cereal, with milk, cream, fruit, yoghourt or – like American grits – a dab of butter.

5

HERBS FROM THE WILD

Most of the cultivated herbs used in the kitchen to-day are derived from wild plants of field and hedgerow, wood and meadow, and many of these are fortunately common and easily found in most districts. First, therefore, I shall describe the wild equivalents of the commonly used kitchen herbs, and in addition introduce you to the joys of some of the lesser-known wild herbs which can bring their own unique flavours to your cooking. A good botany book with colour photographs for identification is a must for these, as a few of them have certain superficial resemblances to other plants of a different family which are poisonous, bitter or otherwise inedible.

The following herbs do not grow wild as native plants: bay, chives, dill, parsley, rosemary and tarragon. Very occasionally you might find the odd plant growing wild as a garden escape. These six plants do not have any related wild equivalent so you will have to use the cultivated varieties where they are essential to a recipe.

ANGELICA

Wild angelica (*Angelica sylvestris*) is common in damp woodlands, fens and marshes, and wet meadowland. It is widespread throughout the British Isles, flowering from July to September. It can grow up to 8 feet (2.45 m.) tall, with smooth, hollow stems, sometimes purplish-tinged. The leaves are very large and deeply cleft, toothed at the edges and set in groups of three or five. The white flower-heads are sometimes, though not always, tinged with pink. An identifying character is the *inflated* sheathing stalks, often purple-tinged, which are a conspicuous feature. Do not confuse this plant with hogweed,

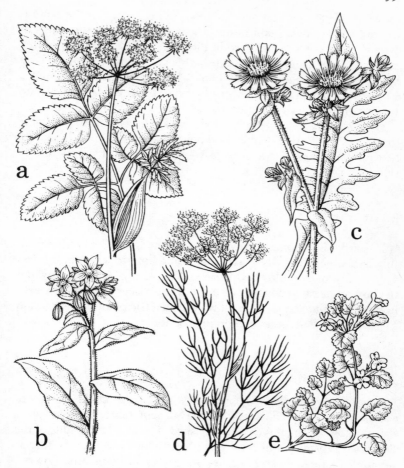

Some common wild herbs: a, Wild angelica (*Angelica sylvestris*); b, Borage (*Borago officinalis*); c, Wild chicory (*Cichorium intybus*); d, Fennel (*Foeniculum vulgare*); e, Ground ivy (*Glechoma hederacea*)

which also grows up to 9 feet (2.70 m.) high or more. Hogweed has *grooved* stems and smells very different from wild angelica.

BALM

Balm (*Melissa officinalis*) is a member of the Labiatae or mint family. Its flowers have a powerful attraction for bees, hence its name of bee balm; another of its names is lemon balm, owing to the lemon-scented leaves. This plant is not a true native but in the south of Britain has become established in the wild, having originally been a garden escape. This most versatile herb has so many uses that it is an essential plant in the wildfood cook's kitchen. It grows to about 2 feet (60 cm.) and has small white flowers set in usual labiate fashion around the square stem at intervals.

The distinctive lemon scent of balm makes it easily distinguishable from the many other white-flowered labiates. Woodlands are the best places to look for it, if it grows in your area. Flowers July to September.

BASIL

Wild basil (*Clinopodium vulgare*) is another labiate, flowering from July to September in dry grassy places and limestone scrub. It is less aromatic than the cultivated variety. The plant is softly downy and the flowers, arranged in whorls around the bases of the upper leaves in typical labiate style, are pinkish-purple. The plant is common in England and Wales, uncommon in Scotland.

BORAGE

Borage (*Borago officinalis*) grows wild on the chalk downs in southern England. It flowers from May to September. The plant gives off an odour of cucumber when crushed. The very bright blue of the flowers is typical in this family of plants which includes the forget-me-not, alkanet, viper's bugloss and other brilliant blue flowers. Borage grows to 3 feet (90 cm.) high. The whole plant is covered with dense hairs.

CHAMOMILE

Wild chamomile (*Anthemis nobilis*), a pleasant-scented herb of the daisy family, is not unlike a number of other members of this family with which it can be confused, notably scented mayweed (*Matricaria odora*), pineapple-scented mayweed (*M. matricarioides*) and others. Many of the distinguishing characters are minor ones as all these plants look very much alike at first glance with their white daisy-like flowers and feathery leaves. Take a good botany book with you when searching for wild chamomile, which flowers from June to September in grassy and heathy places, especially on sandy soils. It tends to have a more prostrate growing habit than the other two mentioned above, which grow more erect. Wild chamomile has *no down beneath the leaves* and smells like apples when crushed. It rarely grows more than 7 or 8 inches (18–20 cm.) high.

CHERVIL

Two wild plants may be used as substitutes for the cultivated chervil. The first of these is the true wild chervil, cow parsley or keck (*Anthriscus sylvestris*), a very abundant plant of the family Umbelliferae. When the hedgerows are frothed with masses of the lacy white flowers and the air is filled with their fragrant, heady scent, you know that spring has truly arrived.

This plant must not be confused with fool's parsley (*Aethusa cynapium*), which is highly poisonous, but fortunately these two plants are easily distinguished by the following characters. The stems of cow parsley are slightly hairy; those of fool's parsley are hairless. Both grow to about 3 feet (90 cm.), but the former is much earlier-flowering: April to June, as compared with fool's parsley which flowers from June to October. A further distinguishing feature is that the white flowers of fool's parsley have long, drooping bracts which give the flowerheads a 'bearded' appearance; the flowers of cow parsley do not have these drooping bracts.

There are several other superficially similar-looking plants in this family which it is as well to be able to recognize at sight. Some are edible; others, such as hemlock, cowbane and hemlock water dropwort, are *extremely poisonous*. Go armed with your botany book when gathering for the kitchen and *do not pick any of this group of plants unless you are absolutely certain of its identity*.

Milfoil, or yarrow, a member of the Compositae or daisy family, is distinctive enough to be easily identified, but in my opinion the taste is much inferior to that of cow parsley. Yarrow is abundant everywhere and grows to a height of 18 inches (45 cm.); the densely packed flowerheads, which have a somewhat misleadingly umbelliferous appearance, may be white, pink, red or even purplish.

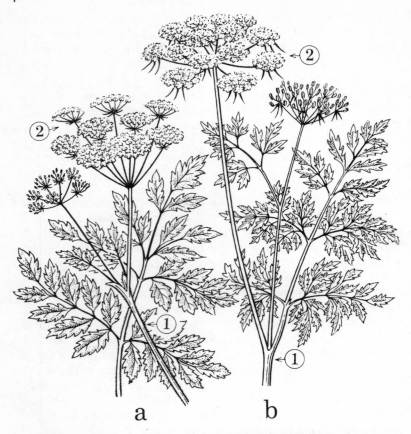

a, Wild chervil (*Anthriscus sylvestris*); b, Fool's parsley (*Aethusa cynapium*)

Warning: Do not confuse (a) which is good, with (b) which is *highly poisonous*.

1 Stems slightly hairy	1 Stems hairless
2 No drooping bracts	2 Drooping bracts, giving a 'bearded' look

CHICORY

The wild chicory (*Cichorium intybus*) bears little resemblance to the cultivated variety but is worth looking for in pastures and grassy places on chalk and limestone soils, flowering from June to September. It grows to about 3 feet (90 cm.) and the leaves are very reminiscent of dandelion leaves but are more deeply indented. The blue flowers are gorgeous and you never see them on the cultivated chicory sold in the supermarket!

CORIANDER

The wild coriander (*Coriandrum sativum*) is not a native plant but an escapee of cultivation which has established itself in a few scattered areas of the British Isles. Richard Mabey, author of *Food for Free* and an expert in this subject, says that it grows alongside the M1, but I doubt if you could spot it from the window of a speeding car!

If you do manage to find it, you will be astonished to find that it is really fetid – it stinks worse than stinking mayweed! Only the fully ripened seeds are aromatic, following the flowering period from June to August. For the record, it grows from about 4 to 10 inches (10–25 cm.) high, and the flowers can be pink or white; the lower leaves have broader segments than the upper. The stem is solid.

FENNEL

In contrast to the foregoing species, this umbelliferous plant, known botanically as *Foeniculum vulgare*, can grow up to 6 feet (1.80 m.) high in the wild (I have seen cultivated fennel in gardens more than 9 feet (2.80 m.) in height). It's a beautiful feathery-leaved plant which looks very decorative even when not flowering. The flowers are bright yellow in typical umbel formation; the stems are shiny-looking, solid at first and becoming hollow as the plant matures. The leaves are sheathed at the base – a common feature in this family. The wild fennel does not smell so strongly of aniseed as the cultivated variety. It flowers from July to September and is most commonly found in bare and waste places, especially in coastal areas.

FENUGREEK

A member of the pea family, wild fenugreek (*Trigonella ornithopo-dioides*) is less aromatic than the cultivated fenugreek, which is a different species, but still worth while using – if you can find it. It's found only in southern Britain, mainly near the coast in dry sandy areas. The flowers, which bloom from late May or early June into July, can be creamy-white or pink, soon producing the pods of seeds which are the part used in cookery. It has a prostrate growing habit and seldom reaches more than a few inches (centimetres) in length. I've found a good many of our native wild plants over the years, including some rarities, but I've never managed to find this one. You may have better luck.

GARLIC

You will have no difficulty at all in locating any of our four common species of wild garlic. These are the true wild garlic, or field garlic (*Allium oleraceum*), crow garlic (*A. vineale*) and ramsons (*A. ursinum*), all of which belong to the lily family, and garlic mustard or Jack-by-the-hedge (*Alliaria petiolata*), which belongs to quite a different family, the Cruciferae or cabbage family.

All these plants smell very strongly indeed of garlic, unlike the cultivated garlic bulbs sold in the shops. However, curiously enough, their flavour is much less pungent than their smell would suggest. The novice wildfood enthusiast will tend to use only a small piece of the plant to flavour the dish and then wonder why it does not taste of garlic! So the rule is: use more than you would if using the cultivated kind. Any part of the plant may be used – bulb, leaf or stem, even the flowers or seeds.

All these plants are common everywhere; field and crow garlics prefer grassy and cultivated areas, while ramsons are found in woods and shady places. Garlic mustard is very common in hedgerows and on grassy banks. If you are approaching a hedgerow full of garlic mustard, you will be able to smell the plants from several yards off, but for additional identification it is white-flowered, with toothed leaves, pointed towards the top of the plant and heart-shaped at the base, and grows up to 3 feet (90 cm.). It flowers from April to June.

The white-flowered ramsons grows up to 16 inches (40 cm.), blooming from April to June; field and crow garlics are taller – up to 30 inches (75 cm.) – and flower later, from June to August, the flowers being pinkish or reddish. The leaves of ramsons are much broader than those of the other two, whose leaves are so narrow as to be grass-like and sheath the stem so that before flowering the plant looks almost like grass. Only the strong smell gives it away!

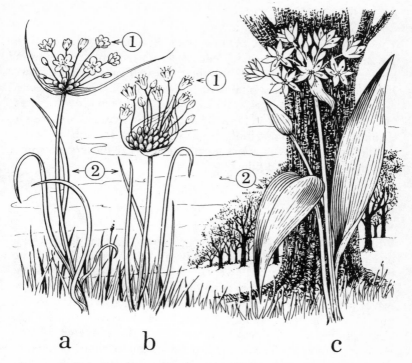

a, Field garlic (*Allium oleraceum*); b, Crow garlic (*A. vineale*);
c, Ramsons (*A. ursinum*)

1 (a) Stamens not protruding
2 (a) and (b) Leaves narrow
grass-like

1 (b) Stamens protruding
2 (c) Leaves broad

HORSERADISH

The horseradish (*Armoracia rusticana*) is an introduced alien which has become naturalized in the wild in damp places and waysides. Its white flowers bloom from May to August. The plant grows to 3 feet (90 cm.) tall and is easily distinguished from others of this family (the cabbage family) by the large glossy leaves, which are a conspicuous feature. It is commonest in south-east England although widely distributed elsewhere except Scotland, where it is a rarity. Its usual habit is to grow in large clumps.

LOVAGE

The native lovage, *Ligusticum scoticum*, is found wild only in Scotland, and on rocky cliff ledges at that, so unless you are a mountaineer you had better use the cultivated variety! This, however, occurs as an occasional garden escape. It is a different species (*L. officinale*) and unlike the native species can often grow to 7 feet (2.15 m.) high or more and usually does, so you're unlikely to miss it if you just happen to find it. It has shiny, bright green leathery leaves, which smell strongly of celery when crushed. The flowers are white and bloom in June and July.

MARJORAM

Wild marjoram (*Origanum vulgare*) grows up to 2 feet (60 cm.) high on chalk downland and limestone soils, and although this is a labiate plant it does not bear its flowers in the usual whorled arrangement typical of this family, but in flowerheads at the top of the stem. The leaves are dark green, oval in shape and toothed. The flowers are purple and may be found blooming from July to October. The slender stems are softly downy. It is related to the cultivated oregano but is less pungent. When it is dried the flavour becomes sweeter, so that it may then be used in a wider variety of dishes.

MINT

There are many kinds of wild mint, all of which can be used in the kitchen. Nine species occur, all commonly and well distributed throughout Britain, except spearmint (*Mentha spicata*) which is confined to the southern half of the country. Each species has its own distinctive scent and flavour. Space precludes a detailed description of the nine species, but you should compare them in your identification book: water mint (*Mentha aquatica*), corn mint (*M. arvensis*), whorled mint (*M. verticillata*), peppermint (*M. piperita*), horsemint (*M. longifolia*), applemint (*M. rotundifolia*), catmint (*Nepeta cataria*) and calamint (*Calamintha ascendens*).

SAGE

The true wild sage (*Salvia sylvestris*) is rare in Britain, and clary (*S. horminioides*) is usually used instead. It is commoner in the south than elsewhere and affects dry grassy places, growing up to 3 feet (90 cm.) high, with irregularly toothed leaves of the greyish hue associated with sage. The pale mauve flowers bloom from June to September; an identifying character is a number of white spots on the lower lip. They are arranged in typical labiate fashion in whorls around the stem. The whole plant is downy.

One of my favourite plants is wood sage (*Teucrium scorodonia*) which can be used in small quantities in cookery. Too much can taste bitter, and in fact it makes a very good substitute for hops when brewing beer. Wood sage is the only labiate with *green* flowers, so it is impossible to mistake it for any other species. It is very partial to chalk downlands near the coast; in Dorset it is abundant even on rock ledges high on the cliffs. It flowers from July to September and occurs most commonly in south-west Britain. Both scent and taste are refreshingly different from ordinary sage, as you will discover if you can get near it for the bees which flock to the blossoms!

THYME

Wild thyme (*Thymus serpyllum*) is a very small, prostrate plant with tiny purple or sometimes pink flowers found, often abundantly, on heathland, dunes and dry grassy places, where it forms mats carpeting the ground among the grass and heather. The flowers, blooming from May to August, with their heady, sweet perfume, are another favourite with the bees. While the scent is no less potent than that of the cultivated variety, the flavour is less strong, so you will need to use more in cooking. The woody-stemmed plants can be hung up to dry in an airy place just like the cultivated kind, but as they are much smaller it is best to hang them up in paper (not plastic) bags. The leaves and blossoms can then be rubbed off the stems between the fingers and stored in air-tight jars. I can confirm from experience that a gathering of wild thyme will produce a certain crop of very stiff joints!

Other wild herbs, although they have no equivalent in the commercially-produced kitchen window-ledge herbs, can contribute their own brand of flavouring delights to your food. All the following are common and distributed over the greater part of Britain, although naturally occurring in the types of habitat most suited to them by reason of the soil and other factors.

GROUND IVY

The ubiquitous ground ivy (*Glechoma hederacea*) is one of the earliest plants to bloom, flowers appearing as early as March and continuing until June and sometimes later. It is, of course, not an ivy at all but a member of the labiate family with round-lobed heart-shaped leaves and a prostrate habit which are very distinctive. It sometimes carpets whole areas of woodland with its blue or violet flowers, and occurs also in hedge banks, bare or waste places and sparse grasslands alike. It frequently turns up as a weed in the garden.

Softly downy and aromatic, the dried leaves make an agreeable herb tea as well as a flavouring for foods that can be improved by adding a herb with a sharp but light fragrance.

HERB BENNET

This member of the rose family, known botanically as *Geum urbanum*, was widely grown as a pot herb in the sixteenth century, when it was added to soups and broths, stews and the simmering stock-pot. The roots have a strong odour of cloves. It grows to about 2 feet (60 cm.) in woods, clearings, hedge banks and other places where there is some shade and a rich damp soil. The small yellow flowers are in bloom from May to August. The leaves are toothed and clasp the stem, and are usually divided into three or five lobes.

LADY'S BEDSTRAW

The masses of tiny yellow flowers of lady's bedstraw (*Galium verum*) smell of honey when fresh, but when dried this is lost and the flowers then smell more like new-mown hay. Pleasant as this is, it is not, to my mind, a particularly good fragrance to incorporate into one's food, but the fresh flowers make a sweet honey-flavoured herbal tea. They bloom from June to September. The plant grows in dry grassy places and although the stems may reach 2 feet (60 cm.) or more in total length they sprawl across the surface of the ground, giving the impression of a much shorter plant.

MEADOWSWEET

The heady perfume of meadowsweet (*Spiraea ulmaria*) is unforgettable, especially when it is growing in masses as it does in many of the fens and marshes of East Anglia and elsewhere. This plant with its fragrant creamy dense clusters of flowers is found also in wet

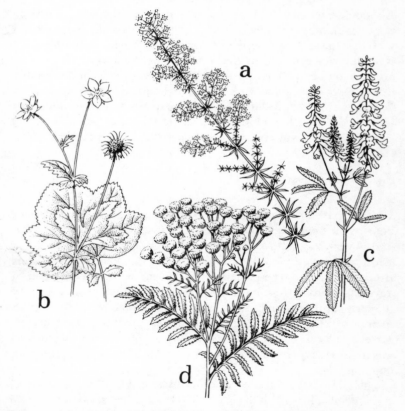

More common wild herbs: a, Lady's bedstraw (*Galium verum*); b, Herb bennet (*Geum urbanum*); c, Melilot (*Melilotus officinalis*); d, Tansy (*Tanacetum vulgare*)

meadows, damp woods and swampy bogs, as well as by river banks. It grows to 3 feet (90 cm.) or more, and flowers from June to August. Its rose-like leaves betray its membership of the rose family.

The flowers can be infused to make a sweet herb tea with soporific qualities said to banish headaches, and the young leaves impart an almond-like flavour to many dishes. The leaves are almost as aromatic as the flowers. The flowers make a wonderful wine – one of the best wines to be made from wild ingredients.

MELILOT

Although melilot (*Melilotus officinalis*) belongs to a different botanical family – the pea family – from lady's bedstraw, it shares with that plant the property of a constituent called *coumarin* which is the substance producing the honey-like perfume when the flowers are fresh and a smell of new-mown hay when dried. The leaves look like those of clovers and trefoils but are longer. It grows up to 4 feet (1.20 cm.) in fields and waste places, on dunes and sandy soils. The long spikes of yellow blooms appear from June to September, and can be used to flavour herb beers as well as some meat dishes.

SWEET CICELY

Here we have another of those lookalike umbellifers which are the bane of the novice botanist to identify! Sweet cicely (*Myrrhis odorata*) is very fragrant, as its botanical name implies; it is also very sweet, and if you use one or two sprigs of the plant when cooking fruit or jam-boiling, you will find you can cut the amount of sugar by anything up to half, so it is a very economical plant to use. Remove the sprigs at the end of cooking time, as you would remove the sprigs of mint which you have cooked with the new potatoes before serving. Sweet cicely can also be added to mollify the flavour of sharp-tasting greens such as sorrel and dandelion – again, remove the sprigs after cooking.

This plant has a number of other uses, including the making of sweet drinks, for which the leaves and the crushed seeds can be used as well as the flowers, and in salads, chopping the leaves for this purpose. The chopped leaves can also be added to various fish and meat dishes and soups, as well as omelets, pancakes, herb butters etc. It can be boiled with root vegetables to add flavour, and the juice can be extracted in an electric juice-extractor to add to other raw vegetable juices. The plant has a tap root which can be boiled and eaten either hot, or cold in salad.

This plant is much commoner in the north than in the south, and grassy roadsides in Scotland are its favourite habitat. It can grow up to 5 feet (1.50 cm.) tall and looks not unlike a very tall cow parsley. The leaves are frequently white-flecked, and smell of aniseed when crushed. The flowering period is from April to June. With such a repertoire of culinary uses it is surprising that it is not cultivated more commonly.

SWEET GALE

This plant, sometimes called bog myrtle, is the *Myrica gale* of botanists and is locally common in bogs, marshes and wet heath-lands in various parts of south-west England, North Wales, Scotland and Ireland. It is a deciduous shrub growing up to 4 feet (1.20 cm.) with dioecious plants – that is, the male and female flowers occur on separate plants. The catkin-like flowers appear before the leaves, the male catkins orange, the female red. The twigs that bear them are reddish-tinged and shiny, and when the leaves appear these are narrow, toothed and greyish-green.

Both leaves and flowers have a sweet, rather resinous smell. Before hops were introduced to Britain the plant was used for the brewing of beer. The catkins appear in April and May. The eucalyptus-like smell is not very conducive to using the plant in food preparation, but gale beer can be brewed if you have the time and the patience for the rather elaborate process necessary.

TANSY

This member of the daisy family, *Tanacetum vulgare*, is common everywhere except in Ireland. Growing up to 3 feet (90 cm.), its yellow flowers appear from July to September. It is most often found in hedgerows, the edges of fields and waste places.

The leaves, which can be chopped into salads, should be taken young, as the older ones can be bitter and even acrid. The smell of the plant is strong and can be a bit off-putting, but this largely disappears in cooking. It can be used in a number of cooked dishes with other ingredients, but it should not be used in anything more than small quantities as it has sometimes been found irritating to sensitive stomachs. In the fifteenth century the juice used to be extracted from the leaves to flavour omelets, and during the same period a dish concocted from the leaves of tansy, green corn, violets, oranges and sugar was popular. It can also be used for wine-making, the flowers being more mildly flavoured than their scent would suggest.

WILD CELERY

Wild celery (*Apium graveolens*) grows in wet places, especially near the sea, and is at its best from June to August. Its leaves look exactly like those of cultivated celery and its smell is the same, but the wild kind does not have the thick stalks of its garden counterpart. Its flowers are white, arranged in umbels with short stalks.

The whole plant can be used, either raw or cooked, and makes a first-class flavouring for soups, stews, sauces, casseroles and other made-up dishes, as well as chopped into salads and eaten raw dipped in salt as an accompaniment to cheese with brown bread and butter. It can also be braised with butter in a fireproof dish with salt and pepper and the addition of chicken stock, cream, grated Cheddar cheese, parsley etc.

The plant grows up to 2 feet (60 cm.) high, which gives one plenty of it for using in the various ways mentioned. The strong smell is greatly reduced by cooking, but the taste is stronger than that of the garden variety, so a little will go a long way.

WOODRUFF

Finally, here we have another plant of the bedstraw family, the Rubiaceae, containing the substance *coumarin* mentioned earlier which produces a strong scent of honey in the fresh plant, changing to the smell of new-mown hay in the dried one. Woodruff (*Galium odoratum*) is a delicate-looking small plant growing up to about a foot (30 cm.) in height. The flowers are white and bloom from April to June, the favoured habitats being moist woodland on chalk and limestone soils, and in thick hedgerows. Beech woods seem to be particularly favourable to the growth of this plant. It is distributed in suitable habitats throughout the British Isles.

Woodruff flowers make a fine honey-scented herbal tea. They can also be made into wine, or used to flavour various other drinks. Richard Mabey must be allowed to have the last word here. He says that a bottle of pure apple juice in which a sprig of woodruff has been allowed to steep for a week or so becomes positively ambrosial . . .

6

USING WILD HERBS

Now for the recipes, since you should now be able to recognize the herbs correctly! Let's start with some heartwarming thick winter soups, followed by some lighter summer ones.

Garlic and Wild Herb Soup

Don't let the quantity of garlic used scare you off – it is considerably less pungent cooked than it is raw. This is the kind of soup that is a filling meal in itself, eaten with hot French bread split down the middle and buttered.

6 wild garlic plants
2 quarts/2300 ml. water
2 teaspoons salt
1 teaspoon black pepper
4 cloves
1 teaspoon chopped fresh sage
1 teaspoon chopped fresh thyme
3 tablespoons fresh parsley, chopped

1 bay leaf
4 egg yolks
1 oz./25 g. butter
1 oz./25 g. grated Cheddar cheese
2 tablespoons single cream

Cut the green stems and leaves off the wild garlic plants, chop them finely and set aside. Remove the skins from the bulbs and slice them thinly.

Put 2 quarts of water in a large saucepan, add the chopped garlic tops and sliced bulbs, salt, pepper, cloves and all herbs. Now bring to the boil, then lower heat and simmer for 15 minutes. Remove bay leaf and cloves.

Beat together the butter with the egg yolks until thick, and pour the mixture into another large saucepan. Place over low heat and gradually pour the soup you have cooked in the other pan into it, stirring all the time. Do not let it boil. When all the soup has been added from the other pan, simmer for a further 5 minutes, still stirring all the time.

Serve hot, with the cream poured over the top in the serving tureen and sprinkled with grated Cheddar cheese.

Wild Celery and Bacon Soup

This is another stick-to-the ribs soup suitable for cold winter evenings.

8 rashers streaky bacon	2 oz./50 g. pearl barley
4 wild celery plants	1 teaspoon salt
10 fl. oz./275 ml. water	½ teaspoon white pepper
10 fl. oz./275 ml. beef broth or stock	

Fry the bacon until crisp, crumble into pieces and set aside. Reserve the bacon fat in the pan. Wash and coarsely chop the wild celery and cook it in the bacon fat over a medium heat for about 10 minutes or until tender. Do not allow it to burn! Set aside when it is ready.

Bring the water and the beef broth or stock to the boil in a big pot and add the pearl barley, then simmer until the barley is tender. Then add the cooked celery, the salt and pepper, bring back to the boil, then lower the heat and simmer for 10 minutes. During the last three minutes of cooking time add about half the crumbled bacon and stir into the soup. Sprinkle the remaining bacon pieces on top of the soup when serving.

Basil and Tomato Soup

This hearty soup is good eaten with a toasted cheese sandwich, which together make a satisfying lunch or supper and may be followed by a chilled fruit dessert or yoghourt.

12 medium-size tomatoes
2 teaspoons finely-chopped
  fresh basil
2 tablespoons chopped chives
2 tablespoons olive oil

1 tablespoon lemon juice
5 fl. oz./150 ml. water
5. fl. oz./150 ml. evaporated
  milk
5 fl. oz./150 ml. beef stock
Salt and black pepper to taste

Heat the oil in a large pot, peel and chop the tomatoes and cook them in the oil together with the chopped chives over a medium heat for about 10 minutes, stirring from time to time to prevent burning or sticking to the bottom of the pan. Add the basil, lemon juice, water and beef stock, salt and pepper, bring to the boil and then lower heat, cover with a lid and simmer for 20 minutes.

Before serving, stir in the evaporated milk, which will make the soup rich and creamy. The milk may be warmed if you wish, but it must not be very hot, much less allowed to boil.

Herb Bennet Soup

10 fl. oz./275 ml. chicken stock
6 oz./175 g. herb bennet leaves
Zest of 1 lemon
1 bunch watercress
2 tablespoons chives (chopped)

Few flowers of herb bennet
2 bay leaves
1 teaspoon salt
½ teaspoon white pepper
5 fl. oz./150 ml. water

Bring the chicken stock and the water to the boil in a large pot. Chop the watercress very finely except for a small portion to be left for garnishing. Chop the herb bennet leaves finely. Add these together with the chives to the stock and water and bring back to the boil, adding the zest of the lemon, bay leaves, salt and pepper. Now reduce the heat and simmer for about 15 minutes, stirring from time to time. When ready to serve, garnish with sprigs of watercress and a few flowers of herb bennet.

Lovage Soup

1 lb./450 g. potatoes, cooked
1 onion
2 tablespoons lovage, chopped
2 pints/1150 ml. stock
½ oz./12½ g. butter

2 teaspoons fresh parsley,
  chopped
½ pint/275 ml. milk
½ oz./12½ g. plain flour
Salt and white pepper to taste

When boiling the potatoes do not allow them to overboil and become mushy. When cool enough, slice them about ¼ inch thick. Peel and slice the onion and sauté this in the butter, then add the potato slices, the lovage and the flour, which should be sprinkled in gradually. Transfer to a big pot and add the stock and seasoning, stirring all the time until boiling-point is reached, then reduce heat and simmer for 20 minutes. Add milk, but do not allow the soup to boil. Put the soup through a blender, then reheat ready for serving. Sprinkle the chopped parsley on top as a garnish.

Borage Soup

½lb./225 g. borage leaves, finely
  chopped
1 oz./25 g. butter
2 oz./50 g. pearl barley (or rice)

2 pints/1150 ml. chicken stock
2 tablespoons single cream
Salt and pepper to taste
Few borage flowers

Cook the barley or rice in the stock until tender. Cook the borage leaves in the butter until they are tender, add to the stock and reboil, then reduce heat and simmer for 10 minutes. Season to taste, then run through the blender before reheating to serve. Top with cream, and sprinkle with the brilliant blue borage flowers. The flowers may be eaten after they have provided a talking-point, and the colour of the soup – a deep green – will provide another one. No pea soup was ever this beautiful shade!

Now for the use of the various wild herbs in meat and fish dishes.

Garlic Herrings with Mustard

1 herring for each person
Flour to dust
Salt and white pepper to taste
2 tablespoons chopped wild
  garlic per 4 herrings

2 tablespoons olive oil
1 tablespoon dry mustard
  powder

Dip the herrings in seasoned flour, first removing head, tail, any fins and guts but leaving the roe, and washing under running cold water. Heat the olive oil in a frying-pan and stir in the chopped garlic. (The leaves of the garlic mustard, finely chopped, are the easiest to use for this recipe.) Drop the floured herrings into the hot oil and fry until crisp on the outside, turning from time to time. When nearly cooked, sprinkle the mustard powder, a little at a time, into the pan and stir it around, turning the herrings in it until they have absorbed all the mustard flavour. Serve with watercress salad and baked potatoes in their jackets each with a dab of butter and a sprinkling of parsley.

Liver and Bacon with Thyme and Sweet Cicely

¾ lb./350 g. lamb's liver
8 rashers streaky bacon
Salt and white pepper to taste
Olive oil to cook
2 teaspoons wild thyme
  (chopped)

2 teaspoons sweet cicely
  (chopped)
Flour to dust

Cut the liver into slices about ½ inch thick, and dust with seasoned flour. Heat the oil in a frying-pan, and fry the bacon until fairly crisp at the edges but not all the way through. Add the chopped herbs and cook until the flavours are absorbed by the oil, then turn up the heat and fry the liver very rapidly so that the outside is crisp and browned but the inside is moist and tender. Serve with sauté potatoes and a green salad.

Herbed Cod in Parsley Sauce

The parsley sauce is made in the usual way but be sure to use *fresh*, coarsely chopped parsley and not dried parsley. This makes all the difference.

4 cod steaks (round)
Butter to cook
2 teaspoons balm, chopped
2 teaspoons marjoram, chopped

2 teaspoons fennel, chopped
Salt and white pepper to taste
Parsley sauce

Ingredients for the parsley sauce:
½ pint/275 ml. milk
¼ pint/150 ml. single cream
1½ oz./37½ g. butter
1 oz./25 g. plain flour

4 tablespoons chopped fresh
  parsley
Salt and white pepper to taste

The cod steaks should be round, i.e. not cut along one side. Sprinkle with salt and pepper and fry gently in butter until cooked right through. The outer skin should be lightly browned and fairly crisp but not stiff. While cooking, add the chopped balm, marjoram and fennel, and stir the herbs around in the butter, turning the cod steaks frequently so that they absorb the herb flavours. When ready they should be served with the parsley sauce, made as follows.

Put the milk, cream, butter and flour in a non-stick pan and whisk them together over a low heat. When smooth and thickened, cook for a further 5 minutes – the heat must be very low and the sauce must not be allowed to boil. Then add the parsley and the seasoning, stir a few times and it is ready to serve.

Chicken with Melilot and Chervil

4 chicken joints
2 oz./50 g. butter
1 medium-size onion
½ pint/275 ml. white wine
2 teaspoons wild chervil
  (chopped)

2 teaspoons melilot (chopped)
2 bay leaves
Salt and white pepper to taste
¼ pint/150 ml. double cream
1 tablespoon lemon juice

Fry the onion, peeled and sliced, in the butter until golden and tender. Do not allow it to become browned or burnt. Season the chicken joints with salt and pepper and fry them in the butter with the onions over a low heat for about 25 minutes until cooked through, turning once. Now transfer all the contents of the pan to a large pot and add the white wine, bay, chervil and melilot. Stir the herbs into the liquid and mix well, and simmer over a very low heat for about 15 minutes, covered with a lid.

When ready, remove the chicken joints, take out the bay leaves and pour the cream into the liquid, adding the lemon juice, stir and bring just up to the boil without actually allowing it to boil. Remove from heat immediately and pour over the chicken joints in the serving dish.

VEGETARIAN MAIN DISHES WITH HERBS

There are so many different vegetarian main meal dishes using wild herbs in various combinations that they would fill the rest of this book! So I have selected some of the most tasty and nutritious ones, choosing as far as possible those using wild herbs that are easy to find.

Stuffed Aubergines

Two medium-size aubergines
Two small onions
Two eggs
4 tablespoons breadcrumbs
2 teaspoons chopped fresh sage
2 teaspoons chopped fresh marjoram
2 oz./50 g. butter
Water to cook
Salt and pepper to taste

Cut the aubergines in half and simmer them slowly for about half an hour or until tender. Remove from water, set aside to cool, and then scoop out the soft inside pulp. Set this aside too.

Fry the onions, peeled and sliced, in the butter until golden and soft, then add breadcrumbs, seasoning, herbs, the aubergine pulp and last of all the yolks only of the two eggs, beaten until frothy (The whites of the eggs can be used to make meringues or in some other dish.) When the mixture in the frying-pan has reached a stiff consistency, spoon it into the aubergine halves and bake at 350°F./ 180°C. (Regulo 4) for 15 to 20 minutes. Check near the end of cooking time to make sure that they do not burn. The top of the stuffing should be just nicely browned.

Avocado Pears with Herb Cream

Two avocado pears
4 tablespoons double cream
Salt to taste
2 teaspoons fresh chopped wild
 horseradish leaves

2 teaspoons fresh chopped wild
 chervil
2 teaspoons fresh chopped wild
 mint leaves (any species)

Mix the herbs and the salt into the cream, and pour over the avocado pears in their individual serving dishes. Each avocado is halved so that two serve four persons.

Baked Potatoes with Chamomile and Sour Cream

4 large potatoes
4 tablespoons sour cream
2 teaspoons chopped fresh
 chamomile leaves

Salt and pepper to taste

Scrub the potatoes, but do not remove the skins. Thread them on a metal skewer from end to end and bake in a pre-heated oven at 425°F./220°C. (Regulo 7) for an hour to an hour and a half according to size. When cooked, serve with the sour cream into which the herbs and seasoning have been well stirred.

Cauliflower au Gratin with Fennel

Enough cauliflower sprigs for 4
Water to cook
Salt for water
2 oz./50 g. breadcrumbs

2 oz./50 g. grated Cheddar
 cheese
5 fl. oz./150 ml. single cream
2 teaspoons chopped fresh
 fennel

Boil the cauliflower sprigs in salted water until tender but not disintegrating. Remove from water and put into an ovenproof dish (no lid is needed) and pour the cream over them. Now mix the grated Cheddar cheese, breadcrumbs and fennel and sprinkle over the cauliflower to form a topping. Bake at 375°F./190°C. (Regulo 5) for 20 minutes, or until the topping is golden-brown.

Herburgers

You make these just like ordinary beefburgers but instead of minced beef you use just herbs and breadcrumbs. Of course you can include meat if you want to – minced beef, lamb, pork leftovers or whatever you have in the fridge to be used, in which case reduce the amount of breadcrumbs by the amount of minced meat you are using, but the quantities of the herbs should be the same. Cooked rice can also be substituted for some of the breadcrumbs, but in my opinion using rice in this recipe does not make the herburgers taste nearly as good. You can adapt the vegetarian recipe or not as you wish.

½ lb./225 g. soft breadcrumbs
1 teaspoon salt
1 teaspoon chopped garlic
½ teaspoon black pepper
1 small onion
1 teaspoon sage

1 teaspoon thyme
1 teaspoon basil
1 tablespoon tomato purée
2 eggs (yolks only)
Oil for cooking

Mix the breadcrumbs, seasoning and herbs in a bowl. Fresh chopped herbs will make the finished product better-tasting than dried ones. Peel and mince the onion finely, and add to the mixture. Now beat the egg yolks until frothy – these are used to bind the mixture together – and add them, with the tomato purée, to the other ingredients. Knead into a large ball ready to be rolled out.

Shape the mixture into 8 burger shapes on a lightly-floured pastry board, and cook in hot oil, turning once, until golden-brown. A deep frying-pan is best for this job. Serve with watercress salad and new potatoes. Resist any temptation to serve them with fattening chips which do absolutely nothing for this dish!

Now for a few ideas for desserts using sweet aromatic herbs, which will lift them right out of the down-to-earth pudding class.

Rhubarb Fool with Angelica

½ lb./225 g. rhubarb
Water to cook
2 tablespoons chopped fresh
  angelica leaves

3 oz./75 g. sugar
5 fl. oz./150 ml. double cream
Few angelica flowers to garnish

Cook the rhubarb with the sugar in water until tender and beginning to disintegrate, adding the angelica leaves about half-way through cooking time. When ready, set aside to cool, then pass through a blender. Mix with the cream, stirring thoroughly, and chill in the fridge. Serve decorated with a few angelica flowers.

Gooseberry Delight with Woodruff

½ lb./225 g. gooseberries
Water to cook
Two full heads woodruff
  flowers

5 fl. oz./150 ml. double cream
3 oz./75 g. sugar

Cook the gooseberries, after topping and tailing, with the woodruff flowers and sugar in water until the gooseberries have disintegrated to a pulp. Remove the woodruff flowers and pass the gooseberries through a blender. Mix with cream, as in the previous recipe, and chill in the fridge.

Tansy Cakes

8 oz./225 g. plain flour
½ teaspoon salt
4 oz./100 g. butter
4 oz./100 g. sugar

1 teaspoon baking powder
2 teaspoons chopped tansy
  leaves
2 eggs
Milk to mix

Sift the flour with the salt and baking-powder, add the sugar and tansy leaves, and mix thoroughly. Rub in the butter. Beat the egg and add this to the mixture with enough milk to make a workable drop-consistency dough.

Grease individual bun tins and drop a tablespoon of the dough into each. Bake at 450°F./230°C. (Regulo 8) for 12 to 15 minutes, and eat hot, split and buttered like scones.

Apple and Meadowsweet Compôte

2 large cooking apples
Water to cook
8 cloves
2 full heads meadowsweet
  flowers

3 oz./75 g. Demerara sugar
Few raisins (seedless)
Pinch nutmeg

Stew the apples, peeled, cored and sliced, in the water with the sugar, cloves, meadowsweet flowerheads and raisins. If preferred, you can stick 4 cloves into each apple and cook peeled but whole; however, they will take longer to cook by this method.

When the apples are nicely stewed (well cooked but not a shapeless mush), remove from heat and stir in the nutmeg. Serve with cream, either hot or cold as preferred. Before serving remove the meadowsweet flowerheads, and if you have cooked the apples by the second method without coring, remove any cores and pips before serving.

Lemon Balm Custard

1 pint/575 ml. milk
2 tablespoons cream
4 eggs
4 tablespoons sugar

1 vanilla pod
2 tablespoons chopped fresh
  lemon balm leaves

Beat together the eggs and milk, then add the sugar and balm leaves, continuing to beat well. Add the cream, stirring the mixture well, and turn into a buttered ovenproof dish (no lid required). Drop the vanilla pod into the mixture. Bake at 300°F./150°C. (Regulo 2) for about half an hour or until set (but not too firmly). If you wish, an optional touch is to sprinkle nutmeg on top, either before cooking or after you take the dish from the oven.

I will end this chapter with some ideas for herbal teas, all of which are easy to make, and some notes on their various properties as a guide. Most of these teas are intended to be drunk without milk, which in many cases would obscure their delicate flavour. Some need to be sweetened, others do not; those that do may be sweetened with light, clear honey rather than sugar, but this is really a matter for personal preference. One or two make good additions to ordinary China tea.

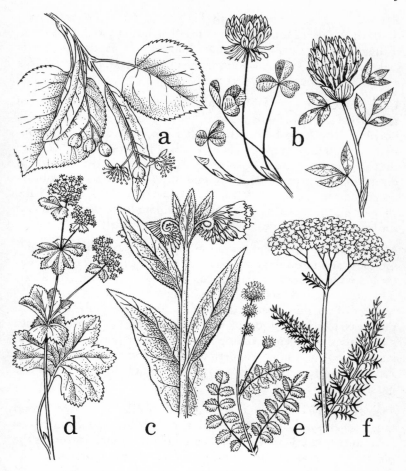

Cup of tea? try these: a, Lime (*Tilia vulgaris*); b, Red and
white clovers (*Trifolium repens* and *T. pratense*);
c, Comfrey (*Symphytum officinale*); d, Lady's mantle
(*Alchemilla vulgaris*); e, Salad burnet (*Poterium
sanguisorba*); f, Yarrow or milfoil (*Achillea millefolium*)

China Tea with Lemon Balm is a good example of this use. The
lemon balm leaves should be chopped and added to the China tea in
the pot. The amount of herb to use is, as a general rule, 3 teaspoons of
the fresh herb per cup, but only half this quantity of the dried herb,
which is twice as strong in this more concentrated form. The infusion

time is from 7 to 10 minutes for the herb by itself in boiling water, less if added to the teapot with China tea. The liquid should be passed through a tea-strainer into the cup. China tea with lemon balm needs little sweetening – a light honey is recommended for this one. It is said to be soothing for the nerves.

Chamomile Tea is probably the best-known of the herb teas. I have never tried it, but the only person I know who has says that it tastes horrible. You have been warned. It's supposed to be drunk unsweetened, and perhaps this is why it was found unpalatable. Like the foregoing, it's said to be soothing to the nerves, and also an aid to digestion and a promoter of sound sleep. Unlike the previously described tea, however, it is the *flowers*, not the leaves, of the chamomile that are used. Perhaps the chamomile tea-drinker infused the leaves instead of the flowers – or used hogweed!

Mint Teas are among the best-testing herb teas. They are light, aromatic and refreshing, can be drunk hor or cold (certain varieties chilled with ice are terrific) and can be used with other ingredients both alcoholic and otherwise to make interesting variations.

Most of the mint species described in this book make very good mint teas, which can be drunk with a sprig of the appropriate species and a thin slice of lemon on top. Serve cold with crushed ice in a tall glass, or hot in a mug. Peppermint may be infused with hot milk instead of water and drunk last thing at night before retiring if one has a cold.

Sage Tea is one I have not tried, but I did try making one with wood sage (*Teucrium scorodonia*) which needed heavy sweetening to be palatable. If you want to try this use only the young leaves, as the older ones are rather bitter. The aroma is absolutely gorgeous.

Wild Thyme is said to make a soporific tea which is also good for colds. The leaves are used, not the flowers.

Ground Ivy, according to Richard Mabey, makes 'one of the more agreeable herbal teas, cooling, and with a sharp, slight fragrance'. He goes on to say that, before the seventeenth century when hops came into use, ground ivy was used in the brewing of ale. The leaves are used rather than the flowers, but I see no reason why the flowers could not be used too – nearly all labiate family flowers are pleasant-tasting. A hundred million bees can't be wrong.

Lady's Bedstraw makes a delicious, honey-flavoured and scented herb tea – the flowers only are used. This needs no sweetening, and I can thoroughly recommend it.

Meadowsweet Tea blossom makes another superb tea – heady and fragrant and light, requiring no sweetening.

Melilot Tea, made from the flowers, is another herb tea which needs no sweetening, having its own honey-scented fragrance and taste. This is another recommended tea.

Woodruff's fragrance readily blends with that of other ingredients in fruit cups and similar drinks. Add a sprig to any fruit juice, or indeed to any cool summer beverage. Steep for as long as possible to obtain the best results. It is also very good added to hot China tea. Added to white wine it is fantastic! Don't use any sugar or you will spoil any drink to which woodruff has been added.

Finally, herbs are not, of course, the only wild plants which can be used to make teas. Other plants can be used such as elderflowers, lime blossom, rose hips etc. These will be dealt with in the chapters which include the plants in question.

7

THE VERSATILE NETTLE

If you can forget that nettles sting – they don't when they are cooked – you have at your disposal a plant that can provide you with any number of tasty dishes, plus wine and beer. Moreover, the plant is available pretty nearly all the year round and is so common that you are virtually certain to be able to find it – and in quantity – practically anywhere you go. After you have cut it, it will grow again more vigorously than before in only a few weeks. It is one of the most mineral- and vitamin-rich 'weeds'. What more could you ask, even of a 'weed'?

As if this were not enough, the nettle also provides several different medicinal and tonic uses, and is also well known for its properties as a hair rinse and conditioner, although these uses are outside the scope of this book. Centuries ago the fibres from the woody stems were also used to make cloth. Dyes were also extracted from the plant as late as during the Second World War, when they were used in the making of camouflage materials. Still, even if we just stick strictly to cooking, we shall still have our work cut out to try out all the different ways in which nettles can add interest and nutrition to our table. Don't forget rubber gloves for picking!

Up to now, I haven't been able to find any reference anywhere to a use for the small, inconspicuous, greenish tassel-like flowers of the stinging-nettle. Only the young leaves should be used, either as they start sprouting in early spring, or the young leaves at the top of the plant – the growing-point plus the next four or five leaves down the stem – later in the year, preferably before flowering. This is because the larger, coarser leaves lower down on the plant do tend to be somewhat bitter. The bitterness, like the sting, is caused by formic acid in the plant tissues, which is much less pronounced in the new, young growth. Cooking completely destroys the stinging properties, but not the bitter quality. Formic acid also has a somewhat astringent effect on the human digestive system, so it is a wise precaution not to eat too many at one time, at least not until you are used to them, or they will give you quite a runaround! A good way to accustom your interior works to the brisk effect of this plant is to combine it in small quantities with other ingredients. But, make no mistake, nettle leaves are richer in iron than spinach, as well as containing more protein than cabbage and more vitamins than many other green vegetables.

The stinging-nettle is not related to the deadnettles of the mint family, which do not sting. The stinging-nettle (*Urtica dioica*) is a member of the family Urticaceae. 'Urticating' is another word for 'stinging', and the specific name *dioica* refers to the fact that the plant is *dioecious*, that is, it bears male and female flowers on separate plants.

Now for the recipes. To cook 'straight' as spinach, just cook the leaves, well-washed, in the water adhering to them after washing for a few minutes with a little salt and pepper. Add a knob of butter when cooked. The taste is indistinguishable from spinach.

However, there are other ways in which nettle leaves can be cooked as a 'side' vegetable. Here are some of them.

Creamed Nettles

Cook the nettles as mentioned above, but add a couple of tablespoonsful of finely-chopped chives, green spring onion tops or shallots. When all are cooked, remove from heat and add top of the milk or single cream – two tablespoonsful if you are serving 4. Stir well but do not re-heat. Serve immediately.

Nettles in Béchamel Sauce

1 ½ oz./37 ½ g. butter	Nettles to serve 4
2 tablespoons plain flour	Salt and white pepper to taste
½ pint/275 ml. milk	

Make the béchamel sauce first by melting the butter in a heavy pan over a low heat and gradually stirring in the flour with a wooden spoon. Add the milk very slowly, stirring all the time until the sauce thickens. Season to taste and continue to simmer over a very low heat. You must keep stirring all the time or the mixture will burn. It will be ready in from 8 to 10 minutes.

The nettles should be chopped very finely (or put through a mincer or blender) and cooked by quickly steaming them in a very small quantity of boiling water in a lidded pan. When cooked, stir into the béchamel sauce. Pour into a serving dish and sprinkle chopped chives on top.

Nettle Balls

Enough nettles for 4
Water for cooking
Salt and pepper to taste
2 tablespoons Parmesan cheese
4 oz./100 g. breadcrumbs

2 tablespoons grated raw onion
1 oz./25 g. butter
1 egg
Oil for frying

Cook the nettles in water in the way outlined in the first recipe with the seasoning, and chop finely. Return to the pan with the butter, the grated onion and Parmesan cheese over a very low heat, stirring the while. Blend in the breadcrumbs and remove from heat. Leave to stand for about 15 minutes to allow the breadcrumbs to absorb the moisture.

Turn the mixture out on to a wooden board or working surface, and form into dumpling-size balls. Roll these in more breadcrumbs, beat the egg, dip the balls into the beaten egg and roll again in breadcrumbs. When well-coated, fry in deep fat for about 3 minutes, or until golden. Serve piping hot with tomato ketchup, home-made with fresh tomatoes.

We come now to several different varieties of soup which can be made with nettles, some relying more heavily on the nettles themselves and others combining this plant with other wildfood ingredients.

Nettle soup

½ lb./225 g. nettle leaves
2 pints/1136 ml. water
2 tablespoons cornflour
Knob of butter

Salt and pepper to taste
Grated Cheddar cheese for
  garnish

Boil the nettle leaves in the water until the latter has become deep green. Sieve the nettle leaves out, leaving just the nettle water (the boiled nettles may be used in another dish). Blend the cornflour with a little cold water until it forms a smooth paste, and stir this into the nettle water, adding seasoning and butter, and return to heat, stirring vigorously. Lower heat and simmer until the liquid is reduced by a third. Serve sprinkled with grated Cheddar cheese.

Cream of Nettle Soup

This is made exactly as in the previous recipe, but when it has reached the ready-to-serve stage, stir in 2 tablespoonsful of double cream. The soup must be removed from the heat before doing this. Serve immediately, sprinkled with grated Cheddar cheese as before.

Nettle Stockpot

This is made in the same way as the first soup recipe but 2 pints of beef stock are substituted for the water. The garnish for this variation is chopped chives, rather than cheese.

Now for some honest-to-goodness main meal dishes.

Nettle Fritters

1 lb./450 g. nettles
2 eggs
4 oz./100 g. breadcrumbs
2 tablespoons grated Cheddar
  cheese

Water to cook
Salt and pepper to taste
Oil for frying

Boil the nettles in the water until tender, then press out the water through a sieve. Chop finely and mix in the seasoning, grated cheese and well-beaten eggs. Form the mixture into flat cakes and coat with breadcrumbs. Fry in oil until golden, and serve piping hot with any sharp sauce such as tartare or horseradish.

Scottish Nettle Haggis

1 lb./450 g. nettles
Water to cook
1 lb./450 g. leeks
1 lb./450 g. savoy cabbage
8 rashers streaky bacon

4 oz./100 g. pearl barley
Salt and pepper to taste
1 tablespoon pork dripping or
 lard

Wash the nettles, slice the leeks and shred the savoy cabbage. Fry the bacon in the dripping or lard until nicely crisp without being burnt. The bacon can be snipped into bite-sized pieces with kitchen scissors, preferably before cooking. Boil the pearl barley in a little water until all the liquid is absorbed and the barley is tender. Barley takes much longer to cook than, for example, rice – be sure to check that it is properly cooked.

Now mix all the ingredients together and season well, and boil in a pudding-cloth in a large pot of water for about an hour. Serve with thick gravy. This recipe serves 8 to 12.

Nettle and Herb Savoury Pudding

1 lb./450 g. nettles
Handful dandelion leaves
Handful sorrel leaves
Handful comfrey leaves
Pinch thyme
Pinch sage
Pinch marjoram

Knob butter
Salt and pepper to taste
2 eggs
1 onion, finely chopped
1 teaspoon minced wild garlic
Water for steaming

Wash and chop the nettles, dandelion, sorrel and comfrey, and mix in a pudding-basin with the sage, thyme, marjoram, chopped onion and minced wild garlic. Beat the two eggs, then blend well into the mixture, adding seasoning and butter. When thoroughly mixed, tie a double-folded pudding-cloth over the top of the basin with string (not a rubber band) and steam for 1½ hours. The easiest way to do this is to place the basin in the top of a perforated steamer, boiling water in the bottom. The lid must, of course, be kept on the top of the steamer. If you do not have a perforated steamer, the pudding can be steamed in an ordinary large saucepan containing boiling water which must not be allowed to bubble up over the top of the pudding-cloth. Keep the lid on but check the water-level from time to time, and top up when necessary. When cooked, serve very hot with a good thick gravy. Serves 8.

Nettle Pasties

½ lb./225 g. plain flour
4 oz./100 g. lard
1 oz./25 g. butter
1 lb./450 g. nettles
Salt and pepper to taste
Pinch grated nutmeg

Pinch ground ginger (optional)
2 eggs
4 oz./100 g. grated Cheddar cheese
Water to cook
½ lb./225 g. mashed cooked potato

Make pastry by cutting lard and rubbing into the flour. Add just enough water to form a workable dough, and roll out to a medium thickness. Cut out circles round a saucer to make the pastry cases for the pasties. Some cooks season the pastry lightly with salt and pepper, if liked, but this is not strictly necessary as the filling is well seasoned.

To make the filling, wash the nettles and cook in boiling water until tender. Chop roughly after draining off the water. Melt the butter in the hot pan and return the nettles to it, adding salt, pepper, nutmeg and ginger (if used). Beat eggs thoroughly and add to the mixture, blending well, then add the cooked mashed potato and the grated Cheddar cheese. Remove from heat.

Spoon this filling on to one half of each of the pastry rounds, then fold over to make the pasties, brushing the edges with beaten egg so that they will adhere. If you have enough beaten egg to use, you may brush over the tops of the pasties lightly if you wish. Bake at 425°F./220°C. (Regulo 7) for 20 minutes, then reduce heat to 375°F./190°C. (Regulo 5) for a further 20 minutes, to finish off. The colour should be a light golden. This quantity makes 8 pasties.

Baked Nettle and Potato Pie

1 lb./450 g. mashed cooked potato
½ lb./225 g. nettles
6 spring onions

2 oz./50 g. butter
½ pint/275 ml. milk
Salt and pepper to taste
Water to cook nettles

Boil the nettles in a little water until tender, then drain off the water. Chop the nettles roughly, chop the spring onions, including their green tops, and mix together with the mashed cooked potato, seasoning to taste, and add the milk, stirring thoroughly to blend all the ingredients. Put the mixture into a buttered baking-dish (no lid is needed) and dot the surface with butter. Bake at 375°F./190°C. (Regulo 5) for about half an hour or until heated through and nicely browned, rather like a shepherd's pie.

Chicken with Nettles and Barley

This is adapted from an old traditional Scottish recipe. I have simplified the recipe considerably in the interests of economy and time in preparation.

One fresh chicken about	2 pints water
2½ lb./1350 g.	Salt and pepper to taste
1 lb./450 g. nettles	Knob of butter
2 bay leaves	2 teaspoons minced wild garlic
4 oz./100 g. pearl barley	1 medium onion

Wash the nettles and chop small, and put into a large heavy pot with the chicken in 2 pints of water. Bring to the boil and add the barley, bay leaves, knob of butter, the onion peeled and chopped, the garlic and the seasoning. Simmer until the chicken is tender and the liquid is reduced to about half. Serves 4 to 6.

Nettles can also be used to make at least two non-alcoholic beverages (see Chapter 17).

8

DANDELION DAYS

As I write these words the dandelions are abundantly in flower. One does not need to go far afield; this plant has successfully colonized even the most built-up areas of the inner cities. This chapter is about the uses of the leaves in cooking. I already mentioned their use in salads in Chapter 2. The roots can also be used to make a substitute for coffee (see Chapter 17).

I mentioned in Chapter 2 that only the young leaves of dandelion should be used, as the older leaves are bitter. The same applies to gathering the leaves for cooking. Avoid the mature, very large leaves as the bitterness is not lost in cooking. The young and tender leaves are most abundant, of course, in early spring, but this is not the only time when one can pick them. Fresh new leaves keep springing up throughout the growing season, and new plants start to grow after the windborne seeds have found even a precarious foothold in the sparse soil of old bombsites, rubbish-dumps and waste ground in urban areas.

Before going on to the recipes, a word of warning will not be out of place here. The somewhat ribald names given to some French dishes based on this plant, which are also reflected in some of the local English names for the plant itself, betray its reputation as a diuretic. It is wise, therefore, to eat it in small quantities, at least to start with, to see how it affects your particular waterworks!

Dandelion Soup

Handful young dandelion leaves
2 pints/1150 ml. water
1 onion, peeled and minced
2 tablespoons butter
2 eggs (yolk only)
¼ pint/150 ml. double cream
Salt and black pepper to taste
Paprika to garnish

Start by sautéeing the minced onion in the butter in the bottom of the pan in which you are going to cook the soup. The onion should be just tender but not browned. If you burn it throw it out and begin again, or you'll ruin the taste of the soup!

When ready, throw in the washed dandelion leaves and pour in the water, and bring to the boil. Season with salt and black pepper, stir well, then lower the heat and simmer until the leaves are disintegrating into the liquid.

While this is cooking, beat together the egg yolks with the cream. Remove the soup from the heat when ready so as to bring it off the boil, and leave it for a short time before adding the beaten egg and cream mixture so that it does not curdle. Stirring all the time, replace the pan over the lowest heat setting and simmer until the mixture thickens. When it has thickened to a smooth, creamy consistency, it is ready. A dash of paprika on top makes a colourful decoration when the soup is in the tureen. Serves 4 to 6.

Buttered Dandelion

Enough dandelion leaves for 4
1 oz./25 g. butter
2 tablespoons chopped chives
(or green spring onion tops)

2 teaspoons chopped parsley
Salt and black pepper to taste
Squeeze of lemon juice

Cook the dandelion leaves in just the water adhering to them after washing. When tender add the butter, salt and pepper, and simmer on a low heat, turning frequently. Add the chopped chives (or spring onion tops) and simmer for a short while longer. Stir well, and remove from the pan. The liquid from cooking should have been absorbed by this time. Serve with a squeeze of lemon juice and garnish with parsley. This makes a particularly good side dish to serve with fish.

Creamed Dandelions on Fried Bread

Enough dandelion leaves for 4
Salt and pepper to taste
Water to cook

2 tablespoons single cream
4 slices bread
Fat for frying

Boil the dandelion leaves in water, adding salt and pepper, and when well cooked pass them through a sieve to make a purée. Blend with the cream, and re-heat over the lowest setting to keep hot while you fry the bread, then pile it on top. I find that the best fat to use is that in which bacon and mushrooms have been cooked.

Now for one or two quiche recipes using dandelions. Since these will not be the only recipes of this kind in the book, this section begins with a basic recipe for the shortcrust pastry used to make the cases. The sugar included when making a case for a sweet flan is optional: the calorie-conscious may omit it. The quantities given will make enough pastry to line a 7- or 8-inch (20 cm.) flan tin. A quiche or flan of this size is just right to serve 4.

Basic Shortcrust Pastry

8 oz./225 g. plain flour
4 oz./100 g. margarine
Pinch of salt
1 oz./25 g. granulated sugar (for
  a sweet flan only)

2 tablespoons (approx.) cold
  water

Sift the flour with the salt into the mixing-bowl. (If you are making a sweet flan and using sugar, include it at this stage.) Cut the margarine into the flour and then rub it in with the finger-tips to form a fine crumbly mixture. Add the cold water very gradually, blending it in with the back of a knife. The dough should be soft yet firm enough to form into a ball. Knead a little, then wrap the ball in foil and chill in the fridge for half an hour before rolling out to line the flan tin, which should be lightly greased beforehand.

A pastry case for a flan or quiche is first baked 'blind' before the filling is inserted and the complete flan or quiche baked. This does involve two baking operations but cannot be avoided, because, if the whole thing were done in one operation, the length of time needed to cook the filling would be far too long for the pastry, which would be burnt black!

To bake 'blind' there are two methods. The simplest one is to prick the dough all over with a fork and line it with greaseproof paper or aluminium foil, and then bake it at the recommended temperature in the recipe for about 10 minutes (in a pre-heated oven). The second method, which is preferred by many cooks as it produces a much crisper pastry, is to fill the flan tin, lined with dough but not with any paper or foil, with beans, rice, lentils or peas (dry and uncooked) and bake for the same length of time at the same temperature, again in a pre-heated oven. The beans or other filling cannot be re-used in cooking, but they can be re-used again and again for the purpose of 'baking blind', and kept in an airtight tin labelled accordingly.

I have been asked several times whether one should first line the dough with greaseproof paper or foil *before* putting in the beans, so I have been consulting the experts, some of whom say you should and others say it does not matter a jot, so I will settle for saying that you can please yourself. Another question I have been asked is whether the greaseproof paper lining you use should be greased or not. A light coating of grease on the side facing the dough will prevent its sticking to the pastry when you remove it. Foil need not be greased as it will not stick anyway.

Flan and quiche cases can be made in advance and then kept until required in the deep-freeze. It saves a lot of time to make up a batch of them at one go. Then, when you have been out on a wildfood-gathering expedition and have brought home something to make into a tasty dish for lunch or supper, all you have to do is to defrost the pastry case while you are putting the filling together.

Dandelion Quiche

A 7- or 8-inch/20 cm. flan case
½ lb./225 g. young dandelion
  leaves
Water to cook
Salt and pepper to taste

6 oz./175 g. curd cheese
2 eggs
Pinch of nutmeg
1 oz./25 g. grated Parmesan
  cheese

Wash the dandelion leaves and boil (or steam if preferred) until tender. Remove from liquid or steamer and drain off any liquid still adhering. When cooled, chop coarsely, season with salt and pepper, and mix with the curd cheese. Beat the eggs until light and frothy, then blend well with the other ingredients. Spoon into the flan case, cover the top with the grated Parmesan cheese and sprinkle with nutmeg. Bake in a pre-heated oven at 350°F./180°C. (Regulo 4) for about 30 minutes. Serve hot or cold. A home-made tomato ketchup, made with fresh tomatoes, goes very well with this one.

Dandelion and Yoghourt Flan

A 7- or 8-inch/20 cm. flan case
½ lb./225 g. young dandelion
  leaves
Water to cook
5 fl. oz./150 ml. carton plain
  yoghourt

¼ pint/150 ml. milk
3 eggs
4 oz./100 g. grated Cheddar
  cheese
Salt and white pepper to taste
Fresh parsley to garnish

Cook the dandelion leaves as in the previous recipe, drain off any adherent liquid, cool and chop coarsely. Arrange the cooked chopped dandelion leaves on the bottom of the flan case. Beat the eggs, add the milk and yoghourt, and season with salt and pepper. Spread the grated Cheddar cheese over the dandelion leaves in the flan case and pour the egg, milk and yoghourt mixture on top. Bake at 375°F./190°C. (Regulo 5) in a pre-heated oven for 30 to 35 minutes, or until set. Decorate with the parsley, and serve hot.

Pissenlit au lard

Handful of dandelion leaves
A few lettuce leaves
2 shallots
1 clove of garlic
Salt and pepper to taste

Olive oil for dressing
2 tablespoons white wine
  vinegar
½ lb./225 g. boiled pork or fat
  bacon

Wash the dandelion leaves and mix with the lettuce leaves, both torn (not cut) into bite-sized pieces. Peel and chop the shallots, crush the garlic, and mix with the leaves in a salad bowl. Dress with the olive oil and toss so that all the ingredients are well coated.

Chop the pork or bacon into good-sized cubes and fry in their own fat in a pan until they are much reduced in size, nicely crisp, and the fat runs out into the pan. Now pour the vinegar into the pan and stir, cooking until the vinegar has mostly evaporated. At this point you should pour the pork or bacon with the fat and liquid from the pan over the salad. Toss together quickly and serve immediately while hot.

9

SORREL IS FOR STARTERS

The most popular starter to a main meal, in Britain at any rate, is soup. In winter the hungry diner looks forward to an honest-to-goodness, down-to-earth, heartwarming soup, substantial enough to take the edge off his – or her – appetite. In summer one still can look forward to soup, but then it should be light and refreshing, even chilled straight from the fridge. One of our commonest waste-ground weeds – sorrel – can provide both.

Sorrel has been used in English cuisine as far back as Tudor times, but it has never enjoyed the popularity it deserves. The French, however, have always valued the culinary joys of this plant, and sorrel figures prominently in many of their national dishes. Just recently it would appear that the British are beginning to appreciate it more, for I have seen it in several of the larger supermarkets and better-class greengrocers' shops, imported from France. This is the cultivated variety, which has a slightly milder flavour than our native 'weed'. However, the young leaves picked from the top of the plant have this same mild flavour; if you prefer the more robust-flavoured lower leaves, go ahead. Unlike some other wild plants, the larger and older leaves are not bitter, though they may be slightly coarser-textured. Use your discretion which kind you use, according to the dish you are making and its mode of preparation.

First, something about the plant. The common sorrel is known scientifically as *Rumex acetosa*. To the botanist, the generic name *Rumex* places it fairly and squarely in the dock family, or Polygonaceae; the specific name *acetosa* betokens its sharp flavour, which has a refreshing citrus-like tang, more like lemon than anything else. It certainly does not taste like vinegar, as some writers aver – writers who, I feel, have never tasted it!

Sorrel is one of the first native wild plants to burst into leaf in

a, Common sorrel (*Rumex acetosa*); b, Bistort (*Polygonum bistorta*)

| 1 Flower spike branched | 1 Flower spike unbranched |
| 2 Leaves arrow-shaped | 2 Leaves narrow-triangular |

spring. The young and tender leaves can be picked as early as February in some areas. Waste places, grassy banks, railway embankments and similar situations are the best places to look for it. It grows up to 2 feet (60 cm.) high and has arrow-shaped leaves which are very distinctive; the lower leaves have long stalks, while the upper ones clasp the stem. The long flower spikes, which ripen in early summer, changing from their earlier green to reddish-brown, are not used in cookery. When the oval seeds ripen they look like clusters of dozens of downwards-drooping 'fingers' – hence the Kent local name for the plant, which is 'Tom Thumb's Thousand Fingers'!

I had my first introduction to sorrel soup twenty years ago, when I was head of biology at a girls' convent boarding school where a nun named Sister Jadwiga, from Olsztyn in Poland, was the cook. While I struggled to imbue my sometimes reluctant students with a love of botany, Sister Jadwiga was cooking, among other things, sorrel soup as one of the delights for our staff lunches. At that time I was not into wildfoods cookery, but this soup was unquestionably the most delicious I had ever tasted. Now, twenty years later and having tasted nearly all the soups described in this book, and survived a number of others which I deemed prudent not to include, I am still of the same opinion.

There are at least a dozen different recipes for making sorrel soup, of which I shall give you the best and easiest ones, starting with the original recipe which I persuaded Sister Jadwiga to let me have for this book. She is now over eighty years old and still lives at the convent, although a younger Sister now does the cooking.

Sister Jadwiga's Sorrel Soup

I have of course adapted the quantities to serve 4, as her original recipe gave quantities to serve the 20 members of staff.

1 lb./450 g. washed sorrel leaves	2 tablespoons plain flour
2 onions	Salt and white pepper to taste
1 bay leaf	2 eggs (yolks only)
2 pints/1150 ml. water	

Chop the washed sorrel leaves coarsely, peel and chop the onions, and put into a large pan with the bay leaf, salt and pepper and the water. (Sister Jadwiga says that if you have some light chicken stock or clear beef broth, you can use that instead of water if you prefer.) Bring to the boil, then reduce heat and simmer for about an hour. Remove bay. Make the flour into a smooth, cream-like paste with a little cold water, and add this to the soup to thicken it, stirring frequently to avoid the flour forming lumps or sticking to the bottom of the pan. Beat the egg yolks until light and frothy, and take the soup off the boil, leaving it to cool slightly before stirring the beaten egg into it, so as to avoid curdling.

Cream of Sorrel Soup

1 lb./450 g. washed sorrel leaves
2 tablespoons breadcrumbs
2 pints/1150 ml. water
2 bay leaves
1 oz./25 g. butter

1 pint/575 ml. single cream
Salt and white pepper to taste
Finely chopped chives to
    garnish
A few croûtons

Chop the washed sorrel leaves and fry them in the butter, then put the leaves together with their juice and butter into a large pan together with the water, seasoning, bay leaves and breadcrumbs (these should be crumbled from a fresh loaf, not the dried 'coating' variety). Simmer for about 40 minutes, then remove from heat, take out and discard the bay, and when the soup has cooled slightly, stir in the cream. Re-heat if necessary but on no account allow it to boil. Serve in individual bowls garnished with chives and croûtons. This quantity serves 4 to 6.

Sorrel Soup (French Style)

1 lb./450 g. washed sorrel leaves
4 oz./100 g. butter
4 cloves garlic
2 pints/1150 ml. chicken stock

Salt and white pepper to taste
2 oz./50 g. plain flour
½ pint/275 ml. double cream

Chop the washed sorrel leaves. Put half the butter into a heavy frying-pan and melt over a low heat. Peel the garlic cloves but do not crush them. Add the whole garlic cloves and fry for about two minutes, then add the chopped sorrel leaves and cook for a further 10 minutes. In the soup pan melt the rest of the butter and add the flour very gradually, stirring all the time. The heat must be at its lowest setting for this operation, which is what the French call making a 'roux', and when you see this term in an English cookbook, that is what you have to do. It's quite tricky to do without ruining the whole thing by burning.

When the roux has reached the right consistency, stir in the chicken stock very gradually, having first pre-heated it without boiling. Bring slowly to the boil and simmer for about 10 minutes. Now add the sorrel and garlic, and season to taste. Mix thoroughly and give the soup a final simmer, then put the whole lot through a blender, return to the heat but do not boil. Remove from heat, and when it has cooled slightly stir in the cream.

Herbed Sorrel and Tomato Soup

1 lb./450 g. washed sorrel leaves
1 lb./450 g. peeled fresh
  tomatoes
1 oz./25 g. butter
2 teaspoons basil

Salt and white pepper to taste
Garlic to taste (optional)
1½ pints/850 ml. chicken stock
½ pint/275 ml. single cream

Chop the washed sorrel leaves and fry lightly in the butter over a low heat until softened. Chop the tomatoes roughly and add to the pan, together with the garlic (chopped) if used. Continue frying for about 8 to 10 minutes, then turn out into the soup pan and add the stock, seasoning and basil. Bring to the boil, then reduce heat and simmer for about half an hour. Remove from heat and allow to cool slightly before stirring in the cream.

Chilled Sorrel Soup

1 lb./450 g. sorrel leaves
2 pints/1150 ml. chicken stock
2 tablespoons chopped fresh
  parsley

2 tablespoons chopped celery
¼ pint/150 ml. plain yoghourt
Salt and white pepper to taste
Cucumber slices to garnish

Wash the sorrel leaves, then chop coarsely and put in a large pot together with the chopped parsley and celery. Add the stock and the seasoning and bring to the boil, then reduce heat and simmer for 45 minutes. Leave to cool, then pour the soup into a large tureen and when quite cold stir in the yoghourt. Chill in the fridge, and when ready to serve, garnish with thin slices of cucumber. Serves 5 to 6.

With all those starters to choose from, it might be understandable to imagine that we have now exhausted the possibilities of sorrel. Not so. We can cook it as a side vegetable, use it in an omelet, make it into fritters, quiches and soufflés, and any number of other tasty main dishes. About the only thing you can't use it for are sweet dishes. Here are some of the best recipes.

Sorrel as a side vegetable

Enough sorrel leaves for 4
Water to cook

Salt and pepper to taste
Knob of butter

Wash the sorrel leaves, chop coarsely and cook in a very little water with the seasoning for 7 or 8 minutes over medium heat. When tender, drain off the moisture and toss in the hot pan with a knob of butter.

Creamed sorrel

Enough sorrel leaves for 4
1 oz./25 g. butter

Salt and pepper to taste
¼ pint/150 ml. single cream

Wash the sorrel leaves, chop coarsely and fry lightly in the butter with the salt and pepper until tender. Remove from heat and allow to cool slightly. Stir in the cream, re-heat and serve immediately.

Herb and Sorrel Omelet

8 eggs
4 teaspoons water
Butter to cook omelets
4 tablespoons finely chopped
  sorrel leaves

2 tablespoons finely chopped
  chives
1 tablespoon finely chopped
  wild chervil

Beat the eggs two at a time for each omelet, adding one teaspoon of cold water to each. Add one tablespoon of sorrel leaves, half a tablespoon of chives and a quarter tablespoon of wild chervil for each omelet. Whisk the mixture until light and fluffy, and cook the omelets in the usual way. When I make this dish I omit the seasoning, allowing each person to season his or her omelet at table according to taste.

Sorrel Fritters

For the batter:

4 oz./100 g. plain flour   1 egg
Pinch of salt   Oil for frying
¼ pint/150 ml. milk

For the filling:

Enough sorrel leaves for 4   Salt and pepper to taste
Water to cook

Sift the flour with the salt and stir in the milk a little at a time. Beat the egg until light and fluffy and fold into the mixture. The consistency of the batter should be a fairly thick but not stiff cream. If it is too stiff, it may be thinned with a little cold water. Stand in a cool place for a little while, and meantime make the filling by cooking the washed sorrel leaves in a very small quantity of water with the seasoning until tender. When cooked, leave to cool and chop coarsely.

Heat oil in a deep frying-pan to 425°F./220°C. Make sure you have a cooking thermometer. It's as essential an item in the kitchen as a wooden spoon. Dip tablespoonsful of the cooked sorrel leaves into the batter, patting them in the spoon so that they stick together, and drop into the hot fat. When one side is golden-brown, turn and cook the other side. Remove from fat when ready and drain on kitchen paper. Serve piping hot with chips and a dab of Worcester sauce. These quantities make 16 fritters – four for each person.

Sorrel Quiche

1 lb./450 g. washed sorrel leaves   Salt and pepper to taste
2 oz./50 g. butter   2 tablespoons grated Parmesan
5 fl. oz./150 ml. double cream   cheese
2 eggs   A 7- or 8-inch/20 cm. flan case.

Chop the sorrel leaves and cook them in the butter until tender, adding the seasoning. When cooked, remove from heat, allow to cool a little and stir in the cream a little at a time. Beat the eggs until light and fluffy, and add to the mixture (do not return it to the heat). Pour the mixture into the pastry case, smoothing the top neatly, and sprinkle with the grated Parmesan cheese. Bake at 400°F./200°C.

(Regulo 6) for 10 minutes, then lower the setting to 350°F./180°C. (Regulo 4) and cook for a further 20 minutes or until set and the topping is golden-brown. This quiche may be served either hot or cold.

Sorrel Soufflé

A lidded frying-pan, a saucepan and a soufflé dish are required to cook this recipe.

1 lb./450 g. washed sorrel leaves	Salt and pepper to taste
2 small onions, peeled and minced	1 oz./25 g. plain flour
	½ pint/275 ml. milk
3 oz./75 g. butter	4 eggs

Soften the minced onions in one ounce of the butter over a very low heat without browning them. Chop the sorrel leaves fairly finely, season to taste and cook in the pan with the onions, covered with the lid. When tender, remove from heat.

In the saucepan melt the rest of the butter and add the flour very gradually. Bring the milk to the boil, and stir this gradually into the flour and butter mixture while just off the boil. Season well and remove from heat. Separate the eggs, and beat the yolks, adding to the mixture. Now add the sorrel and onion mixture from the other pan, and stir well.

Beat the egg whites until very stiff (I use a hand-held electric blender for this). Fold into the mixture and pour into a greased soufflé dish. Bake at 400°F./200°C. (Regulo 6) for the first two minutes (in a pre-heated oven) and then lower the setting to 375°F./190°C. (Regulo 5) and cook for a further 20 to 25 minutes. Serve hot.

Sorrel Pasties

Enough sorrel leaves for 4	4 oz./100 g. plain flour
1 onion	Salt and pepper to taste
2 oz./50 g. lard	Oil for frying

Wash the sorrel leaves, chop fairly finely and mix with the onion, peeled and minced. Mix the flour, lard and seasoning to make a

dough (adding a little cold water) and roll out thinly. Cut into rounds
approximately 4 inches (10 cm.) in diameter. Season the sorrel and
onion mixture and spoon into the centre of each round of dough,
folding the latter over and pressing the edges together to form
pasties. Drop into hot oil and fry, turning once, until each side is
golden-brown. Serve hot. This quantity makes about 12 pasties.

OTHER PLANTS IN THE SORREL FAMILY

The bistort (Polygonum bistorta) is an easily-recognizable relative of
sorrel. It has a single unbranched flower-spike of dense pink flowerlets, blooming from June to October. The leaves are triangular,
rather narrow, the upper ones heart-shaped at their bases where they
join the stem. Meadows, woods and roadsides are the main habitats,
but the plant is common only in the north, becoming more scattered
and intermittent in its appearance in other areas of the country. It is
not found on limestone soils and occurs only sporadically in Ireland.
Where it does occur, however, it forms large patches, up to 2 feet
(60 cm.) high.

This is the plant, called 'Easter ledges' in northern England, which
is the main ingredient of the famous 'Easter Ledges Pudding', a
traditional dish in those regions. There is an immense variety of
recipes for this pudding, according to the locality. The following one
comes from the Lake District.

Easter Ledges Pudding

Good handful of bistort leaves	2 eggs
A few nettle tops	Salt and pepper to taste
Some lady's mantle leaves	1 oz./25 g. butter
Water to cook	

Wash all the green leaves and chop coarsely, and boil for 10 minutes,
then strain off the liquid. Beat one of the eggs well and add to the
cooked leaves. Hard-boil the other egg, then chop very small and add
this, too. Season with salt and pepper, and mix in the softened butter.
Transfer the mixture to a pudding-basin and tie a pudding-cloth over
the top. Boil for 40 minutes. This pudding was – and I believe still is –
traditionally eaten with veal, much as Yorkshire pudding is traditionally eaten with roast beef.

Lady's mantle (*Alchemilla vulgaris*) is a member of the rose family which grows from 8 to 14 inches (20–35 cm.) tall in grassy places, flowering from May to September. It is much commoner in the north. If you cannot find this plant to use as a subsidiary constituent of Easter Ledges Pudding, don't worry. Another north-country recipe substitutes young dandelion leaves for lady's mantle. Yet another recipe, from Yorkshire, says that you can 'add one or two other green herbs if you like' without specifying which. Some that grow in your area could be the easiest choice.

If you always thought that dock leaves were useful only to relieve the irritation from stinging-nettles, you may be surprised to know

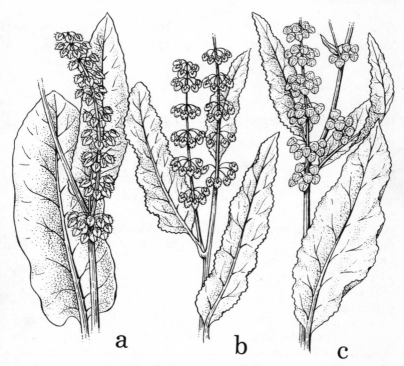

a, Broad-leaved dock (*Rumex obtusifolius*); b, Curled dock (*R. crispus*); c, Northern dock (*R. longifolius*)

(a) Leaves broad oblong
(c) Leaves broad with wavy margins

(b) Leaves narrow with wavy margins

that they have a certain limited culinary use. Only the very young leaves can be used, as the large ones are very bitter. Our three common species all belong to the genus *Rumex*, like sorrel. Unfortunately the taste is quite dissimilar. Their taste more resembles that of vine leaves, as used by the Greeks and Greek-Cypriots in cooking stuffed vine leaves, one of their national dishes. I give here two recipes of this ilk using dock leaves. The three species to look for are *Rumex obtusifolius*, the broad-leaved dock, which is common everywhere on bare and waste ground and needs no description; *R. crispus*, the curled dock, with wavy edges to the leaves, an equally common weed especially in cultivated areas; and *R. longifolius*, the northern dock, also wavy-edged but occurring only in the northern parts of Britain. The first-named flowers from May to October, the second species from June to October, and the northern species during June and July only. All grow anything up to 3 feet (90 cm.) tall.

Stuffed Dock Leaves

Enough young dock leaves for 4
A little olive oil
2 onions
2 oz./50 g. cooked brown rice
Salt and pepper to taste
1 oz./25 g. butter

2 tablespoons double cream
1 egg (yolk only)
1 teaspoon chopped fresh sage
1 teaspoon chopped fresh marjoram
Oil for frying

Wash the dock leaves, then pour boiling water over them and leave them thus for a short time; this helps to dispel any slight bitterness and also softens them. Afterwards drain off the water and dry by patting with a clean tea-towel, and brush lightly on both sides with olive oil.

Peel and mince the onions and fry in the butter over a low heat until soft but not browned. Remove from heat and stir in the cream a little at a time, season to taste, add the herbs and blend with the cooked rice. Turn out into a dish. Beat the egg yolk and incorporate this into the mixture to bind it.

Place a spoonful of the stuffing mixture in the centre of each dock leaf and roll it up, tucking the ends in to form little parcels. If you like you can tie them up with cotton to ensure that they do not fall apart during cooking. Then drop into hot oil, in which they will take only a few minutes to cook. Serve hot with horseradish or soy sauce.

Dock and Minced Meat Parcels

Enough young dock leaves for 4
A little olive oil
1 medium onion
2 oz./50 g. breadcrumbs (soft)
6 oz./175 g. minced meat
Salt and pepper to taste

2 teaspoons fresh wild garlic
1 egg (yolk only)
1 teaspoon chopped fresh
  parsley
1 teaspoon chopped fresh thyme
2 oz./50 g. butter
Oil for frying

Treat the dock leaves exactly as in the previous recipe. Fry the onion in the butter just as described in the last recipe. Without removing from heat, stir in the minced meat, salt and pepper and garlic, and continue stirring over low heat until the meat is cooked. Now remove from heat and transfer to a basin, add the herbs and the soft breadcrumbs, and mix to form a stiff paste. Beat the egg yolk and use to bind the mixture, as before.

Place spoonsful of the stuffing in the dock leaves and wrap as in the previous recipe to form parcels, tying with cotton for safety before frying in hot oil for a few minutes. Serve with home-made tomato ketchup, made with fresh tomatoes, or with a dash of Worcester sauce.

A NOTE ABOUT WOOD SORREL

Wood sorrel (*Oxalis acetosella*) is not related at all to the sorrel mentioned earlier in this chapter but is a member of an entirely different family, the Oxalidaceae. It has a taste very similar to sorrel and can be used in all the recipes in which sorrel is used, as well as raw in salads. The whole plant can be used, including the stems and the flowers. This plant, however, contains oxalic acid, which although poisonous in large quantities is perfectly harmless if only small quantities are used.

Wood sorrel is found in woods and shady places, especially in pinewoods. It is common throughout Britain and flowers from April to June. The flowers, which have five petals, are white, usually veined delicately with mauve, occasionally purple. Like the flowers, the leaves are borne on slender, delicate stems. The leaves are trefoil, like a clover, and frequently close up as shown in the illustration. These tiny plants seldom grow more than 4 inches (10 cm.) high, but usually form a carpet over the ground where they occur.

This plant was known as a salad vegetable as long ago as the fourteenth century, and later was cultivated in gardens for salad use. Because of the necessity to avoid eating large quantities, wood sorrel is better used in salads than cooked as a vegetable or used as a substantial ingredient in a main dish.

10

BACK TO YOUR ROOTS

Compared with the wealth of recipes using leaves, stems, flowers, fruits, nuts and seeds, the number of dishes that can be prepared from wild roots is sparse indeed. Added to this is the complication that it is now illegal to dig up wild plants, unless growing on private property, or abundant weeds. I am therefore omitting all those plants which can be considered rare, uncommon or of sporadic occurrence. Those used include common widespread weeds, and also plants which may quite possibly be found growing in your own garden or on privately owned land. In the latter case the best course of action is to ask the owner of the farmland or other private ground for permission to dig up a few of the desired plants. When I have on occasion done this I have never yet been refused permission. One or two of the wild plants described have cultivated varieties which can be substituted if necessary.

Three of the plants described are spiny and thistle-like (one is a true thistle) so you may not want to dig one of those up anyway!

Roots should be harvested in the autumn if possible, because the longer the plants are left growing during the summer, the more time they will have to build up reserves of starch in their roots, and from our point of view, therefore, the later we leave them in the ground, the more succulent they will be.

ARUM LILY (ARUM MACULATUM)

This plant also goes by a number of other names such as cuckoo-pint, lords and ladies, Jack-in-the-pulpit etc. The name 'arum lily' is a misnomer, as this plant is not a lily and belongs to quite a different family, the Aroideae. 'Wild arum' would, perhaps, be a better name

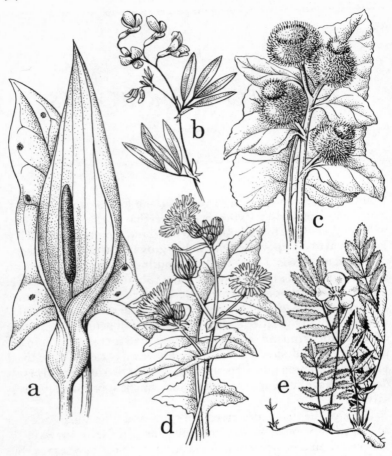

Plants with edible roots: a, Arum lily (*Arum maculatum*);
b, Bitter vetch (*Lathyrus montanus*); c, Burdock (*Arctium
lappa*); d, Sow-thistle (*Sonchus oleraceus*); e, Silverweed
(*Potentilla anserina*)

for it. The plant is common everywhere in shady places, the deep
shade of woods being its favourite habitat, but it is almost as
frequently found in overgrown hedge bottoms and on grassy banks
overshadowed by vegetation.

The arrow-shaped leaves appear early in spring, and as they
mature they become blotched with purple to a greater or lesser
degree. In April and May the flower appears, a pale greenish-white

spathe or hood, enclosing the conspicuous purple spadix. The fruit is a cluster of brilliant orange berries which is a familiar hedgerow object later in the year.

Although all parts of the plant contain a very poisonous alkaloid, this substance is entirely destroyed by baking at a high temperature. Only the root is used, and if it is thoroughly baked right through, the toxin is rendered harmless.

In the past the roots of this plant were baked and ground into flour, which was known as 'Portland arrowroot' because the trade in this product was centred around Portland in Dorset. It was used as a substitute for arrowroot or sago.

BITTER VETCH (LATHYRUS MONTANUS)

This plant, sometimes also known as bitter vetchling, is everywhere abundant, except in East Anglia. It prefers heathy areas, scrub and open woodland. It can be recognized by the leaves ending in points and not tendrils, and by the small spikes of from two to six flowers, which are reddish-purple fading to blue at the bases of the flower-spikes. The flowers bloom from April to July and are followed by reddish-brown pods of seeds.

Don't let the name put you off – the root is perfectly edible and has no bitter taste. Gerard, in his 16th century *Herbal*, likened the taste to that of chestnut. The roots are simply boiled and eaten and have sometimes been used in Scotland as a subsistence crop, either raw or dried.

BURDOCK (ARCTIUM LAPPA)

This abundant weed of waste places is related to the thistles but is not a true thistle, as the leaves and stems are not spiny. The flowerheads are not spined but are surrounded by hooked bracts (burs), and these flowerheads, being compact, globular and purple in colour, give the plant a thistle-like appearance. The huge leaves, however, are more reminiscent of rhubarb – hence its local name of wild rhubarb in Somerset and pig's rhubarb in Dorset. This conspicuous plant grows up to about 3 feet (90 cm.) high and flowers from July to September. In the USA this same species grows up to 10 feet (3 m.) high!

The root of this plant is very tasty and can be used either as a side vegetable to accompany a main dish or as a main dish in its own right. Here are some recipes from America, where the burdock seems to be more popular than it is here. I am indebted for the recipes to my Mennonite friends Maria van Booys and Neltje Kaufman.

Parsleyed Burdock Root

½ lb./225 g. burdock root
3 tablespoons butter
Salt and freshly ground black
  pepper to taste

3 tablespoons chopped fresh
  parsley
Water to cook
Few drops lemon juice

Peel the burdock root, cut into slices and boil until tender. Drain off the water and put the burdock slices back into the pan with the butter, salt and pepper, parsley and lemon juice. Toss in the pan until they are well coated with the seasoned parsley butter, and serve hot.

Burdock Root Patties

½ lb./225 g. burdock root
2 onions
Water to cook
1 egg
4 tablespoons soft breadcrumbs

Salt and pepper to taste
1 tablespoon chopped fresh
  parsley
Butter for frying

Peel the burdock root and boil till tender, then mince or pass through a blender. Peel and mince the onion (chop very finely if you do not have a mincer). Mix the burdock, onions and breadcrumbs, add the seasoning, and bind with the well-beaten egg. Turn out on to a board and shape into patties. Sprinkle the parsley on the surface of each patty (both sides) and press into the surface. Fry the patties in the butter, turning once, until golden brown. This quantity makes 4 to 6 patties.

Burdock Root in Orange Sauce

½ lb./225 g. burdock root
6 fl. oz./175 ml. orange juice
  (natural unsweetened)
1 tablespoon light brown sugar
1 tablespoon cornflour

Pinch of salt
Water to cook burdock and to
  mix cornflour
Thin slices of orange for garnish

Peel burdock root and boil with salt until tender, and cut into bite-sized pieces. Simmer the orange juice and the sugar for 5 minutes in a heavy pan. Mix the cornflour with water to make a smooth cream-like paste, and add to the orange juice and sugar mixture, stirring all the time. Add the burdock root pieces and simmer a further 10 minutes. Serve hot garnished with orange slices.

Burdock Root with Pineapple Tidbits

½ lb./225 g. burdock root
1 small can pineapple tidbits
2 tablespoons butter
1 tablespoon light brown sugar

1 teaspoon lemon juice
1 tablespoon cornflour
Water to cook

Peel the burdock root, boil until tender and slice into rounds. Melt butter in a heavy frying-pan, stir in the brown sugar and lemon juice and set aside. Drain the pineapple syrup from the can of tidbits and mix with the cornflour smoothly, then add to the butter and sugar mixture. Reduce heat and stir continuously until the mixture has thickened. Add burdock root rounds and pineapple tidbits to the mixture and heat through. Serve hot.

Glazed Burdock Slices

1 lb./450 g. burdock root
2 tablespoons honey
2 tablespoons light brown sugar
2 oz./50 g. butter

2 oz./50 g. long-grain rice
2 tablespoons chopped fresh
  parsley
Water to cook

Peel burdock root, boil until tender and slice into rounds. While still hot, pat dry in kitchen paper towels. Mix sugar and honey and roll the burdock rounds in the mixture. Melt butter in a heavy frying-pan and fry the burdock rounds gently over a very low heat, turning often until completely glazed. Serve on a bed of hot rice which should be cooking while you are preparing the burdock. Garnish with parsley. Serves 8.

CHICORY (CICHORIUM INTYBUS)

This plant, the 'succory' of the old herbalists, grows anything up to 4 feet (1.20 m.) in height, and is one of the easily recognized members of the Compositae or daisy family on account of its brilliant corn-flower-blue flowers and its dandelion-like leaves. It is common in the southern part of England on roadsides and waste places, flowering from July to October. It is more abundant on chalk and limestone soils than elsewhere.

The roots are used to make a substitute for coffee, or to add to real coffee. Used alone it is rather bitter, but when added to real coffee it imparts the flavour known commercially as 'French style' coffee.

Wash the roots, cut them into small pieces and lay them out on a baking-sheet. Roast in a very slow oven until dark brown. Turn frequently so that they are roasted right through. Then put them through a coffee grinder, a mill or a food processor, and use as coffee, or add a proportion to ordinary ground coffee, as much or as little as you like.

In Middle Eastern countries the roots of chicory are boiled and eaten as a vegetable.

COUCHGRASS (AGROPYRON REPENS)

Believe it or not, you can eat grass – at least its roots, if you choose this particular species which, as I'm sure you know, is a noisome perennial weed and the bane of gardeners – it's 'twitch' to them. No one is going to mind in the least if you dig the stuff up – rather the reverse. Surprisingly, the root is sweet-tasting when peeled and boiled, and one source states that it was 'a staple food of medieval peasants' – though it does not specify where.

Couchgrass is better known, however, as a source of root 'coffee'. It is peeled, cut into pieces and roasted in exactly the same way as chicory or dandelion root, and then used to make 'coffee'. The plant is very rich in minerals, and the old herbals give a good many medicinal uses for it, though these are outside the scope of this book.

DANDELION (TARAXACUM OFFICINALE)

The dandelion needs no description. Common everywhere, it is one of our most useful and versatile plants. The flowers make a very fine wine, the leaves are good in salad and can also be cooked in a variety of ways, and the roots are well known for being the source of dandelion 'coffee'. I never fail to be amazed at the way in which all the writers aver that this beverage tastes like real coffee. It doesn't; it has a distinctive flavour of its own. To me it tastes exactly like ground-up digestive biscuits. So, if you like liquid digestive biscuits, go ahead and make the stuff. As for me, if I want something to taste like a digestive biscuit I'll eat a digestive biscuit. I prefer my coffee to taste like coffee.

To make this brew, peel, chop and roast in the usual way. One writer says you should not peel them; all the others say you should. Do not grind too finely – a coarse grind is best.

If you would like to try dandelion root cooked as a vegetable, Japanese style (it's popular in Japan, where it's called *nituke*), scrub the roots clean of soil – apparently they don't peel them – and slice into thin rounds. Sauté these in vegetable oil, then add a small amount of water, a pinch of salt and a dash of white pepper. Cover the pan and stew until the roots are soft and most of the moisture has been absorbed in the cooking. Serve with a dash of soy sauce.

FENNEL (FOENICULUM VULGARE)

This plant can grow up to 8 feet (2.50 m.) tall if conditions are to its liking. It is common around the English and Welsh coasts, also inland in the south-east. I saw a very tall and luxuriant specimen growing wild in Dorset which was 10 feet (3 m.) high. It was growing by the roadside about 2 miles from a small village, and may have been a garden escape. Waste places, grassy clifftops and coastal road verges seem to be favoured. It has very beautiful feathery leaves and a distinct aniseed smell, rather like liquorice. The bright yellow flower-heads appear from July to October.

Herbed Fennel Relish

½ lb./225 g. fennel root
¼ oz./6 g. cucumber
2 oz./50 g. celery
½ teaspoon chopped fresh
  borage

½ teaspoon chopped fresh basil
1 teaspoon chopped fresh chives
Salt and pepper to taste
1 tablespoon lemon juice
1 tablespoon olive oil

Scrub the fennel root, cut off any discoloured or stringy parts, and chop into small pieces. Chop the cucumber into small cubes (do not peel). Remove any stringy portions from the celery and chop into small pieces. Put into a bowl, beat the oil with the lemon juice, season with salt and pepper and pour it over the vegetables. Add the borage and the basil and stir well. Sprinkle chives over the top as a garnish.

Fennel Sauce

¼ lb./100 g. fennel root
½ pint/275 ml. water
1 oz./25 g. butter

1 oz./25 g. cornflour
Salt and pepper to taste

Scrub the fennel root, chop roughly and boil in the water until tender. In a separate pan melt the butter and stir in the cornflour, cooking over a very low heat for about two minutes, stirring all the time so that it does not burn. Now add the fennel and the water in which it has been cooking, and season to taste. Simmer on a low heat, stirring constantly, until the sauce is thickened and smooth. Serve with fish.

FLOWERING RUSH (BUTOMUS UMBELLATUS)

This is not a true rush but belongs to a quite separate family, the Butomaceae. It is quite common growing in and around shallow fresh water in the southern parts of Britain and in a few places in the Midlands. It grows up to 5 feet (1.50 m.) and may be recognized by the long, rush-like leaves being three-cornered in section. The bright pink flowers bloom from July to September. This plant is also popular with gardeners for planting in and around ponds.

The root is edible, but I can find no reference in the literature of the plant to its mode of preparation. I can only presume that it can be cooked and eaten as a vegetable. However, I'm sure it would be jolly difficult to dig up a root that grows under water anyway.

GARLIC (VARIOUS WILD SPECIES)

The uses of various species of wild garlic have been described in Chapter 6, but in additon you might like to have this recipe (from America) for garlic vinegar, the use of which provides an easy way to add controlled amounts of garlic flavouring to salads and vegetable dishes. I am indebted to Laura Kroy for this recipe.

Garlic Vinegar

6 wild garlic bulbs
1 quart/1150 ml. white wine
  vinegar
1 teaspoon salt

1 teaspoon ground cloves
1 teaspoon caraway seed
Freshly-ground white pepper to
  taste

Wash and peel the garlic bulbs, and crush with pestle and mortar. Put this crushed garlic into a large glass storage jar which has a tightly fitting lid. Add the salt, pepper and ground cloves. Crush the caraway seed and add to the other ingredients. Heat the vinegar just to simmering point (do not boil) and pour into the jar, cover tightly and let it stand for a week in a cool place, stirring occasionally. At the end of that time strain through muslin or cheesecloth and pour into sterile bottles with tightly fitting caps. This keeps well – Miss Kroy has some which she has kept for over a year and is just as good as when she made it.

HERB BENNET (GEUM URBANUM)

The culinary uses of the roots of this plant go back to the sixteenth century when it was well known as a potherb and cultivated in gardens for this purpose. In addition it had a great many medicinal uses in the old herbals. The root tastes and smells strongly of cloves and can be used in almost any dish in which cloves would normally be used. It is strongly moth-repellent and used to be hung in closets until the advent of more modern chemicals. Why not use herb bennet roots instead of these? It must be much nicer to have one's clothes smell of cloves rather than mothballs!

The plant is a member of the rose family and grows in woods and shady places on fertile soils throughout Britain except in the far north of Scotland. It attains a height of 4 feet (1.20 m.), and the attractive five-petalled yellow flowers bloom from May to September. The leaves look just like the rose-bush leaves – this is a good aid to identification. The rose family has several other yellow-flowered species such as the cinquefoils, etc., but their leaves are very different.

The roots should be washed and cut into pieces before adding to soups, stews, puddings, pies etc. It is particularly good to substitute the roots of this plant for cloves in pickles, but they should be boiled first to soften them.

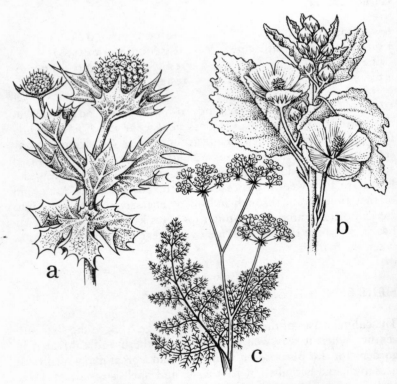

More plants with edible roots: a, Sea holly (*Eryngium maritimum*); b, Marshmallow (*Althaea officinalis*); c, Spignel-meu (*Meum athamanticum*)

MARSHMALLOW (ALTHAEA OFFICINALIS)

This pretty pink-flowered perennial grows to about 3 feet (90 cm.) and prefers saltmarshes and other maritime habitats. It occurs in southern and eastern coastal districts of England, south Wales and parts of Ireland, and flowers in August and September. The whole plant is covered with a velvety down, and even the flowers are velvety; the plant is easily identified from this feature alone. The roots are used to make the sweetmeat of the same name, which bears no resemblance to the synthetic concoctions made nowadays and known as 'marshmallow' which are made from starch, sugar and gelatine, plus the usual additives, artificial flavourings, chemical preservatives and what not. In bygone days there was a flourishing trade in the real thing, when fishermen's wives in East Anglia used to go out collecting the plants in the salt marshes along the coast.

Marshmallow

Marshmallow roots   Icing sugar
Water to cook

Scrub the roots and peel off any discoloured parts, cut into cubes and boil until tender. Remove from water, drain off the liquid and pat dry with kitchen paper towels, and dip into a bowl of icing sugar until completely coated. You can flavour them with vanilla if you like by dropping a vanilla pod into the water while boiling.

PARSNIP (PASTINACA SATIVA)

The wild parsnip is the ancestor of our cultivated variety and is much smaller, so you will have to gather more roots than you would need if you used the garden kind. The wild parsnip is quite common in southern and eastern England on waste ground and grassy places, especially on chalk and limestone soils. Where it occurs it is usually locally abundant. It grows to about 18 inches (45 cm.) high and produces umbels of chrome-yellow flowers from June to September. The plant is strong-smelling, and the roots are stronger-flavoured than those of the cultivated variety.

As far back as in the Middle Ages the wild parsnip was eaten both as a vegetable *per se* and as a component of soups, stews and the stockpot. Owing to the sweetness of this root (a characteristic which is more pronounced after the late autumn frosts have chastened it) it was used extensively in sweet dishes also and figured prominently in recipes for cakes, pies and puddings.

The wild parsnip has one disadvantage not shared by the culti-vated kind – the root has a hard woody core. The roots should be washed, peeled and boiled until the outer parts are quite soft – this takes about 45 minutes. The middle will never soften however long you boil it, so when using it as a straight boiled vegetable be prepared to leave the hard central core behind after scraping off the edible portions.

To use in pies etc, you can mash the roots to form a sort of purée and then press this through a coarse-meshed sieve in order to remove the hard fibrous parts. The purée can be mixed with flour and used in baking the crust of the pie. Another use is to mix with flour, season with salt, pepper and herbs of your choice, and fry in butter after shaping into small patties. A dash of nutmeg on top adds a nice finishing touch.

Mix the purée with flour and suet when making the dough for a suet pudding, to enclose either a meat filling or a sweet one such as apples, blackberries etc. It is quite a novelty to find a vegetable that can be used in either sweet or savoury dishes, so use it in both – after all, you couldn't do that with a cabbage.

PIGNUT (CONOPODIUM MAJUS)

There used to be quite a tradition in the old days in the country of 'grubbing for pignuts' – a pastime of which the children of the rural areas were particularly fond. The 'nuts', which are really tubers, were eaten raw, after scraping or washing. They can also be boiled as a vegetable and eaten with butter and salt. They are rather difficult to dig up, but in case you'd like to have a go, it's fairly easy to distinguish from other species of this family (the Umbelliferae) because the leaves are much narrower than those of most others of this group. They are so thin as to look almost thread-like, and present a characteristic spindly appearance which is rendered all the more distinctive because the leaflets are very sparse. The white flowers bloom from May to July, and the plant is found commonly every-where in Britain except on chalk soils. Woods, fields, and shaded grassy places are its favoured habitats. It grows to about 18 inches (45 cm).

RAMPION (PHYTEUMA TENERUM)

This plant is rare except in southern Britain on limestone soils where it can often be locally abundant. It grows to about 2 feet (60 cm.) high, and the very dark blue round heads of flowerlets blossom from late June or early July to the end of August. Dry grassland, woods and thickets are the places to look for it. The plant figures so widely in medieval recipes that it must have been much more common and widespread several hundred years ago. It was served as a vegetable, the thick, fleshy roots being chopped, boiled in water and served with vinegar. The young leaves were also incorporated into salads.

REST HARROW (ONONIS ARVENSIS)

Rest harrow is very common on dry chalk grassland, flowering from June to September. It looks rather like a sort of wild sweet pea. Although said to grow to about 18 inches (45 cm.) or so, in Dorset I have seen thick shrubs of this plant at least 2 feet (60 cm.) or more high. However, I did not dig any up to chew the roots raw, which is, apparently, what people used to do in bygone days, especially in the north of England, and maybe still do for all I know. The root tastes like liquorice.

This plant attracts a good many of our less common butterflies and moths to its blossoms, and the leaves afford a pabulum for a number of interesting larvae. It is a very pretty plant, too.

SALSIFY (TRAGOPOGON PORRIFOLIUS)

This plant is not very common, but the recipes I am going to give you can be used employing the cultivated kind (also known as scorzonera) which is sold in some specialist greengrocers' and supermarkets. The cultivated variety is, of course, much bigger than the wild root, but even that is of no mean proportions. The wild salsify grows in waste places near the sea and reaches a height of about 18 inches (45 cm.). The dull purple flowerheads bloom from April to June. A closely related species, goatsbear (*Tragopogon pratensis*) is more common and its long white tap root tastes the same, so it could be used instead. Goatsbeard has yellow flowers instead of purple but they open only in morning sunshine, thus accounting for the name by which this plant is often known, John-go-to-bed-at-noon. It also has a later flowering season, from May to August. Grassy places, wasteland, dunes, meadows and roadsides are all home to this plant.

The flavour of the root of salsify, scorzonera or goatsbeard is so distinctive that it makes a good vegetable dish in its own right. Here are the recipes (any of the three kinds can be used).

Buttered Salsify

½ lb./225 g. salsify root
Water to cook
2 oz./50 g. butter

1 tablespoon lemon juice
1 teaspoon salt
Dash of black pepper

Peel the salsify root, cut into bite-sized pieces and boil them in the water, adding the lemon juice while boiling. When tender, transfer to a pan containing melted butter over a very low heat, add the seasoning and cook until the butter is almost absorbed. Serve hot.

Salsify Fritters

½ lb./225 g. salsify root
1 egg
1 tablespoon plain flour

Salt and pepper to taste
Water to cook and to make batter
Fat for frying

Peel the salsify root, cut into small pieces and boil until tender. Pass through a blender or mincer to make a purée. Beat the egg, stir in the flour and add cold water until a smooth batter is obtained. Shape the root purée into round patties (you can add a little flour to bind if the mixture is not stiff enough) and dip in batter. Fry in the fat (which must be very hot) until golden. Serve with salt and pepper at table. These fritters served with chips make a very tasty vegetarian meal (but slimmers beware!). The quantity given makes 6 to 8 fritters.

Salsify Relish

Enough salsify root for 4
Water to cook
Salt and pepper to taste
1 tablespoon olive oil
1 tablespoon lemon juice

1 tablespoon fresh chopped
parsley
1 tablespoon fresh chopped
chervil
1 tablespoon fresh chopped
marjoram

Peel the salsify root, slice in rounds and boil until tender. Drain off the liquid and pat dry wtih kitchen paper towels. Place in a bowl, add the chopped herbs and seasonings and the lemon juice and olive oil. Mix thoroughly. Serve chilled as an accompaniment to meat or fish.

Grilled Salsify with Cheese

½ lb./225 g. salsify root
2 oz./50 g. butter
Water to cook

Salt and pepper to taste
4 tablespoons grated Cheddar
cheese

Peel the salsify root, cut into slices and boil until tender. Drain off the liquid and pat dry with kitchen paper towels. Place in a buttered dish and dot with more butter. Sprinkle the grated Cheddar cheese generously on top, and place under the grill until the cheese is browned and bubbling. This dish is fantastic served with a green side salad of wildfood leaves (see Chapter 2). Season at table.

Salsify in Garlic Sauce

½ lb./225 g. salsify root
1 oz./25 g. butter
1 tablespoon olive oil
1 tablespoon chopped fresh
parsley

1 tablespoon minced wild garlic
(any species)
Salt and pepper to taste
Water to cook

Peel the salsify root, cut into slices and boil until tender. Drain off the liquid and pat dry with kitchen paper towels. Sauté the root in a mixture of butter and olive oil in a heavy frying-pan, adding the garlic, parsley and seasoning. Serve hot with tiny little new potatoes and a sprig of wild mint of any kind.

SEA HOLLY (ERYNGIUM MARITIMUM)

You are going to have your work cut out digging up this one. The plant is horrendously spiny all over, like a thistle. It is a very beautiful plant withal, being a blue-green or blue-grey (icy blue according to one book) and the flowers are powder-blue (according to the same book). Not many plants have this particular colour combination.

It's hard to believe that this plant is actually a member of the Umbelliferae or carrot family, several species of which have been mentioned earlier in this book such as wild chervil, pignut and fennel. I think it's too beautiful a plant to dig up, although it's quite common growing on sand and shingle by the sea shore. In any case some of these roots can go down as much as six feet (1.80 m.), so you'd need the strength of King Kong to get them out. It grows above ground to an average of 2 feet (60 cm.), flowering in June and producing more blooms until September. You'd be forgiven for thinking it is a thistle.

In olden times people used to candy the root. It was boiled first so that it could be peeled, as the outer covering was too hard to peel off otherwise. The stripped root was then cut into pieces and boiled again, this time with its equivalent weight of sugar until the latter turned into a thick syrup, when the roots were removed and laid out to cool. They then crystallized into the 'candied eryngo root' of Elizabethan times. I don't doubt that they tasted good, but is it worth it?

SILVERWEED (POTENTILLA ANSERINA)

You cannot mistake this common 'weed' for any other plant. A member of the rose family, its leaves are silver on the underside, and it is the only wild plant with silver leaves which has yellow flowers. It is a creeping plant and never grows much above 6 inches (15 cm.), and can be found in abundance in damp grassy places, waste land, dunes, fields and moors and by the roadside. It is also a weed of cultivation and can often be found in the vicinity of arable land. The long white or cream-coloured roots are quite difficult to dig up, but in a ploughed field you will often find them up-ended on the surface along with the other weeds that the plough has turned up, thus saving you quite a hard job.

Until the potato was introduced to Britain, silverweed was cultivated as a root crop – records go right back to late prehistoric times. The roots were boiled, baked in the embers of the fire or even eaten raw. They have a slightly sweet, parsnip-like flavour. The roots were also dried and ground for use as meal and used in breadmaking and to make a kind of porridge.

Recipes for using the roots of this plant are legion. I give you some of the easiest ones.

Silverweed Bannocks

Silverweed roots enough for 4
Water to cook
2 tablespoons fine oatmeal

Pinch of salt
Knob of butter
3 fl. oz./75 ml. milk

Wash the roots, cutting off any discoloured portions, and chop roughly into pieces. Parboil for about 5 minutes. Remove from water and spread out to dry in the sun (preferably) or in a very slow oven. When quite dry and brittle, pound them to a powder in a pestle and mortar, or grind them in a grain mill or coffee-grinder. Mix the powder with oatmeal, add salt and rub in the butter, and put into a mixing-bowl, making a hole in the middle of the mixture into which you should pour the milk very slowly, a little at a time, stirring the while until you have a stiff paste. Roll out into a Swiss-roll shape and then cut off rounds about half an inch thick, starting at one end.

The Scots use a 'bannock slab' (Scotland is where this recipe originated) on which they toast the bannocks in front of a roaring log fire, turning once. The next best thing to use is a heavy cast iron flat griddle with no lipped edges such as is used to make chapatis in India. You could probably find one in an Asian kitchenware shop. If you must make do with something else then I suggest the best compromise is a *very* heavy cast iron frying-pan. Whatever you use, no fat is put on to the slab, griddle or pan. With care the bannocks can be toasted without burning either them or the utensil you are using. They do not take long to do. If you use fat you will ruin the taste of the bannocks. The quantity given makes 6 to 8 bannocks.

SOW THISTLE (SONCHUS OLERACEUS)

Several thistles have culinary uses but this is probably the best one. Identify it by the arrow-shaped points of the leaves where they clasp the stems, the pale yellow flowers forming a loose cluster, and the terminal lobe of the leaf being much longer than the others. The plant flowers from May to November and is a weed of cultivation occurring abundantly in bare and waste places, growing up to 5 feet (1.50 m.) high. The leaves are dull grey-green in colour.

In spring the tender young leaves can be used in salads if cooked first to get rid of the spines, but it is the roots that make the best dish from this plant. Cook exactly as described for salsify, in any of the dishes using that plant. The taste is not the same, but the sow thistle has a distinctive taste of its own which is quite interesting if somewhat mild. If left in the ground until winter the roots of this plant can be quite substantial and take a bit of good hard digging.

SPIGNEL-MEU (MEUM ATHAMANTICUM)

Only Scottish readers will be able to try this one, as the plant does not grow anywhere else. It occurs only in mountain pasture. The plant is an umbellifer with the typical white-flowered umbels (hence the name of the group) and is very strongly aromatic. The flowering season is June and July. It can grow to 5 feet (1.50 m.) though it is usually shorter. The root tastes like parsnip and can be used in exactly the same way.

STAR OF BETHLEHEM (ORNITHOGALUM UMBELLATUM)

This member of the lily family has a beautiful pure white flower and long, slender grass-like leaves, which are grooved and bear a central white stripe. There is a green stripe on the underside of each petal. It occurs, flowering in May and June, locally commonly in grassy places in southern and eastern Britain. It is extensively cultivated in gardens and often occurs as a garden escape in cultivated areas. It grows to about a foot (30 cm.) in height. The flowers do not open on dull days.

The bulbs are cooked and eaten as a vegetable and are very popular in America and the Middle East.

WILD TURNIP (BRASSICA RAPA)

The wild turnip is very closely related to the cultivated turnip and has been used as food for thousands of years. The wild variety produces quite good-sized swollen roots and can be used in exactly the same way as the kind sold by the greengrocer. The young leaves can also be used just like cultivated turnip tops.

The wild turnip is common on bare and waste ground, especially near streams and in cultivated areas. The plant grows to about 3 feet (90 cm.) and the yellow flowers bloom from May to August. The leaves clasp the stem. The plant has a very slender appearance. After flowering it produces long, slender pods. By this time the roots will have attained a good size and can be used for soups, stews, casseroles and buttered as a vegetable.

11

A GATHERING OF ELDERS

The elder (*Sambucus nigra*) is one of our commonest hedgerow trees and needs no description. It is also one of the best known to the wildfood enthusiast. Both the flowers and the berries can be used in making a large assortment of delicious foods and drinks; the latter include both wines and non-alcoholic beverages. I shall describe the non-alcoholic beverages in Chapter 17; this chapter is concerned with the various food recipes.

Perusal of any of the old herbals will reveal that for the last three hundred years or more this plant has been used in one way or another medicinally for anything from curing a cough to encouraging the flow of milk in nursing mothers. Small wonder, then, that a plant as versatile as this should also be equally versatile in the kitchen. We shall start with the unopened flower buds, which make a piquant and unusual pickle. This was popular in the eighteenth century, and I see no reason why it could not regain its popularity now – it is not at all difficult to make.

Pickled Elder Buds

1 lb./450 g. elder buds	2 tablespoons allspice
2 pints/1150 ml. water	2 tablespoons root ginger
6 oz./175 g. salt	2 tablespoons peppercorns
2 pints/1150 ml. malt vinegar	1 small chilli
2 tablespoons cloves	

Cut off stalks and put the buds into a basin. Make a brine with the salt and water, pour over the buds and leave, covered with a cloth, for 7 days. After this time remove from the brine, draining off the liquid, but do not rinse.

Make the spiced vinegar by putting all the spices into a pan with the vinegar. Heat slowly until boiling point is just reached, with the lid on the pan. Then keep over the lowest possible heat for two hours, remove from heat and leave to cool.

To make the pickle, put the elder buds into a pan, pour the spiced vinegar over them and bring to the boil slowly. When boiling-point has been reached pour the pickle into jars and seal, and allow to cool. *NOTE:* Aluminium pans should not be used for recipes in which vinegar is used, as aluminium reacts with vinegar to produce a harmful substance. Use only enamel or stainless steel pans.

Elderflower Fritters

There are several recipes for elderflower fritters. I think that this one from America is one of the most tasty versions. Gather two or three heads of elderflowers for each person, and make the batter as follows:

4 oz./100 g. plain flour	1 tablespoon honey
1 teaspoon baking powder	1 teaspoon vanilla essence
1 teaspoon salt	⅓ pint/190 ml. milk
2 eggs	

Beat the eggs. Sift together the flour, salt and baking powder. Add the milk, a little at a time, and stir in the honey and vanilla essence. When thoroughly mixed, blend in the beaten eggs. Whisk until a medium-stiff batter is obtained. (A blender can be used if preferred.)

Snip off the stalks from the elderflower heads, but do not separate the individual flowers from the heads. Dip the heads into the batter and fry in hot fat until golden brown. Drain on absorbent kitchen paper, dust with sugar with a dash of cinnamon (optional) and serve with whipped cream.

Elderflower Pancakes

The following recipe makes 6 thick or 8 thin pancakes. For each pancake gather one elderflower head. Strip the individual flowers from the heads, removing all stalks. Make the batter as follows:

¼ pint/150 ml. milk   Pinch salt
2 eggs   3 oz./75 g. plain flour

Beat the eggs. Sift the flour with the salt, blend with the milk and whisk the beaten eggs into the mixture (or use a blender) until a creamy batter is obtained. Now stir the elderflowers into the mixture, ensuring that they are evenly distributed.

Cook the pancakes in the usual way, using a non-stick pan with a dab of butter for each pancake. The butter should be hot so that a minimum of time is needed to fry each side, then remove, roll up and serve with a slice of lemon and a dusting of sugar.

Elderflower Mousse Dessert

8 elderflower heads   2 oz./50 g. sugar (any kind)
1 pint/575 ml. milk   1 tablespoon cornflour
2 eggs   2 oz./50 g. castor sugar

Strip the individual flowers from the heads, removing all stalks, and simmer in the milk for about 10 minutes, taking care not to allow the milk to boil. Separate the eggs, and whisk or blend the yolks with the sifted cornflour. Add the hot milk, after first straining out the elderflowers, stirring all the time. It is best to add the milk gradually rather than all at once. Pour back into the pan and stir continuously over a very low heat until the mixture thickens. Pour into individual glasses and leave to cool.

Beat the egg whites with the castor sugar until very stiff and standing in peaks, then spoon this mixture on top of the cooled mixture in the glasses. Dust with sugar and serve chilled.

Iced Elderflower Cream

8 elderflower heads   4 fl. oz./100 ml. single cream
6 oz./150 g. castor sugar   1 egg (white only)
3 lemons   ¼ pint/150 ml. milk

Strip the elderflowers from the heads, removing all stalks. Bring to the boil slowly in the milk, adding the castor sugar and the grated rind and the juice of the lemons. Simmer over very low heat for about

10 minutes, taking care not to allow the mixture to boil. Ensure that the sugar has dissolved, then strain through muslin and allow to cool. When almost cold add the cream, blending thoroughly, and freeze for about an hour.

Beat the egg white stiffly until it is standing in peaks, then fold into the half-frozen mixture, beat well together and re-freeze. Use in the same way as regular ice cream.

Gooseberry and Elderflower Fool

12 elderflower heads
1 lb./450 g. gooseberries
4 oz./100 g. sugar

½ pint/275 ml. water
4 fl. oz./100 ml. single cream

Dissolve the sugar in the water to make a syrup by boiling together for about 5 minutes. Drop in the gooseberries and the elderflowers (stripped from the heads and with stalks removed), lower the heat and cook for about 10 minutes. Cool, then pass through a blender, then blend in the cream by hand-operated whisk. Serve chilled. Serve in individual glasses and decorate the top of each with a small sprig of elderflowers. These are perfectly edible raw.

Gooseberry and Elderflower Jam

Gooseberries and elderflowers have a special kind of affinity. You can preserve this by making jams and jellies with them. The products will combine the tart sweetness of gooseberries with the heady, muscatel-like fragrance of elderflowers. The quantities below will make about 6 pounds of jam or jelly.

4 lb./1800 g. gooseberries
12 elderflower heads

4 lb./1800 g. white sugar
2 pints/1150 ml. water

Tie the elderflowers in a muslin bag and boil them with the gooseberries and the sugar in the water until setting point is reached (use a jam thermometer and you can't go wrong). Remove the bag of elderflowers, give the jam a good stir with your wooden spoon and have ready your sterilized hot jars and transparent covers. Remove from the heat and spoon into the jars, filling them to the brim. Cover with waxed circles and transparent covers (held on with rubber bands) and label.

Gooseberry and Elderflower Jelly

4 lb./1800 g. gooseberries   8 elderflower heads
Water to cook   4 lb./1800 g. white sugar

Cook the gooseberries with enough water to cover them until they are soft, and strain through a jelly-bag overnight so that the liquid drips into a large basin or jug (this must be big enough to hold 4 pints). *NOTE: Do not* press or squeeze the fruit in the bag in an effort to extract more juice, or the jelly will be cloudy.

The next day, remove the liquid to a large pan. Tie the elderflowers (with stalks removed) in a muslin bag and immerse in the liquid. Add the sugar, and boil rapidly until setting-point is reached (again, you will need a jam thermometer, which virtually cuts out all risk of under- or over-boiling). Remove from heat and take out the muslin bag containing the elderflowers; again, do not press or squeeze this – just hold it until it has stopped dripping. Allow to cool a little before potting up into sterilized glass jars, sealing and labelling in the usual way. The test of a good jelly is to hold it up to the light; you should be able to see clear through it. Various fruit jellies (see Chapter 13) produce an amazing diversity of translucent glowing colours. Holding these pots up to the light will make your reputation as a wildfoods preserve-maker long before their contents are spread on your guests' bread and butter.

Gooseberry and Elderflower Cheese

The pulp left in the jelly-bag after you have made the gooseberry and elderflower jelly need not be wasted. You can make a delicious potted 'cheese' (a kind of fruit curd) with this. Just put it through a sieve to remove the seeds and any skins, and then into the blender. To every pint of pulp add half a pound (225 g.) of castor sugar, and two elderflower heads (fresh – not the ones you used for making the jelly) tied in a muslin bag. Put the pulp, sugar and elderflower heads into a pan and heat *gently* up to boiling-point. You *must* stir all the time with your wooden spoon, or the mixture will burn. Cook until thick, then remove the elderflower bag. Pot into small jars, seal and label. Flavourings such as cinnamon or nutmeg may be added if desired, but do not be too heavy-handed with these or you will destroy the delicate elderflower flavour and fragrance.

We come now to the berries of the elder which hang in the same profusion in late summer and early autumn as the heavy flowerheads did in the spring. One thing about this plant, it is never stingy! Usually you can gather as many as you require – either flowers or fruit – from just one tree or large bush. However, if there are several trees or bushes together, it is always better to gather some from each rather than all from only one of them, of course. In the cases where I have gathered from one tree only, it has always been so prolific that after the gathering the tree looked just the same as it did before I started. And I had gathered enough to make two gallons of wine as well as some for cooking!

Elderberry Soup

1 lb./450 g. elderberries
1½ pints/850 ml. water
1 tablespoon cornflour

3 oz./75 g. sugar
1 lemon

Wash the berries and strip them from the stalks. Put them into a pan with the water, grate the zest from the lemon (avoiding grating off the white pith, which is bitter) and add to the pan with the juice of the lemon and the sugar. Bring to the boil and simmer until the berries are tender. Remove from heat and when cooled pass through a sieve, and put it back into the saucepan.

Blend the cornflour with a little water to make a thin cream, and stir into the mixture. Now bring once more to the boil, but at that point do not allow to boil any more but reduce heat to as low as possible and simmer, stirring continuously, until the soup thickens. Serve hot with croûtons or, if preferred, chill in fridge and serve with dabs of soured cream.

Elderberry Chutney

I was hard put to it to choose a recipe for elderberry chutney from among the 14 different ones I have. Eventually I chose this one from

America. It was sent to me by Deborah Turner from the Wooden Shoe commune in Ohio.

1 lb./450 g. elderberries
½ pint/275 ml. vinegar
1 medium onion
4 oz./100 g. Demerara sugar
½ lb./225 g. large seedless raisins
2 chillies

1 teaspoon salt
½ teaspoon ground ginger
½ teaspoon cayenne pepper
1 teaspoon mustard powder
1 teaspoon allspice
Pinch nutmeg

Strip the stalks from the berries, and mince them. Mince the onion and the raisins. Put all the minced ingredients into a saucepan and add the vinegar, sugar, salt and all the spices. Simmer gently until thick, stirring from time to time, and when ready spoon into hot sterilized glass jars, seal and label in the usual way.

Elderberry Ketchup

1 lb./450 g. elderberries
8 shallots
½ teaspoon salt
6 cloves

1 blade mace
1 slice root ginger
20 peppercorns
¾ pint/425 ml. vinegar

Boil the vinegar and pour over the elderberries (stripped of their stalks) in a bowl or dish, and cover with a cloth. Stand overnight on the bottom shelf of an oven at its very lowest setting (200°F./95°C. or Regulo ¼). The next day strain off the liquid and boil it for 10 minutes with all the other ingredients. When quite cold, bottle. This ketchup keeps indefinitely and improves with keeping. Try to keep it for at least a year before use.

Elderberry Capers

For this recipe (which was also sent me by Deborah from America) you need to go picking at just the right time to catch the *unripe* berries while they are still green. The 'capers' taste delicious! They can be used to make caper sauce and any other dishes in which regular capers are normally used.

½ lb./225 g. unripe green
  elderberries
1 tablespoon salt
5 fl. oz./150 ml. water

5 fl. oz./150 ml. cider vinegar
2 tablespoons sugar

Wash the berries (stripped of all stalks) and drain off excess water.
Place in a bowl and cover with a brine made from the salt and water.
Cover with a cloth and leave to stand for two days.

Have ready enough sterilized hot glass jars. Drain off the liquid
from the berries and place in the jars, evenly distributed. Boil the
vinegar with the sugar until the sugar is completely dissolved, and
pour into the jars, filling them right to the top. Seal immediately, and
label.

Elderberry Syrup

Originally a cough mixture, this can also be used, diluted with hot
water, as a soothing bed-time drink if you have a cold.

1 lb./450 g. elderberries
1 lb./450 g. sugar

8 cloves

Leave the berries in an ovenproof dish in the bottom of a warm oven
(for example, after you have finished cooking in the oven and turned
off the heat). The juice will gradually be released by the warmth.
Pour this off into a pan as it appears, until no more is released.
Squeeze any juice still left out of the berries and add to the pan. Add
the sugar and the cloves and simmer for half an hour. Remove from
heat, strain through muslin, and bottle.

Elderberry and Blackberry Jam

2 lb./900 g. elderberries
2 lb./900 g. blackberries

4 lb./1800 g. sugar
1 lemon

Strip the elderberries from their stalks and put into a preserving-pan
with the blackberries, sugar and the juice of the lemon. Bring to the
boil (the juice will start to flow copiously as soon as heat is applied,
thus obviating the need for adding water to prevent the fruit from

burning and then having to boil the water out again). Stir from time to time and when boiling-point has been reached boil rapidly (what the cookbooks call 'a fast rolling boil') until your jam thermometer informs you that setting-point has been reached. Skim off any scum and seeds that rise to the surface. Have ready enough sterilized hot jars, and fill to the top with the jam before sealing and labelling in the usual way.

Elderberry and Crab-Apple Jelly

2 lb./900 g. elderberries
2 lb./900 g. crab-apples

4 lb./1800 g. sugar
2 pints water

Strip the stalks from the elderberries and chop the crab-apples (but do not peel or core). Simmer in a preserving pan with the water until soft, then put into a jelly-bag and leave this to drip overnight into a large bowl or other vessel (big enough to hold four pints). Pour the juice into a pan with the sugar and boil until setting-point is reached, and leave to cool slightly before filling the hot sterilized jars, sealing and labelling.

The pulp left in the jelly-bag can be used to make a potted fruit 'cheese' in the same way as the gooseberry and elderflower cheese (recipe on page 116) was made from the left-over pulp after making gooseberry and elderflower jelly.

ALWAYS remember NEVER TO PRESS OR SQUEEZE a jelly-bag or your jelly will be cloudy! More jellies have failed to make it to the county show or Women's Institute competition for this reason than for any other!

In any future recipes for fruit jellies you may use the left-over pulp to make fruit cheeses or curds. Just follow the recipe on page 116.

You may like to make elderberry curd in the same way as lemon or orange curds are made, i.e., using eggs and butter. Here is the recipe.

Elderberry Curd

2 lb./900 g. elderberries
½ lb./225 g. butter
1 lb./450 g. sugar

8 eggs
Water to cook

The berries should be stripped of their stalks and cooked until soft in only just enough water to prevent burning the bottom of the pan. The cooked berries should then be sieved to remove the seeds, and put into a double boiler with the butter and sugar. Keep the water in the bottom pan boiling well and topped up when necessary. Stir the elderberry mixture frequently to ensure that the sugar is dissolved and that there are no lumps of butter which have not blended. Beat the eggs well and add to the mixture, stirring all the time until the curd thickens. Then pot, seal and label in the usual way.

We come now to some delicious recipes for pies and other desserts made from fresh elderberries, as opposed to preserving them.

Elderberry and Crab-Apple Pie

1 lb./450 g. elderberries   ¾ lb./350 g. sugar
1 lb./450 g. crab apples   8 cloves

To make pastry:
6 oz./175 g. plain flour   Pinch of salt
1½ oz./37½ g. butter or   Cold water to mix
  margarine
1½ oz./37½ g. cooking fat or
  lard

For the glaze:
Small quantity milk   Small quantity castor sugar

Make the pastry first, so that when you have made the dough you can wrap it in foil or clingfilm and leave it to cool in the fridge while you are preparing the fruit. This helps to avoid the rolled-out pastry splitting as you transfer it from the pastry-board to the pie-dish, and also helps prevent shrinkage during the actual cooking process.

For light pastry the golden rule is to keep everything, including your hands, as cool as possible, and to *sift* the flour (in other words, get as much air into it as you can). So, *sift* the flour into your mixing-bowl, don't just pour it in out of the packet. Cut the fats into the flour with a knife, and when the pieces are small enough start rubbing them into the flour *lightly* with your finger-tips. Just prior to this operation sprinkle in the salt and mix.

When the mixture is crumbly, add the water and mix with the

blade of the knife. About 4 tablespoons should be right, but it may need slightly less or more. When you have mixed the dough to the right consistency, roll in flour to form a ball and place in the fridge to cool while you prepare the pie filling.

Grease an 8-inch (20 cm.) pie-dish and put a china or earthenware pie-funnel in the middle. (Don't laugh, but I actually knew a beginner cook who used a funnel made of *plastic*!) Peel, core and slice the crab-apples and strip the elderberries from their stalks, mix together and place in the dish. Sprinkle the sugar over them. I use Demerara sugar for this dish but you can use white if you prefer. If you cannot find crab-apples use ordinary cookers. Add the cloves, distributing them evenly around the fruit.

By now your pastry should be ready to roll out on a floured board to make a crust to fit over the top of the pie. Roll it out one inch larger all round than the dish, then cut a strip an inch wide off each edge. Brush these strips on one side with milk and stick them all round the edge of the dish. Then brush them again on the upper surface and press the crust all round the edge to fit on top of the brushed strips closely. The milk will make the crust stick to the strips and the strips stick to the dish so that the pie does not come adrift during cooking. Flute the edges with a fork to decorate, and brush the whole crust with milk. Make a small hole in the middle over the funnel to allow steam to escape; this will avoid spoiling the appearance of the pie by having fruit juice running out all over the pastry. Sprinkle lightly with castor sugar, and bake in a pre-heated oven on the top shelf for 10 minutes at 375°F./190°C. (Regulo 5), then reduce heat to 350°F./180°C. (Regulo 4) and resite the pie on the middle shelf. It should now take from 25 to 30 minutes to cook through, and the crust should be a light golden-brown. A pie this size serves up to 6. Serve with cream.

Elderberry and Blackberry Pie

The recipe for this is exactly the same except that you need less sugar – half a pound will suffice. You can also omit the cloves unless you particularly like the flavour they impart. Cloves, to my mind, are an essential adjunct of cooking with apples but are not always necessary with other fruits.

Elderberry Crumble

1 lb./450 g. elderberries   6 oz./175 g. sugar

For the topping:
6 oz./175 g. plain flour   4 oz./100 g. Demerara sugar
3 oz./75 g. butter   Pinch bicarbonate of soda

Strip the elderberries from their stalks and place in an oven-proof dish. Sprinkle with the sugar.

To make the crumble topping, sift the flour with the bicarbonate of soda. (Some people like to add a pinch of salt at this point, but this is optional.) Cut the butter into the mixture and then rub in with the fingertips until you have a fine crumbly texture. Now mix in the sugar, and then sprinkle the topping over the elderberries and cook at 375°F./190°C. (Regulo 5) for about 35 minutes, or until the topping is golden-brown. Serve with cream.

You can, if you like, use half elderberries and half apples, in which case the amount of sugar used in the fruit itself should be raised to 8 oz./225 g. Or you could use half elderberries and half blackberries (6 oz./150 g. sugar). If using apples, the odd clove or two will bring out the flavour.

Elderberry Ice Cream

1 lb./450 g. elderberries   10 fl. oz./275 ml. double cream
6 oz./175 g. castor sugar   2 eggs
2 oz./50 g. icing sugar

Strip the berries from their stalks and pass through a blender. Remove the seeds by running the purée through a sieve. Now put back into the blender with the castor sugar. Whip the cream with the sifted icing sugar until thick enough to stand in points, and fold into the purée. Separate the whites from the yolks of the eggs (the latter can be used for some other dish). Whisk the whites until stiff and fold into the mixture. Freeze in a covered container.

Elderberry Fool

1 lb./450 g. elderberries   ½ pint/275 ml. water
1 lemon   2 eggs (whites only)
6 oz./175 g. sugar   5 fl. oz./150 ml. single cream

Strip the berries from their stalks and pass through a blender. Sieve to remove pips, then return to the blender with the sugar. Add the juice of the lemon and the water, put into a pan and boil rapidly for about 5 minutes. Freeze the mixture for about an hour, after first cooling.

Separate the whites from the yolks of the eggs (use the yolks for something else) and beat until stiff. Fold the whites together with the cream into the half-frozen mixture and whisk together vigorously. Return to the freezer container but this time do not freeze, just chill for half an hour in the fridge. Serve chilled. A few elderberries (raw) may be put on top of the mixture in individual glasses, for decoration. This quantity makes 6 to 8 glasses.

12

GATHER YE ROSEBUDS . . .

Flowers, as we have already seen, make attractive additions to salads and can also be used to make a diversity of herbal and floral teas, or *tisanes*, as the French call them (see Chapter 17). However, these are not their only uses. Let us start by looking at what we can do with the common wild rose, or dog rose, of the hedgerow. Its fruits are used to make rose-hip syrup as well as other products described in the next chapter, but what can we do with the flowers?

Rose Petal Honey

The petals of 2 dozen wild rose   1 ½ lb./675 g. clear honey
  flowers   1 lemon
2 pints/1150 ml. water

Make rose water by putting the rose petals into a bowl, covering them with boiling water and leaving them to stand, covered with a cloth, for 4 or 5 hours. *NOTE:* In all recipes where rose petals are used any white portions at the base of the petals must be removed, or the resulting product will taste bitter.

Strain the rose water through a sieve, pressing the petals to extract all the juice. Leave to cool. Meanwhile bring the honey to the boil, add the lemon juice and finally the rose water. Simmer for about 10 minutes, then bring back to a rapid boil. Stirring all the time with a wooden spoon, boil hard until the mixture becomes thick and syrupy. Remove from heat and cool a little, but stir from time to time. Strain once more, then pot, seal and label in the same way as other preserves.

Rose Petal Syrup

The petals of 24 to 30 wild rose   ½ lb./225 g. white sugar
  flowers   1 lemon
½ pint/275 ml. water   1 orange

Dissolve the sugar in the water over a medium heat. Do not allow it to boil. Add the juices of the orange and the lemon, strained to remove any pips or flesh. Turn the heat to the lowest setting and simmer for about half an hour, adding the rose petals a few at a time. Continue simmering for a further 15 minutes after the last of the rose petals have been added. Remove from heat, cool a little and strain. Pour into glass jars, seal and label. This syrup makes a very good accompaniment to ice cream.

Rose Petal and Rhubarb Jam

1 lb./450 g. wild rose petals   2 lbs./900 g. white sugar
2 lbs./900 g. young rhubarb   2 lemons

Cut the rhubarb into one-inch pieces and place in a large bowl. Sprinkle with the juice of the lemons, and cover with the sugar. Leave to stand overnight, covered with a cloth.

The next day place in the preserving-pan with the rose petals, stir well and bring to the boil. Do not reduce the heat but boil rapidly until setting-point has been reached, as shown on your jam thermometer. Remove from heat, cool slightly and pot in sterilized hot jars, seal and label.

Rose Petal Jelly

1 lb./450 g. wild rose flower   ½ pint/275 ml. water
  petals   1 sheet leaf gelatine
1 lb./450 g. sugar

Dissolve the gelatine in the water over a medium heat, and stir in the rose petals and the sugar until the latter is dissolved. Simmer over a low heat until the mixture thickens to a syrupy consistency. Strain through a jelly-bag or muslin overnight into a basin. The next day place in a saucepan and boil rapidly until setting-point is reached, and pot in clear glass jars, seal and label.

Crab-Apple and Rose Petal Jelly

2 lbs./900 g. crab-apples
1 lb./450 g. wild rose flower petals

2 lbs./900 g white sugar
Water to cook

Peel, core and chop the crab-apples and cook in enough water until they are tender. Strain through a jelly-bag or muslin overnight. The next day, put in a pan over a low heat and add the sugar, stirring until it is completely dissolved. Then add the rose petals and bring to a rapid boil. Strain through muslin, then reboil until it reaches setting-point. Remove from heat and cool slightly before potting into sterilized hot glass jars. Seal and label in the usual way.

Rose Petal Vinegar

This is simplicity itself and scarcely warrants a 'recipe' as such. All you do is to steep a few wild rose petals in a bottle of white wine vinegar for a few days, and you have rose petal vinegar.

Rose Petal Yoghourt

This is another simple way of using wild rose petals. Two or three flowers are required to a 5-fl. oz. (150 ml.) carton of plain yoghourt. Remove the petals and put them into the blender with the yoghourt, and serve chilled, decorated with a rosebud or small flower.

Crystallized Rose Petals

These can be used to decorate a number of desserts, so I will give you the method now; then, when these are required for a recipe, I will just say 'crystallized rose petals'.

Beat the white of an egg until stiff. The petals have to be dipped into this, so hold them with tweezers. When both sides are covered, sprinkle with castor sugar, then lay them all out on a baking-tray, taking care that they are not touching or they will stick together. Place this at the bottom of the oven at its very lowest setting (Regulo ¼) 200°F./95°C. and leave for several hours. Store in airtight glass jars.

Most flowers can be crystallized in this way, either whole or just the petals, and a row of glass jars containing various flowers and petals crystallized by this method looks most attractive.

Candied Rose Petals

The method for candying varies slightly from that for crystallizing. This time you have to make a syrup from sugar and water and dip the flowers or petals into this. The syrup reaches the right consistency at 240°F./125°C. Use half a pound (225 g.) of white sugar to a pint (575 ml.) of water. After the petals have been dipped, sprinkle with castor sugar and leave them to dry spread out on a tray or other flat surface in a current of air – they do not have to be dried in the oven. Once again their storage containers must be airtight – and once again various kinds make an attractive display in a row of glass jars.

Rose Petal Ice Cream

½ lb./225 g. wild rose petals
4 oz./100 g. castor sugar
Water to cook
½ pint/275 ml. double cream

3 oz./75 g. icing sugar
3 eggs (whites only)
Crystallized wild rose petals

Put the rose petals, castor sugar and a little water into a blender and liquidize smoothly. Beat the egg whites until standing stiffly in peaks. Beat the cream with the icing sugar until thick, and stir in the rose petal mixture. Fold the beaten egg whites into the mixture, put into freezer containers and freeze. Garnish with crystallized wild rose petals.

Rose Petal and Strawberry Yoghourt Delight

12 fl. oz./350 ml. plain yoghourt
½ lb./225 g. strawberries
2 tablespoons rose water (p. 125)

2 eggs (whites only)
6 oz./175 g. castor sugar

Put the strawberries, rose water and sugar into the blender to make a purée. Add the yoghourt and stir thoroughly; then freeze for about an hour (in the freezing compartment, not the fridge). Beat the egg whites until standing in stiff peaks. Fold into the half-frozen mixture and re-freeze. Serve very cold, garnished with crystallized wild rose petals (optional) or with fresh wild rose flowers, if preferred.

Rose Petal Custard

1 pint/575 ml. milk
4 eggs (yolks only)
4 oz./100 g. castor sugar
1 teaspoon vanilla essence

½ pint/275 ml. double cream
2 tablespoons rose water (p. 125)
The petals of 20 wild rose flowers

Beat the egg yolks with the sugar until thick. Add the milk and bring to the boil, stirring all the time. Remove from heat when a thick custard has been produced. Flavour with vanilla essence and chill in the fridge. When quite cold, add the cream, stirring well. Liquidize the rose flower petals with the rose water by passing them through the blender, and strain through a sieve. Add to the custard, whisking lightly with a hand-operated whisk, and chill. A few of the wild rose flowers may be reserved for decoration, if desired.

Rose Petal Flan

1 8-inch/20 cm. flan case (pp.77–8)
12 fl. oz./350 ml. plain yoghourt
3 tablespoons rose water (p.125)

½ pint/275 ml. double cream
2 eggs (yolks only)
4 oz./100 g. castor sugar
Crystallized wild rose petals

Whip the cream until thick and add the yoghourt and castor sugar. Beat the egg yolks and blend well into the mixture, finally adding the rose water. Chill the mixture in the fridge just long enough to start it setting firmly. Before it sets completely pour it into the flan case, and bake in a pre-heated oven at 325°F./170°C. (Regulo 3) for 45 minutes to an hour, or until the filling is set and the pastry case is golden-brown. Chill in the fridge, and sprinkle the top with crystallized wild rose petals before serving.

The wild rose flower adapts itself most readily to a variety of uses which are not always possible with some other wild flowers. However, a number can be so used, or at least for some of the recipes. You can experiment with other fragrant blossoms such as honeysuckle (*Lonicera periclymenum*), meadow-sweet (*Spiraea ulmaria*), may or hawthorn blossom (*Crataegus monogyna*) and so on, but you may find that some flowers are less suitable for use in these dishes than others. This is because they have tougher petals which disintegrate and blend less easily than the delicate petals of the rose, or because in some cases they may contain hard parts which are difficult to remove, either before or after cooking.

The vast majority of wild flowers can be used to make fragrant and tasty beverages, either herbal or floral teas (*tisanes*) or wines. However, it is the fruits and berries which follow the blossoms that will be found to be the most versatile, and it is these which must now claim our attention.

13

HEDGEROW FRUITS AND BERRIES

This chapter gives recipes only for those hedgerow fruits and berries which are common enough to justify their use. Other kinds which are rare or found locally in only one or two localities, should not be used. Some other kinds are locally abundant but are so small that vast quantities would need to be gathered to make picking worth while; these, too, I shall pass up. The wild raspberry and the wild strawberry are examples of the latter category. Gather these only in small numbers, to be eaten fresh with cream – if you can find them! They are elusive at the best of times, and one has to be in just the right place at the right time, which is not always possible.

Now for the more familiar plants whose fruits and berries can be used to make a large variety of delicious dishes.

BILBERRY (VACCINIUM MYRTILLUS)

This plant is common on moorland and in mountainous areas in most parts of Britain except the south-east. The dark blue berries (hence the name blueberry in some areas, and blaeberry in Scotland) appear earlier than many other wild fruits, being found from July on into September. The plant does not grow very tall – under two feet (60 cm.) in height on average. It is a member of the heather family or Ericaceae. Other local names include blaeberry, whortleberry, huckleberry, etc. The bilberry stains fingers and clothes a deep purple, and these stains are very difficult to remove, so don't spill the juice on your best damask tablecloth! Eating them raw while picking is also fraught with danger: your lips and tongue will be stained in the same way. The berries do taste very good fresh, however, and perhaps the best method is to pick them wearing disposable plastic

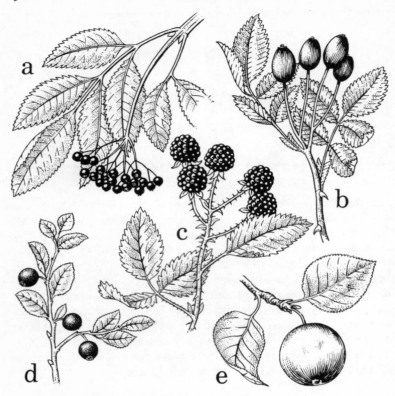

Fruits of the hedgerow: a, Elder (*Sambucus nigra*); b, Rose hips (*Rosa canina*); c, Blackberry (*Rubus fruticosus*); d, Bilberry (*Vaccinium myrtillus*); e, Crab apple (*Malus sylvestris*)

gloves, put them into a dish with sugar and cream, and eat them with a spoon.

So, when you are setting out to make some of the following dishes, be careful where you put the bilberries. Spread white plastic bags over all the surfaces you are going to use, and on the floor too if you are a butterfingers like me.

Bilberry Soup

A dark blue soup will make a fine talking-point for your guests! It also tastes delicious, and they are certain to come back for more.

1 lb./450 g. bilberries
1½ pints/850 ml. water
5 fl. oz./150 ml. single cream

1 tablespoon cornflour
2 oz./50 g. sugar
Pinch of nutmeg

Wash the berries and put into a pan with the water and sugar, bring to the boil and simmer until tender. Put the whole lot through the blender to liquidize; a sieve will do if you haven't a blender. Mix the cornflour with a little water to form a thin cream, add this to the soup in the pan and bring back to the boil, stirring all the time until the soup has thickened. When ready remove from heat and blend in the single cream. Serve in individual soup-bowls with a sprinkling of nutmeg on top. It can also be chilled and served cold.

Pickled Bilberries

1 lb./450 g. bilberries
½ pint/275 ml. wine vinegar
6 cloves

1 chilli
1 lb./450 g. sugar
1 tablespoon allspice

Wash the berries and put them in a pan with the wine vinegar, sugar, cloves, chilli and allspice. Bring to the boil and simmer for about half an hour. Remove from heat and strain through a sieve, but do not press or squash the berries. Reserve these while you re-boil the juice until it becomes thick and syrupy. Return the berries to the juice and mix well, but do not re-boil. After removing from the heat allow to cool slightly before bottling in glass jars, sealing and labelling. This pickle is very good with cold roast beef and makes a welcome change from the ubiquitous horseradish sauce. It is also a very tasty relish to eat with traditional boiled beef and carrots.

Bilberry and Crab Apple Jelly

1 lb./450 g. bilberries
1 lb./450 g. crab apples

1½ lbs./675 g. sugar
Water to cook

Peel, core and chop the crab apples and put into a pan with the washed bilberries and enough water only to cover. Boil for about an hour, then strain through a jelly-bag overnight. Put the juice into a pan with the sugar and boil rapidly until it reaches setting-point, then pour into sterilized hot glass jars, seal and cover.

Bilberry and Red Currant Jelly

This is made in exactly the same way as the preceding recipe, substituting red currants for the crab apples and reducing the sugar by 4 oz. (100 g.) The jelly can be used with meat, in the same way as red currant jelly pure and simple, or it can be used as a tea-time delicacy with thin bread and butter, scones etc.

Bilberry Jam

This jam never sets very firmly, but for a firmer-setting jam include another fruit in equal proportions. I will give one recipe for the plain bilberry jam and one recipe for a half-and-half version (you can substitute another kind of fruit for rhubarb if you wish).

4 lbs./1800 g. bilberries   1 lemon
4 lbs./1800 g. sugar   ¼ pint/150 ml. water

Put the bilberries, sugar and water into the preserving-pan with the grated zest and the juice of the lemon, and bring to the boil. Continue at a rolling boil until setting-point (220°F./140°C.) is reached, then bottle in sterilized hot glass jars, seal and label. This quantity makes 6 to 7 lbs. of jam.

Bilberry and Rhubarb Jam

2 lbs./900 g. bilberries   4 lbs./1800 g. sugar
2 lbs./900 g. rhubarb   ¼ pint/150 ml. water

Cut the rhubarb into one-inch pieces and put it into the preserving pan with the washed bilberries, water and sugar, and boil until setting-point is reached. Bottle, seal and label as previously. This quantity makes about 5 lbs. of jam.

Bilberry Pudding

1 lb./450 g. bilberries   5 oz./150 g. sugar
1 tablespoon arrowroot   1 pint/575 ml. water

Put the washed bilberries through a blender, then put into a pan. Blend the arrowroot with a little cold water to make a thin cream, then stir this into the bilberry juice in the pan, add the sugar and water, and bring slowly to the boil over a medium heat, stirring continuously with a wooded spoon. As soon as the mixture thickens and takes on a translucent appearance it is ready. Serve piping hot with double cream.

Bilberry Cake

½ lb./225 g. self-raising flour	Pinch of salt
4 oz./100 g. white sugar	5 fl. oz./150 ml. milk
4 oz./100 g. butter	1 egg
4 oz./100 g. bilberries	

Beat the butter and sugar until creamy. Beat the egg well and beat this into the butter and sugar mixture. Stir in the milk and the bilberries. Fold in the sifted flour, adding the salt at this stage, and finally whisk lightly, just long enough to ensure that all the ingredients are well blended. Pour the mixture into a well-greased 7- or 8-inch (20 cm.) round cake tin and place on the centre shelf of a pre-heated oven. Bake for about 30 minutes at 375°F./190°C. (Regulo 5). Leave to cool before turning out.

Using a loose-bottomed cake tin saves a lot of aggro when turning out cakes. They should also always be turned out on to a wire cake-stand so that the air can get to them, not put on a plate at this stage.

Bilberry Fritters

1 lb./450 g. bilberries	Castor sugar for dusting

For the batter:

4 oz./100 g. plain flour	1 tablespoon white sugar
1 teaspoon baking powder	Few drops vanilla essence
1 teaspoon salt	⅓ pint/190 ml. milk
2 eggs	

Beat the eggs. Sift together the flour, salt and baking powder. Add the milk gradually, stirring in the sugar and vanilla essence. When thoroughly mixed, blend in the beaten eggs, either in a blender or with a hand-operated whisk, until a medium-stiff batter results.

Wash the bilberries and drain off excess water, and mix them into the batter. Drop tablespoons of this into hot fat and cook until golden brown on both sides. Drain off the fat on absorbent kitchen paper, and serve sprinkled with castor sugar. Whipped cream may also be served with the fritters. This quantity makes 8 to 10 fritters.

Bilberry Compôte

1 lb./450 g. bilberries	2 tablespoons water
½ lb./225 g. sugar	1 lemon

Boil the washed bilberries in the water with the juice and grated rind of the lemon and the sugar until the liquid thickens and becomes syrupy, then cool and stir well, chill in the fridge and serve with whipped cream.

Bilberry Pie

1 lb./450 g. bilberries	½ lb./225 g. sugar

For the pastry:

6 oz./175 g. plain flour	Pinch of salt
1½ oz./37½ g. butter or margarine	Cold water to mix
1½ oz./37½ g. cooking fat or lard	

For the glaze:

Small quantity milk	Small quantity castor sugar

Make the pastry first, so that you can wrap the dough in foil or clingfilm and leave it to cool in the fridge while you are preparing the fruit (see page 121).

Sift the flour with the salt into a basin and cut the fats into it with a round-ended knife, and when the pieces are small enough rub them *lightly* into the flour with your finger-tips. When the mixture is crumbly, add the water and mix with the blade of the knife. About four tablespoons should be enough, but you may need slightly less or more. When the dough has reached the right consistency roll it into a ball, in flour, wrap and cool in the fridge while you prepare the pie filling.

Grease an 8-inch (20 cm.) pie-dish and put an earthenware or china pie-funnel in the middle. Put the washed bilberries, mixed with the sugar, in the dish. Remove the dough from the fridge and roll out on a floured board to make a crust to fit over the top of the pie. The crust should be rolled out one inch larger all round than the dish, and an inch-wide strip cut off each edge. Brush these strips on one side with milk and stick them all round the edge of the dish; then brush them again on the upper surface and press the crust all round the edge to fit closely on top of the brushed strips (see p. 122).

Flute the edges with a fork to decorate, and make a small hole in the middle over the funnel to allow steam to escape; this avoids fruit juice running out all over the pastry and spoiling the appearance of the pie. Brush the whole crust with milk, sprinkle lightly with castor sugar, and bake in a pre-heated oven on the top shelf for 10 minutes at 375°F./190°C. (Regulo 5), then reduce heat to 350°F./180°C. (Regulo 4) and resite the pie on the middle shelf. It should now require about 25 minutes or so to cook through, and the crust should be a light golden-brown when the pie is cooked. Serve with cream. A pie this size serves 6.

Bilberry Ratafia Dessert

1 lb./450 g. bilberries
½ lb./225 g. castor sugar

1 packet ratafia biscuits
½ pint/275 ml. double cream

Stew the bilberries with the sugar and leave to cool. Chill in the fridge and serve with ratafia biscuits and double cream. If you are unable to locate ratafias, which sometimes take some finding, you can use the sponge biscuits called 'boudoir fingers', or trifle sponges, but ratafias are better if you can find them as they have a most delicious almond flavour which the others lack.

Bilberry Suet Pudding

2 lbs./900 g. bilberries

1 lb./450 g. sugar

To make suet crust:
½ lb./225 g. self-raising flour   Pinch of salt
4 oz./100 g. shredded suet   Cold water to mix

Sift the flour and salt into a bowl, add the suet and mix lightly with a
rounded knife blade. Sprinkle in cold water a little at a time as you
continue to mix with the knife, until a soft elastic dough is formed.
Sprinkle with flour lightly to stop the dough sticking to the bowl.
When the dough is ready, lift it out on to a floured board and leave it
for about five minutes to settle, then roll out to about half an inch
thick.

Grease a medium-size pudding basin and line it with the suet
pastry, leaving some to make the lid. Fill the lined basin with the
bilberry and sugar mixture, dab the edges with water (use a pastry
brush) and fit the lid on top, pressing the edges together. Tie a
pudding-cloth over the top with string (do not use a rubber band as
this usually snaps during cooking) and boil the pudding, basin and
all, in a large covered saucepan, taking care that the boiling water
does not bubble over the top of the pudding. This is, in effect,
steaming the pudding. Check regularly that the water is kept topped
up, since the pudding will need two hours' cooking.

This is a most delicious pudding that is perfect to round off a meal
on a misty early autumn day, or evening, served with thick, rich
cream.

Bilberry Crumble

1 lb./450 g. bilberries   ½ lb./225 g. sugar

For the topping:
6 oz./175 g. plain flour   4 oz./100 g. Demerara sugar
3 oz./75 g. butter   Pinch bicarbonate of soda

Put the bilberries in an ovenproof dish and sprinkle with the sugar.
Make the crumble topping by sifting the flour with the bicarbonate
of soda (a pinch of salt is optional). Cut the butter into the mixture
and then rub in with the fingertips until you have a fine crumbly
texture. Now mix in the sugar and sprinkle the topping over the
bilberries. Cook at 375°F./190°C. (Regulo 5) for about 35 minutes,
or until the topping is golden-brown. Serve with cream.

Bilberry Fool

1 lb./450 g. bilberries
1 lemon
6 oz./175 g. sugar

½ pint/275 ml. water
2 eggs (whites only)
5 fl. oz./150 ml. single cream

Put the bilberries with the sugar through the blender. Add the juice of the lemon and the water and boil rapidly for about 5 minutes. Freeze the mixture for about an hour, after first cooling.

Beat the egg whites until standing in stiff peaks. Fold into the half-frozen mixture together with the cream and whisk together vigorously. Return to the freezer container but this time do not freeze, just chill in the fridge for half an hour or so. Serve chilled. A few bilberries (raw) may be used for decoration when the mixture is divided into individual glasses. This quantity makes 6 to 8 glasses.

Bilberry Ice Cream

1 lb./450 g. bilberries
6 oz./175 g. castor sugar
2 oz./50 g. icing sugar

10 fl. oz./275 ml. double cream
2 eggs (whites only)

Put the bilberries with the sugar through the blender. Whip the cream with the sifted icing sugar until thick enough to stand in peaks, and fold into the purée. Separate the whites from the yolks of the eggs. Whisk the whites until stiff and fold into the mixture. Freeze in a covered container.

Bilberry Yoghourt

The purist may prefer to eat raw bilberries with plain yoghourt and honey, but if you prefer something more closely approaching the commercial-type 'fruit yoghourt' but without the additives, flavourings and preservatives, stew the bilberries lightly with a little honey or sugar and leave to cool, then run through the blender, reserving a few of the cooked berries 'unblended' to put at the bottom of the tub, à la commercial-style, and mix the blended fruit-sugar combination with plain yoghourt. Pour into the tub over the fruit at the bottom. Chill in fridge.

The same method may be used with a good many other wild fruits, and any variations in method necessary in any individual case will be pointed out as I go along – for example, some fruits must have pips, skins, etc. removed first.

BLACKBERRY (RUBUS FRUTICOSUS)

The blackberry is too familiar to need any description. It has been used by man for thousands of years and is probably the most commonly used wild plant in Britain. In this case, however, familiarity most definitely does *not* breed contempt, for, despite its commonness, it is undoubtedly one of the most delicious of all our wayside fruits. Yet I am constantly amazed whenever I go blackberry-picking to see so few other people doing the same thing despite a superabundance of the fruit Nature has provided for our bounty.

Blackberries abound on all the Greater London area commons such as Barnes, Putney and Wimbledon, and the Surrey commons such as Bookham, Oxshott etc.

Baked Apples Stuffed with Blackberries

4 large cooking apples   16 cloves
½ lb./225 g. blackberries

Core but do not peel the apples. Stuff the hollow where the core has been removed with blackberries, pressing well down as you go along. Arrange on a baking-tin with two or three tablespoons of water to prevent the bottom of the tin from burning and the apples sticking to it. Bake at 350°F./180°C. (Regulo 4) for 25 minutes, or until the apples are just beginning to split. Do not leave them any longer, or the blackberry juice will run out and end up on the bottom of the baking tin. Serve hot with light-brown soft sugar and thick cream.

It is really optional whether you use cloves or not; many people prefer to leave them out, saying that the taste and fragrance of the cloves mask the taste of the blackberries. If you want to use them, stick four into each apple more or less equidistant from each other along an imaginary line running round its middle.

Blackberry Junket

I'm now going to quote Richard Mabey for this one, as it's one I've not tried yet. It sounds delicious, and I'm sure Richard would not mind my sharing it with you.

'The most delicious blackberry product I know', says Richard Mabey, 'is a junket made from nothing other than blackberry juice. Remove the juice from the very ripest berries with the help of a juice extractor, or by pressing them through several layers of muslin. Then simply allow the thick, dark juice to stand undisturbed in a warm room. Do not stir or cool the juice, or add anything to it. In a few hours it will have set to the consistency of a light junket, and can be eaten with cream and sweet biscuits'.

Pickled Blackberries

1 lb./450 g. blackberries	2 tablespoons allspice
1 lb./450 g. sugar	1 chilli
1 pint/575 fl. oz. white wine vinegar	½ oz./12½ g. ground ginger

Put the blackberries and the ginger into a bowl and pour the vinegar over them. Allow to stand for about 12 hours. Then tip the lot into an enamel or stainless steel (*not* aluminium) pan and bring to the boil. Turn the heat to a low setting and simmer for 30 minutes. When cold, add the allspice and the chilli. Dissolve the sugar in a very little hot water and add, stirring all the time until thoroughly mixed. Cool, bottle and seal.

Blackberry Vinegar

This is a delicious bedtime drink and especially good for a sore throat or cough.

1½ lbs./675 g. blackberries	1¼ pints/725 ml. white wine vinegar
1 lb./450 g. Demerara sugar	

Place the blackberries in a bowl and pour the vinegar over them. Let them stand undisturbed, covered with a cloth, for a week. Then strain through muslin, put the juice and vinegar mixture into a non-aluminium pan with the sugar, and boil for 5 minutes. Stir well to ensure that the sugar is completely dissolved. Cool and bottle. To make the soothing syrup dilute half and half with hot water.

Blackberry Summer Pudding

Half a large white sliced loaf	½ lb./225 g. sugar
1 lb./450 g. blackberries	½ pint/275 ml. water

Cut the crusts off the slices of bread and line a pudding-basin with them. Overlap the slices where necessary to ensure that there are no gaps left. Put the blackberries and the sugar into a pan with the water, bring to the boil and cook gently for about 5 minutes. Pour the contents of the pan into the pudding-basin, and cover the top with another layer of bread. Place a saucer or small plate on the top to press it down, and something on top as a weight – I use a small jug filled with water. Leave overnight in the fridge. The next day remove the weight and the plate or saucer, and turn the pudding out into a serving-dish. Serve chilled with thick, rich cream.

Blackberry Preserve

3 lbs./1350 g. blackberries	A little butter
3 lbs./1350 g. sugar	

Grease the bottom of the preserving-pan with the butter and put in the blackberries over a low heat. When they begin to come up to simmering-point, pour in the sugar (this can be warmed by standing it in a bowl in a pre-heated oven at its lowest setting for a little while, to some advantage). Now you'll have to stir continuously with your wooden spoon for about 30 minutes. The blackberries will burn if you don't, so be warned!

At about the end of that time, the blackberries and the sugar will be ready for potting. It goes without saying, of course, that during all this moil and toil with your wooden spoon the heat must be at its lowest setting, or you'll *still* burn the fruit. It's this process which makes all the difference between a preserve and a jam, which requires fast boiling. While you can under-boil or over-boil jam, it's almost impossible to burn it.

The potting is done in the usual way, using sterilized hot glass jars, waxed circles and transparent covers, and labels. I finish off mine with the traditional circles of gingham fabric.

Blackberry Jam

4 lbs./1800 g. blackberries   2 lemons
4 lbs./1800 g. sugar   2 tablespoons water

Put the blackberries, sugar and water into the preserving-pan together with the grated zest of the lemons and their juice. Bring to the boil, then continue rapid boiling until setting point is reached. Pot in the usual way.

Blackberry and Apple Jam

4 lbs./1800 g. blackberries   4 lemons
4 lbs./1800 g. sugar   4 tablespoons water
4 lbs./1800 g. cooking apples

This quantity makes about 10 lbs./4500 g. of jam. The reason why I use cookers rather than crabs is because much more sugar is needed when crabs are used to offset their sourness. The Bramley cooker ensures a sweet jam without using more sugar. Granny Smiths can be used if you prefer.

Peel, core and chop the apples and put them into the preserving pan with the blackberries, sugar and water. Grate the zest of the lemons and add together with their juice. Bring to the boil, fast-boil up to setting-point and pot as usual.

Bramble Jelly

6 lbs./2700 g. blackberries   2 lemons
6 lbs./2700 g. sugar   Water to cook

Put the blackberries into the preserving-pan with just enough water to cook. Bring to the boil and simmer until all the juice has run out. Remove from heat and leave to cool, then put into a jelly-bag and leave to drip through overnight. Remember – *do not squeeze or press the bag*!

The next day put the juice into a pan and add the sugar together with the strained lemon juice (not the zest this time) and bring to the boil, then boil rapidly for about half an hour, remove from heat, pot and seal.

Some people prefer to add the lemon juice at the blackberry-boiling stage. This does save time straining out the flesh and pips, but otherwise it makes no difference which method you use.

Blackberry Ketchup

2 lbs./900 g. blackberries
½ teaspoon salt
4 oz./100 g. Demerara sugar
½ teaspoon mustard powder
4 cloves

1 chilli
1 teaspoon mixed spice
Dash of nutmeg
½ pint/275 ml. wine vinegar

Simmer the blackberries in their own juice (do not add water) until soft. You will of course have to keep stirring all the time so that they do not burn, but do not be tempted to add water – you will ruin the whole thing if you do. Then put them through the blender. Sieve to remove the pips, then put into a pan with all the other ingredients, and simmer on a medium low heat for about 15 minutes. Sieve once more to remove the solid ingredients (cloves, chilli and mixed spice). If you prefer, you can eliminate this second sieving process by trying the three ingredients mentioned in a little muslin bag, then all you have to do is to fish out the bag.

Bottle in sterilized heated jars or bottles, seal and label.

Blackberry Ice Cream

1 lb./450 g. blackberries
½ pint/275 ml. double cream
3 oz./75 g. icing sugar

4 eggs (whites only)
Pinch of salt

Put the blackberries and the sugar into the blender. Then sieve to remove the pips. Whip the cream and fold into the blackberry purée, then whip the egg whites, with a pinch of salt, until very stiff. Fold into the blackberry and cream mixture. Put into a covered container and freeze.

Blackberry Syrup

This is a very useful and delicious syrup to pour over vanilla ice cream, plain blancmanges, ground rice moulds and similar desserts.

2 lbs./900 g. blackberries   12 oz./350 g. sugar
½ pint/275 ml. water

Put the blackberries into a pan with the water and bring to the boil, then simmer for 45 minutes. Remove from heat, cool and strain through muslin (or a jelly-bag). Put the juice into a pan and simmer for a further 10 minutes over a very low heat. Remove from heat and add the sugar, stirring continuously until all the sugar is dissolved. This sounds tedious, but if you dissolve the sugar by boiling the mixture the syrup will not be clear. You do, however, have to simmer it again – but *after* the sugar has dissolved! Then you can remove from the heat (after about 20 minutes), cool a little, bottle, seal and label.

Blackberry Curd

4 lbs./1800 g. blackberries   1 lb./450 g. butter
4 lemons   12 eggs
3 lbs./1350 g. castor sugar

Wash the blackberries and cook over a low heat until soft (do not add water – the few drops still adhering after washing will keep them from burning). Sieve to remove the pips. Into the top of your double boiler (or pan within a pan in lieu thereof – I usually make large quantities at a time so I use a 1½-gallon pot standing in my preserving-pan to contain the boiling water. For some reason proper double boilers all seem to be far too small) put the blackberry pulp, the juice of the lemons (not the zest), the butter and the sugar, and enough water in the *bottom* of the boiler (to be kept topped up as necessary) to boil at a brisk rate but not *too* much or it will boil into your curd and spoil it. Stir the curd with a wooden spoon until all the sugar is dissolved and the butter has melted and blended into the mixture. Now beat the eggs and add to the mixture, stirring from time to time and ensuring that the water is kept merrily boiling, and eventually the curd will thicken into just the right consistency for the curd – you don't need a thermometer for this one.

Pot into sterilized hot jars, seal and label.

Blackberry Cheese

You've probably been wondering what to do with the pulp left in the jelly-bag after making jelly. No need to waste it – make blackberry cheese.

Just add about a quarter pint of water to each pound of pulp and run it through the blender. Sieve to remove the pips, and put into a pan with half a pound of sugar to each pound of pulp. Cook on a low heat until the sugar is dissolved, then continue cooking for a further 10 to 15 minutes until the mixture thickens. Remove from heat, cool a little, pot and seal.

Blackberry Crumble

No cookbook would be complete without a recipe for this traditional favourite dish.

1 lb./450 g. blackberries   6 oz./175 g. sugar

For the topping:
6 oz./175 g. plain flour   4 oz./100 g. Demerara sugar
3 oz./75 g. butter   Pinch bicarbonate of soda

Place the blackberries in an ovenproof dish and sprinkle with the sugar.

To make the crumble topping, sift the flour with the bicarbonate of soda. If you wish to add a pinch of salt, as many people do when making crumble toppings, this is the point at which to do so, but it is entirely optional, which is why I did not include it in the list of ingredients – I never use salt in anything unless I have to. Cut the butter into the mixture and then rub it in with the fingertips until you have a fine crumbly texture. Now mix in the sugar, and then sprinkle the topping over the blackberries and cook at 375°F./190°C. (Regulo 5) for about 35 minutes, or until the topping is golden-brown. Serve with cream.

If you like, you can use half blackberries and half cooking apples, in which case the amount of sugar used in the fruit itself should be raised to 12 oz. (350 g.). A clove or two can be added, if desired.

Blackberry Pie

1 lb./450 g. blackberries	½ lb./225 g. sugar

For the pastry:

6 oz./175 g. plain flour	Pinch of salt
1½ oz./37½ g. butter or margarine	Cold water to mix
1½ oz./37½ g. cooking fat or lard	

For the glaze:

Small quantity milk	Small quantity castor sugar

Make the pastry first. For method, see page 77. Then refer to pages 136–7 for the method of making the actual pie, substituting blackberries for bilberries. The *mode d'emploi* is exactly the same. You can make a blackberry and apple pie by substituting half-and-half (the weight of the apples should be measured *after* they have been peeled, cored and chopped). Cookers (Bramleys or Granny Smiths) are best for this dish. Raise the sugar to ¾ lb. (350 g.) and add two cloves (optional).

A pie this size serves 6. Serve with double cream.

Blackberry Shortcake

This recipe comes from America and was sent to me by Angela Fearon of Poughkeepsie, N.Y.

1 lb./450 g. blackberries	½ lb./225 g. castor sugar

For the shortcake pastry:

6 oz./175 g. plain flour   Pinch of nutmeg
1 tablespoon baking powder   1 egg
4 oz./100 g. butter   ½ pint/275 ml. single cream
½ teaspoon salt   Butter to grease baking-tin

Dredge the blackberries with castor sugar and leave in a bowl. To make the shortcake pastry, sift the flour with the baking-powder, salt and nutmeg and cut in the butter. Rub with the finger-tips until a fine crumbly consistency is reached.

Beat the egg, fold in the cream and mix lightly into the biscuit dough mixture. Roll out on a floured board and cut in half. Shape each half into a round to fit an 8-inch (20 cm.) tin. Grease the tin with butter and put one of the halves of the shortcake into it. Brush the top with melted butter. Now lay the other half on top. Bake in a pre-heated oven at 450°F./230°C. (Regulo 8) for about 20 minutes or until golden and cooked through.

Remove from oven and allow to cool slightly before turning out. Split the shortcake into the two halves (buttering the top of the lower half aids this). Pile half the fruit between the two halves and the rest on top, and serve hot with whipped cream (or sweetened sour cream if liked). Serves 6.

BULLACE (PRUNUS DOMESTICA)

The bullace, which is a member of the plum family, is not a very common tree except in the Midlands; even there it is not as common as all that, but where it occurs you usually find a few in close proximity, making it worth while gathering the fruit. These clumps most often occur on the edges of woodland or in hedgerows. The tree, or bush, looks rather like a blackthorn (the species that bears sloes) but is larger and has bigger flowers. The fruits, too, are bigger than sloes, normally bluish-black with a pronounced matt 'bloom', but occasionally yellowish (this is a variety derived from an imported sub-species). The fruits are fully developed in October and November, and a touch of frost does much to mollify their astringent taste (the same goes for sloes). The bullace is less astringent than the sloe, though still too much so to admit of its being eaten raw. This astringency is considerably lessened by cooking and is lost completely when wine is made from them.

Bullace Jam

4 lbs./1800 g. bullaces   Water to cook
4 lbs./1800 g. sugar

This is a fruit that needs no lemon juice to help the jam to set – it has more than enough acidity already! Pick the bullaces as late as possible to catch them after the first frosts have taken the edge off their astringency.

Remove stalks, and simmer in just enough water to cover until soft. Skim off any pips which rise to the surface, both at this stage and later when boiling. Add the sugar, stirring until it has dissolved, then bring to a rapid boil, continuing until setting-point is reached, and pot, seal and label in the usual way.

Bullace Cheese

4 lbs./1800 g. bullaces   Water to cook
4 lbs./1800 g. sugar

Remove stalks, and simmer in just enough water to cover until the bullaces are soft. Remove from heat, cool and put through a blender, then sieve the pulp to remove skins and pips. Add the sugar to the purée and boil until setting-point is reached, and pot in the usual way.

CRAB APPLE (MALUS SYLVESTRIS)

Malus sylvestris means 'the apple of the woods' and this is where you will find it, as well as in hedgerows and on deciduous heathland. I was quite surprised to find it growing on Barnes Common cheek by jowl with oak, hawthorn, gorse and broom. Unfortunately the 'apple of the woods' is sour indeed – much too sour to eat from the tree. But it makes superb jelly and can also be used in a number of other interesting dishes. The apples are rather small and, like all apples, are full of pectin, and thus jelly made from them needs no lemon juice to provide acidity for setting. I will start with this recipe as it is the traditional one for which the fruit is famous.

Crab Apple Jelly

5 lbs./2250 g. crab apples   5 pints/2875 ml. water
5 lbs./2250 g. white sugar

Chop the crab apples but do not peel or core. Cook in the water until they are soft and mushy. Remove from heat, cool and put into a jelly-bag to drip overnight. The next day, boil the juice and sugar for about 20 minutes, stirring well from time to time, until setting-point is reached. Then remove from heat, cool slightly and bottle in sterilized hot jars, seal and label.

Pickled Crab Apples

5 lbs./2250 g. crab apples   Muslin bag of various spices
3 lbs./1350 g. white sugar
2 pints/1150 ml. white wine
  vinegar

Remove stalks from crab apples. Make a syrup with the sugar and vinegar and add the muslin bag containing spices of your choice (for example, ginger, cloves, cinnamon, garlic, allspice, nutmeg etc). Put the apples into an enamel pan and pour the spiced hot syrup over them. Cook gently until the apples are tender, but not too long or their skins will burst and spoil their appearance. Pack the apples into sterilized hot glass jars, pour the syrup over until the jars are full, seal and label.

Crab Apple and Cinnamon Cheese

3 lbs./1350 g. crab apple pulp   2-inch stick cinnamon
  left over from making crab   Water to cook
  apple jelly
3 lbs./1350 g. castor sugar

Mix the pulp with enough water to thin it to a consistency suitable for the blender, and pass through. Sieve afterwards to remove pips. Put into a pan with the sugar and heat on a medium-low setting to boiling-point, stirring to dissolve the sugar. Cook until the mixture thickens, then add the cinnamon towards the end of cooking-time, removing when ready. Pot into sterilized hot glass jars, seal and label.

Crab Apple Butter

3 lbs./1350 g. crab apples   1 pint/575 ml. water
3 lbs./1350 g. white sugar   8 cloves

Chop the crab apples without peeling or coring them and cook them in the water until soft and pulpy. If the water seems insufficient, a little more may be added but do not overdo it or the boiling-out process will take far too long. Some people use cider instead of water in this recipe, but this is entirely optional and I consider the results equally good, having tried both.

Run the mixture through the blender, then sieve to remove pips and solid parts. Then put into a pan with the sugar and the cloves (tie these in a little muslin bag, then you will not need to spend ages fishing the cloves out separately with a spoon) and bring to the boil. Cook until the mixture thickens, remove cloves, pot and seal in the usual way.

Crystallized Crab Apple

1 dozen sound crab apples   ½ pint/275 ml. water
1 lb/450 g. white sugar   ¼ teaspoon cream of tartar

To make the crystallizing syrup, stir the sugar and water over a low heat until the sugar is dissolved, add the cream of tartar and boil rapidly until the thermometer reaches 275°F./120°C. At this point, remove the pan from the heat and immediately plunge it into a larger pan of cold water.

Dip the apples into the hot syrup and then place on a baking-tray and cook in the oven at 325°F./160°C. (Regulo 3) for about 10 minutes. Remove to a wire rack for cooling. When completely cold store in airtight jars.

DEWBERRY (RUBUS CAESIUS)

The dewberry is a very close relative of the blackberry and can be used in exactly the same way as its cousin. The fruit of the dewberry is smaller, with fewer segments and a more pronounced bluish 'bloom'. The dewberry is also much less common than the blackberry but is quite widespread in southern and eastern areas of Britain, especially on limestone soils.

HAWTHORN (CRATAEGUS MONOGYNA)

This is the tree or bush which produces 'haws', the red berries that stud the hedgerows in late autumn and throughout the winter and which provide such an abundance of nourishment for the birds when at year's end there is little else to provide them with sustenance. One of our commonest hedgerow and woodland species, the hawthorn can also provide us with an abundant harvest of fruit which can form the basis of a number of tasty dishes.

Haw Ketchup

3 lbs./1350 g. haws
12 oz./350 g. sugar
1½ pints/850 ml. wine vinegar

1 teaspoon salt
Dash cayenne pepper

Wash the berries, removing any stalks and cook (in an enamel pan) with the vinegar, simmering for about half an hour. Put through a blender and then sieve to remove pips. Return to the pan with the sugar, salt and pepper, and boil for 15 minutes, stirring well. The mixture will thicken slightly, and this is the stage at which to remove it from the heat, bottle, seal and label.

Jelly bag

Haw Jelly

For some reason jam made solely from haws does not turn out particularly interesting, unless blended with other fruits. Haws do, however, make quite a good jelly, although in my view it is not so good as jellies made from some of the other wild fruits.

| 3 lbs./1350 g. haws | 3 pints/1725 ml. water |
| 3 lbs./1350 g. sugar | 3 lemons |

Put the haws in a pan with the water, simmer for an hour and leave to drip through a jelly-bag overnight. The next day, put into the preserving-pan with the sugar and the juice (not the zest) of the lemons. Boil until setting-point is reached, then put up in jars in the usual way.

To make a jelly using other fruits in combination with haws, such as crab apples, blackberries, bilberries, hips etc, use the haws half-and-half with the other fruit. The method used is exactly the same.

JUNIPERUS COMMUNIS (JUNIPER)

The juniper is an evergreen shrub or small tree belonging to the cypress family. The greyish-green leaves, in whorls of three, are spiny-tipped. The berries can be either green or blue-black, or both at the same time. Only the blue-black berries should be picked. The

Juniper (*Juniperus communis*)

Leaves spine-tipped, in whorls of 3; fruits in small clusters plant is widespread but nowhere really common except on upland moors in Scotland and northern England.

Juniper berries, however they are used, have a distinct resinous taste which may not be to everyone's liking. Those who like the resinous-tasting Greek wines such as *retzina* and *ouzo* will probably like them, but it is quite definitely an acquired taste.

Juniper Vinegar

½ pint/275 ml. juniper berries   1 blade mace
2 pints/1150 ml. cider vinegar   1 bay leaf

Simmer the berries in the cider vinegar for a few minutes, adding the mace and bay leaf, then remove from heat, fish out the mace and bay leaf and strain the berries through muslin. Bottle the vinegar and keep for at least a month before use.

Juniper Preserve

½ lb./225 g. juniper berries   Water to cook
1½ lbs./675 g. sugar

Cook the berries in the water until tender but not long enough for them to lose their shape or burst the skins. Add the sugar and stir until dissolved over the very lowest possible heat. Gradually bring to the boil until the syrup thickens, then pot and seal in the usual way.

Juniper Butter

24 juniper berries   1 lemon (juice only)
2 medium onions   1 tablespoon parsley
2 cloves garlic   Salt and pepper to taste
4 oz./100 g. butter

Peel and mince the onions and fry over a low heat in the butter until soft, then add the garlic, minced or crushed, juniper berries, lemon juice, parsley and seasoning. Stir continuously while cooking for a few minutes longer, then pot and seal as usual.

Juniper-Flavoured Potatoes

Peel or scrape the potatoes, which should be small new ones for choice, and parboil for 5 minutes. Melt some butter in a heavy frying-pan and add the potatoes, previously drained. Fry gently and, as they become cooked through, season with salt and pepper to taste and sprinkle with a few crushed juniper berries. Turn frequently so that the potatoes become nicely sautéed all round, and serve when ready in the juniper-flavoured butter in which they were cooked. The number of potatoes will depend on the number to be served, and also the size of the potatoes. Taking an average new potato 2 inches in length, allow 4 to 6 per person.

If you prefer, you can cook new potatoes by boiling in the usual way, and re-heat the juniper butter (see previous recipe) to pour over them at table. These juniper dishes are supposed to go with fish, veal etc.

Rowan (*Sorbus aucuparia*)

Leaves pinnate; berries orange, in clusters

ROWAN (SORBUS AUCUPARIA)

The rowan or mountain ash is a tree of beauty, and its berries make a superb jelly. The brilliant orange clusters of berries can scarcely be confused with the fruits of other tree species, and the tree is as common in urban areas as in rural ones – perhaps more so since it is being increasingly planted by councils with an eye to beautifying city streets. It is common throughout the length and breadth of Britain except on limestone soils. The fruits often remain on the trees well past Christmas, but it is better to gather them before the birds do! Thrushes, in particular, are inordinately fond of them.

The jelly made from the berries of the rowan has a sharp tang like marmalade and a luscious deep orange colour. It goes well with lamb, venison, pheasant etc.

Rowan Jelly

4 lbs./1800 g. rowan berries   2 lemons (juice only)
3 lbs./1350 g. white sugar   1½ pints/850 ml. water

Remove all stalks from the berries and put them into a preserving pan with the water and lemon juice. Simmer until soft, then leave to drip overnight through a jelly-bag. Put the juice with the sugar into a pan and boil until setting-point is reached, bottle, seal and label. The lemon juice supplies the pectin (setting-agent) which is lacking in these berries.

Rowan and Crab Apple Jelly

This is made using the recipe for crab apple jelly on page 150 substituting half rowan berries for half the crabs and adding the juice of two lemons. The two fruits together make a particularly interesting blend, and the jelly looks as good as it tastes.

Spiced Rowan and Crab Apple Jelly

Make this as above but including a little muslin bag containing a few allspices and cloves during the cooking time, removing this at the appropriate stage.

ROSE (ROSA CANINA)

The fruits of the wild rose (or dog rose) are, of course, hips. Rose-hip syrup is well known to all. The value of this plant in providing a rich source of Vitamin C in its fruits was recognized during World War II, when rose-hip syrup began to be manufactured in vast quantities — though it was not unknown to botanists, herbalists and wildfood enthusiasts before that time. Rose-hip syrup is, of course, still made commercially, but it might be fun for you to try making your own — and certainly a lot cheaper. You must, however, be *very* careful in ensuring that the sharp-pointed prickles attached to the seeds are entirely eliminated, as these could cause injury to the delicate membranes of throat, stomach or bowels. I would advise the use of a *double* thickness of very fine muslin for the jelly-bag which has to be used to strain out the juice. Here is the recipe. Only an enamel or stainless steel pan must be used when making rose-hip products since contact with aluminium or iron turns the hips black and destroys their Vitamin C content.

Rose Hip Syrup

3 lbs./1350 g. hips   3 lbs./1350 g. white sugar
6 pints/3450 ml. water

Boil 4 pints/2300 ml. of the water. Slice the hips and add, bring to the boil and cook until soft (about half an hour). Cool and leave to drip through a jelly-bag overnight. Reserve the liquid.

Boil the pulp left in the jelly-bag with the remainder of the water for half an hour. Cool and strain this, too, through the jelly-bag.

Combine the two lots of liquid and boil until reduced by about half, then add the sugar, bring back to the boil and cook until all the sugar is dissolved. Continue boiling until the liquid has reached the consistency of syrup, then remove from heat and leave to cool, covered. When quite cold, bottle and seal. The syrup should be stored in the dark, otherwise the Vitamin C is lost.

You will note that in all the following recipes the hips, as when making the syrup, have to be put through muslin, for the reason already described. Even the jam cannot be made without using a jelly-bag. Better be safe than sorry!

Rose-Hip Jelly

4 lbs./1800 g. rose hips   2 lemons (juice only)
3 lbs./1350 g. white sugar   Water to cook

Simmer the rose-hips in water for two hours, then leave to drip through a jelly-bag overnight. The next day put the juice into a pan with the sugar and boil until setting-point is reached, having previously added the lemon juice after the sugar has dissolved. Remove from heat, pot, seal and label as usual.

Rose-Hip Jam

Rose-hips will not have enough 'body' if used alone to make jam, since the pulp has to be left behind owing to the prickly seeds. It is therefore necessary to add another fruit – ordinary cooking apples seem to produce the best results. Do not use crabs – their tart sourness will swamp the flavour of the hips, which ordinary 'cookers' do not seem to do.

4 lbs./1800 g. rose-hips   Water to cook
2 lbs./900 g. cooking apples   2 lemons (juice only)
5 lbs./2250 g. white sugar

Treat the rose-hips exactly as described in the previous recipe, reserving the juice. The next day peel, core and chop the apples and cook to a pulp in just enough water to cover. Add the rose-hip juice, lemon juice and sugar and boil until setting-point is reached, pot and seal in the usual manner.

Rose-Hip Table Cream

1 lb./450 g. rose-hips   3 tablespoons cornflour
½ lb./225 g. white sugar   5 fl. oz./150 ml. single cream
1½ pints/850 ml. water

Boil the hips in the water until soft. Put through a blender and then sieve through a double thickness of very fine muslin to remove the prickly seeds. Boil the purée with the sugar until a syrupy consistency is reached. Blend the cornflour with a little water to make a thin cream, and add to the rose-hip syrup in the pan, reducing the heat and simmering until the mixture thickens, stirring all the time. Remove from heat when ready and allow to cool slightly, then fold in the cream and put into individual moulds, or one large one if preferred. Serve with cream.

Rose-Hip Delight

This recipe will require half a pound of rose-hip jam (page 158) and four tablespoons of rose-hip syrup (page 157). In addition to the above, you will need:

Juice of one lemon
2 tablespoons clear honey

Whites of 2 eggs

Reheat the jam until soft, then add the lemon juice, honey and rose-hip syrup. Stir well and remove from heat when thoroughly blended. Beat the egg whites until very stiff and fold into the mixture. Spoon into individual glasses and chill in the fridge. Serve with cream.

Chilled Rose-Hip Soup

This is a light, refreshing summer recipe from America, sent to me by Dorothy Cierpiala of New York City. Dorothy, a schoolteacher, comes from a long line of farming women who enjoyed making tasty dishes from wild foods.

½ lb./225 g. rose hips
Water to cook
2 pints/1150 ml. water to add later

4 tablespoons white sugar
2 tablespoons cornflour
½ pint/275 ml. double cream

Cook the hips in just enough water to cover, and bring to the boil. Continue boiling for about 15 minutes. Strain through a jelly-bag. This process may take some time, so it may be advisable to do this part of the preparations the night before the soup is required.

The next day put the liquid into a pan with 2 pints of water, add the sugar and bring to the boil. When the sugar has completely dissolved, stand the pan off the heat. Mix the cornflour with a little water, blending thoroughly, and stir into the soup. Return the pan to a medium heat and cook until the soup has thickened. Remove from the heat, leave to cool and when nearly cold fold in the cream to make a marbled pattern throughout the soup, and chill.

All this double cream reminds me of a book I read when I was in America called *Be Fit, Not Fat*, in which there was a rather natty couplet:

> A moment on the lips –
> A lifetime on the hips!

Somehow I don't think it was *rose* hips the author was referring to ... After all, anything with that much Vitamin C can hardly be fattening!

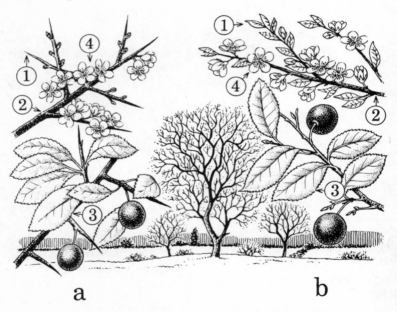

a, Sloe (*Prunus spinosa*); b, Bullace (*Prunus domestica*)

a	b
1 Prominent pointed thorns	1 No thorns
2 Black twigs	2 Brownish twigs
3 Leaves pointed-oval, toothed	3 Leaves much larger
4 Flowers appear *before* leaves	4 Flowers appear *with* leaves

SLOE (PRUNUS SPINOSA)

The sloe is the fruit of the blackthorn, a widespread and abundant shrub which can grow up to 12 feet (3.60 m.) in height, with oval, plum-like leaves (it is a member of the plum family) tiny white blossoms in the spring and small round dark blue berries in the autumn. The flowers appear *before* the leaves, which are toothed along the edges. The bush grows in hedgerows, woods and scrub through the British Isles but is less common in the north of Scotland.

The sloe is very acrid and cannot be eaten off the tree, but it makes superb jelly and can also be used in several other ways. Leave the picking of sloes until as late as possible. After the first frosts of autumn the berries lose some of their acerbity, although never to the extent of enabling the gatherer to eat them raw.

The specific name *'spinosa'* is of course self-explanatory and I advise you to wear leather gloves when picking sloes. Rubber gloves and those plastic disposable ones are useless for this purpose. They will only become torn by the sharp spines, and then you are back to square one.

Sloe Jelly

4 lbs./1800 g. sloes   Water to cook
4 lbs./1800 g. sugar

Put the sloes into a pan with just enough water to cover, and simmer until soft (about an hour should suffice). Strain through a jelly-bag overnight. The next day put the liquid into a pan with the sugar and cook over a low heat until the sugar is dissolved; then bring rapidly to the boil and continue boiling until setting-point is reached. Pot, seal and label in the usual manner.

Sloe and Apple Jelly

2 lbs./900 g. sloes   6 lbs./2700 g. sugar
4 lbs./1800 g. cooking apples Water to cook

Do not use crab apples for this recipe – the sloes are bitter enough without adding the sourness of crabs to compound an already difficult situation! Use Bramleys or Granny Smiths.

Peel, core and chop the apples and put them into the preserving-pan with the sloes. Add water just enough to cover, and boil to a pulp. Strain through a jelly-bag overnight.

The next day put the liquid into a pan with the sugar and bring to the boil. Boil rapidly until setting-point is reached, pot, seal and label.

Sloe and Blackberry Jelly

This is made in exactly the same way as the preceding recipe, substituting 4 lbs./1800g. blackberries for the apples. The amount of sugar remains the same. You may have to add a little more water than in the previous recipe, but do not overdo it: you will only have to boil it out again, which will make the boiling take longer.

14

ARE YOU A HARD NUT CASE?

Nuts are high in nutrients but against this they are somewhat limited in application to food purposes. In this country there are only five nut-bearing trees whose products are of much use, unlike the United States of America with its variety of regional climates and consequent proliferation of trees, which include many more nut-bearers than our species do. In this chapter I am also including two products which are not nuts but which seem to fit in here better than in other chapters. The first to be described is one of these.

ASH (FRAXINUS EXCELSIOR)

The ash tree is common on chalk soils but is also frequently planted in other areas throughout Britain. The winged seeds, which look like bunches of keys, must be familiar to everyone who takes even a passing interest in the trees of town and country, since they are very conspicuous. These seeds can be used to make a delicious pickle. They should be gathered in June or July while still young and tender.

Pickled ash keys

2 lbs./900 g. ash keys   Water for boiling
2 oz./50 g. mixed pickling spice
4 pints/2300 ml. distilled white
  malt vinegar

Boil the keys in three changes of water until tender. There is no short cut to changing the water – if you don't the pickle will be bitter.

Remove from water, drain and pack into glass jars which have been sterilized by boiling in water and left upside down to drain on a clean kitchen towel. (Wooden tongs are best for removing the jars from the boiling water.)

To make the spiced vinegar, which you can do while the keys are being boiled, pour the vinegar into an enamel saucepan (*not* aluminium, which reacts with vinegar) and bring to the boil. Throw in the mixed pickling spices and boil for about 10 minutes. Then pour the hot spiced vinegar into the jars containing the boiled ash keys. The vinegar must fill the jars right up to the top. (The addition of salt is optional – some people add a little salt to the vinegar when at the boiling stage and some do not.) Screw-top lids which have to come into contact with vinegar must be made of plastic, not metal. If your jars have only metal lids, seal them with waxed or greaseproof paper and rubber bands instead. I save coffee jars for pickles as all these have plastic screw-on lids.

BEECH (FAGUS SYLVATICA)

The smooth grey bark is one of the distinguishing features of this stately forest tree. In autumn the leaves turn to every shade of russet, gold and red as well as bronze; these are the leaves which are so useful for preserving to make winter decorations as a foil for everlasting flowers, honesty and various red berries. The triangular brown nuts are encased in rough-surfaced greenish four-sided cases and can be gathered in September and October. There are four nuts in each case. Towards the end of the season the outer cases turn brownish and fall to the ground, and under a large tree these may form a thick carpet easily gathered. However, you should get there before the squirrels, mice and other woodland creatures beat you to it!

Beech nuts are tasty raw – I remember eating lots of them as a child when on my nature rambles – but they can also be eaten salted or roasted.

The only other use I know of for these nuts is grinding them in a mill to press out the oil which forms a large part of them. Beech-nut oil is rich in protein and fat. It should be filtered to remove solid particles and then stored in sealed airtight containers. It is said to store much longer than many other vegetable oils. It can be used for salads or for cooking. A pound of nuts will yield 3 fluid ounces of oil.

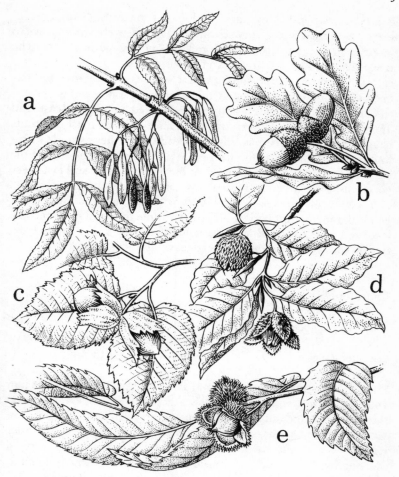

They're nuts! a, Ash keys (*Fraxinus excelsior*); b, Oak acorns
(*Quercus robur*); c, Hazel cobs (*Corylus avellana*); d, Beech
nuts (*Fagus sylvatica*); e, Sweet chestnuts (*Castanea sativa*)

CHESTNUT (SWEET) (CASTANEA SATIVA)

The sweet chestnut should not be confused with the horse chestnut
(*Aesculus hippocastanum*) which belongs to a different family and
whose nuts ('conkers') are poisonous. The sweet chestnut is a
member of the Fagaceae – the same family as the beech – and, like the

beech, has smooth grey bark. It does not have the 'five-fingered' leaves so typical of the horse chestnut. The sweet chestnut grows to 90 or 100 feet (27 to 30 m.), with reddish, narrow-pointed buds. The tree grows throughout Britain and is found in most areas, though it is certainly not one of the commoner trees. It is not a native but has become naturalized after its introduction from southern Europe.

The familiar brown chestnuts are encased in a spiny case and appear in the autumn. Everyone must have enjoyed roast chestnuts round the fire at Christmas – they are ready when they explode with a loud pop – dabbing them into a little pile of salt on the side of the plate after peeling them. Even when burnt black, they still taste very good! But there are lots of other ways of using chestnuts.

If you want to risk competition with the squirrels and leave gathering them until November, by that time they will have become loosened from the husks as these split open, and will be found lying free on the ground among the dead leaves at the base of the trees.

Chestnut Purée

2 lbs./900 g. peeled chestnuts
1 head celery
Bouquet garni

2 oz./50 g. butter
Salt and pepper to taste
Stock or water to cook

Place the chestnuts, celery (cut into short lengths) and herbs in a pan and pour in just enough stock or water to cover. Cook gently – no fast boiling – and simmer for about an hour, or until the nuts are tender. Lift out with a slotted spoon and run through the blender with a little of the stock. Add the butter and seasoning, mixing thoroughly. The purée can be used as a vegetable accompaniment to a meat dish or as a base for other dishes such as the following.

Chestnut Spread

1 pint/575 ml. chestnut purée
10 fl. oz./275 ml. cream cheese
2 tablespoons sour cream
3 tablespoons grated raw
  chestnuts

Salt and pepper to taste
2 tablespoons finely chopped
  fresh parsley
Dash of mustard powder

Blend the cream cheese with the sour cream, then blend with the purée and the grated nuts and chopped parsley. Season to taste and pack into jars. This spread must be kept refrigerated, and used within 4 or 5 days.

Chestnut Stuffed Eggs

8 hard-boiled eggs
8 tablespoons chestnut purée
8 teaspoons sour cream

8 teaspoons grated raw chestnut
Salt and pepper to taste

Halve the hard-boiled eggs and remove the yolks. Mash these and add to the chestnut purée and sour cream. Season to taste. Replace the yolks with this mixture, slightly heaping it in the egg halves, and season to taste. Sprinkle with grated raw chestnut.

Chestnut Soup

1 lb./450 g. chestnuts
2 medium potatoes
1 pint/575 ml. water
5 fl. oz./150 ml. single cream

2 bay leaves
Yolks of 2 eggs
Salt and pepper to taste

Shell and skin the chestnuts and put into the pan with the water, diced uncooked potato, bay leaves, salt and pepper. Simmer until tender, then sieve or pass through a blender, and reheat but do not allow to boil. Just before serving, add the cream and the beaten egg yolks. The soup must have been taken off the heat when these two ingredients are added. Stir well and serve garnished with a sprig or two of watercress if available. Serves 5 to 6.

Chestnut Stuffing (for turkey or chicken)

The quantities given first are for an average-size turkey; the quantities in brackets are for an average family-size chicken.

2 lbs./900 g. (1 lb./450 g.)
chestnuts

1 lb./450 g. (½ lb./225 g.)
sausagemeat

2 onions (medium)

4 oz./100 g. (2 oz./50 g.)
sultanas

1 tablespoon (½ tablespoon)
sugar

Pinch cinnamon (optional)

2 oz./50 g. butter

Salt and pepper to taste

A little tomato juice to moisten

Boil the chestnuts until soft and peel and skin them. Slice the onions and fry in the butter until golden, then add the sausagemeat and cook gently for a few minutes. Do not allow the onions to turn brown or the mixture to burn. Add the tomato juice, sugar, salt and pepper, and cinnamon (if used). Stir together until well blended, then add the chestnuts, previously minced, and the sultanas. Mix well, and allow to cool sufficiently to enable you to stuff the bird.

Chestnut Stuffing (vegetarian)

2 lbs./900 g. (1 lb./450 g.)
chestnuts

4 oz./100 g. (2 oz./50 g.) butter

2 eggs (1 egg)

Juice of 2 lemons (1 lemon)

Salt and pepper to taste

2 tablespoons port

Boil the chestnuts until tender, peel and skin them, and mince. Add melted butter, lemon juice and seasoning. Beat the egg (or eggs) and add the port. Blend well, and when sufficiently cooled stuff the bird.

Braised Chestnuts

1 lb./450 g. chestnuts

Beef stock to moisten

Bouquet garni

1 head of celery

2 oz./50 g. butter

Salt and pepper to taste

Boil the chestnuts until tender, then peel and skin them carefully so as to avoid their disintegrating. For the same reason, it is best not to boil them too long for this particular recipe. Lay them in a buttered ovenproof dish with the chopped celery, the bouquet garni and seasoning, and pour in enough stock just to cover. Cook, with a lid, in a slow to moderate oven (325°F./160°C. or Regulo 3) for about 40 minutes. Serve as a vegetable accompaniment to a meat dish.

Chestnut Mousse

1 lb./450 g. chestnuts	½ pint/275 ml. single cream
½ pint/275 ml. water	2 eggs (whites only)
6 oz./175 g. sugar	Vanilla essence to taste

Boil the chestnuts, peel and skin them and pass them through a blender. Put into a saucepan with the water, sugar and vanilla essence, and bring to the boil, stirring continuously until the mixture is smooth. Remove from heat and when cool beat the egg whites until stiff and whip the cream and blend these into the mixture. Chill in fridge before serving.

Chestnut Preserve

4 lbs./1800 g. chestnuts	1 ½ pints/850 ml. water
3 lbs./1350 g. sugar	

Dissolve the sugar in the water over a low heat, then bring to the boil until it reaches 220°F./114°C. Peel and skin the chestnuts and boil them in the syrup until tender. Reduce the syrup by further boiling if necessary. When the syrup is thick, bottle the preserve in hot sterilized jars, seal and label in the usual way.

If you like, a vanilla pod can be boiled in the syrup (and removed after boiling), but this is entirely optional.

HAZEL (CORYLUS AVELLANA)

Hazelnuts (sometimes called cobnuts or filberts) can be ready for gathering at any time from late August to November, according to the season. The hazel is a common hedgerow and woodland tree, a native of Britain and found throughout the country. The bark is reddish-brown and smooth, the leaves pointed oval and downy when young. The tree does not normally grow very tall – usually to about 18 or 20 feet (5.50 to 6 m.) – and is frequently coppiced under woodland management schemes. The nuts don't taste too bad raw (though in my view far inferior to beech-nuts) but are infinitely better roasted. To roast hazel-nuts, remove them from their husks and lay them on a baking-tray and put this into a pre-heated oven at

350°F./180°C (Regulo 4) for about 15 minutes or until golden-brown. Roll them around a bit with a metal implement from time to time so that they roast equally on all sides. When they are ready, allow them to cool. Sprinkle with salt while still hot if you wish to store them as a savoury nibble or to use in savoury recipes; to store them for use in sweet recipes, omit the salt.

These nuts are extremely high in protein value and are absolutely irresistible to squirrels, wood mice etc. If you want to beat your competitors to it you had better start looking round about the third week in August.

Cob-nut Butter

Have your blender at the ready if you want to make this wild substitute for peanut butter, and at the same time you can congratulate yourself that the wild product is considerably superior to peanut butter in protein content. You will need the salted cob-nuts for this recipe. Melt a little butter and put it into the blender with the cob-nuts, and just keep blending until it is the right texture. A smooth butter will need longer blending than a crunchy variety – it's all a matter of taste.

Try the butter to see whether it needs more salt (but try to avoid overdoing it). Pack into airtight jars with screw-top lids, and store in cool conditions. There is no need to refrigerate. The butter will keep for three months if the lid is replaced firmly after use.

Herbed Hazel Spread

1 lb./450 g. cob-nuts
2 teaspoons finely chopped chives (or green spring onion tops)
2 teaspoons finely chopped parsley

6 oz./175 g. butter
Salt and pepper to taste

Use the salted cobs for this recipe. Pound them to a paste with a pestle and mortar and mix in the herbs and seasoning, gradually blending in the butter. This makes a tasty spread to use with cheese crackers or as a dip with cheese straws.

Hazel-nut Biscuits

4 oz./100 g. roasted cob-nuts
12 oz./350 g. plain flour
2 teaspoons baking-powder
½ lb./225 g. butter
½ lb./225 g. sugar

2 eggs
2 tablespoons milk
1 teaspoon vanilla essence
½ teaspoon salt

Unsalted cob-nuts should be used. Chop them as finely as possible, to about the usual size of nut chips as used in biscuits. Cream the butter with the sugar, and beat the eggs well. Add these to the mixture together with the milk and the vanilla essence, then the chopped nuts. Sift together the flour, baking-powder and salt, and add to the mixture by folding in until thoroughly blended.

Roll small balls of the mixture, place on a baking sheet and flatten into rounds with the palm of the hand. The sheet should be well greased or the biscuits will be difficult to remove whole. Bake at 400°F./200°C. (Regulo 6) for 10–15 minutes. Remove to a wire rack for cooling. This quantity makes about 45 biscuits.

Hazel-nut, honey and ginger squares

1 lb./450 g. roasted cob-nuts
12 oz./350 g. self-raising flour
4 eggs
4 tablespoons clear honey

4 teaspoons ground ginger
½ lb./225 g. sugar
Pinch of salt

Chop the nuts finely to biscuit chip size. Beat the eggs well and add the sifted flour and salt a little at a time until a dough is formed. Roll out the dough and cut into strips about ½ inch thick and about 2 inches wide. Cut across the strips at 2-inch intervals to make squares. Put the honey into a pan with the sugar and the ginger and bring to the boil. Drop in the squares (only one or two at a time) and cook over a low heat. Do not stir, or over-cook. Lift out with a slotted spatula when the squares have turned golden-brown. Place them on a flat tin, sprinkle with the chopped nuts and pour the remaining syrup over them. Leave to cool; by the time the squares are cold they will have set. They should be levered carefully off the tin with a spatula, and stored in an airtight cake tin lined with greaseproof paper. Eat like biscuits or cakes. This quantity makes about 20.

OAK (QUERCUS ROBUR)

The nuts produced by the oak are, of course, familiar to all as acorns. These have few applications for the wildfood enthusiast, although they are relished by pigs, squirrels and other animals. They are very bitter, owing to the large amount of tannin they contain, but this can be boiled out to a great extent. The acorns can then be ground into flour – if you want to be bothered – for making bread, cakes, muffins etc. I think stone-ground wholemeal flour tastes a lot better and will do you more good; still, in case you want to experiment, this is what to do.

Remove the acorns from their cups and boil them for two hours. Throw out the water and re-boil them for another two hours. Keep on doing this until the water you throw out is no longer dark-coloured. The gas or electricity you use for all this boiling will probably cost you more than a bag of wholemeal flour, and the time you would save could be put to far more productive use.

The next step after the boiling is to drain the acorns and dry them in the oven. This operation can be combined with roasting them for about an hour at 300°F./150°C. (Regulo 2), spreading them out in shallow pans and turning from time to time so that they are evenly roasted. You then grind them in a mill. It's said that this flour makes good bread, cakes etc.

I've managed to unearth two American recipes from an eighteenth-century cookbook. Apparently they were used by early pioneers in America when wheat flour was difficult to obtain or cost more than the pioneers could afford.

Hard Times Bread

This sounds straight out of Dickens, but apparently it was being made before he was born.

1 lb./450 g. acorn flour	2 teaspoons salt
4 tablespoons butter	2 eggs
4 oz./100 g. maize meal	½ pint/275 ml. buttermilk
1 teaspoon baking soda	

Sift together acorn flour, maize meal, baking soda, salt; beat the eggs well; melt the butter over a low heat. Add the buttermilk to the dry ingredients in the mixing bowl, then the butter, and lastly the beaten eggs. Knead the dough until it is of a fairly soft dropping consistency, like a *very* stiff batter, but not sloppy. Grease a large griddle (a really big heavy cast-iron frying-pan will do if you have no griddle) and cook over the heat, turning once, until both sides are golden-brown. You will note that the recipe does not give gas or electric settings, because the pioneers used wood-burning stoves or even open fires. A medium-high heat should do the job. They do not take long to do; the easiest way is to divide the mixture into large blobs and cook as you would chapatis.

Hard Times Muffins

1 lb./450 g. acorn flour	2 eggs
4 oz./100 g. maize meal	½ pint/275 ml. milk
3 teaspoons baking powder	4 tablespoons melted bacon
1 teaspoon salt	drippings

Sift together the acorn flour, maize meal, baking powder and salt. Beat the eggs with the milk, and stir in the bacon drippings. Add the liquid to the dry ingredients and stir until just moist; do not over-mix. Pour the mixture into muffin tins and bake in a hot oven for about 15 minutes or until browned and crusty. This quantity makes about 30 muffins.

Many of the pioneers built their own ovens from oil drums, old tins and even stones, but perhaps you, like me, have an automatic modern cooker, so at an educated guess I'd say set your oven for 425°F./220°C. (Regulo 7) — 15 minutes at this temperature (pre-heated) would be about right.

Roasted ground acorns can also be used as a substitute for coffee. The recipe for this bizarre experiment will be found in Chapter 17. Apparently it was used during World War II in some European countries when coffee was unobtainable at any price even on the black market.

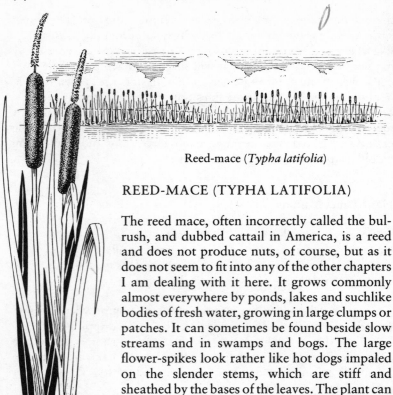

Reed-mace (*Typha latifolia*)

REED-MACE (TYPHA LATIFOLIA)

The reed mace, often incorrectly called the bulrush, and dubbed cattail in America, is a reed and does not produce nuts, of course, but as it does not seem to fit into any of the other chapters I am dealing with it here. It grows commonly almost everywhere by ponds, lakes and suchlike bodies of fresh water, growing in large clumps or patches. It can sometimes be found beside slow streams and in swamps and bogs. The large flower-spikes look rather like hot dogs impaled on the slender stems, which are stiff and sheathed by the bases of the leaves. The plant can grow to 6 feet (1.80 m.) tall, though it does not always reach this height.

The most popular part of the plant to use in wildfood dishes, especially in the States, is the pollen. The ripe flowerheads or spikes are covered with a protein-rich pollen which is easily shaken off into a container held underneath, or brushed off with a good-sized brush. It makes a very good flour, especially for pancakes and muffins (so beloved of Americans) and the pollen is simply substituted for ordinary flour in the relevant recipe. An American pancake recipe is given below. This has been adapted from a recipe in one of Bradford Angier's backpacking manuals.

Cattail Pancakes

½ lb./225 g. cattail pollen
2 teaspoons baking powder
2 eggs
2 tablespoons sugar

½ teaspoon salt
1 pint/575 ml. milk
Butter to cook and to serve
Maple syrup to serve

Make the batter just as you would for ordinary flour pancakes, by sifting the pollen with the baking powder and salt, also the sugar. Beat the eggs well and add the milk, blending thoroughly. Add this to the dry ingredients. Pour the batter into a sparingly buttered pan, which has been pre-heated until just short of smoking hot. Turn once only. The second side takes only half as long to cook. Serve steaming hot with butter and maple sugar. This quantity makes 4 to 6 pancakes according to the size of pan used to cook them.

If after all that wading in muddy stream beds you'd like to have something more than just pollen for all your toil and trouble, you can go in spring and dig up a *few* roots (only where there is a vast reed-bed). You will find shoots growing up the stem from the base of the root which look exactly like asparagus. Cut off and peel these shoots, and cook and eat just like asparagus. They can also be sliced and used raw in salads. It is important to gather this part of the plant for use before the plant has grown to 2 feet (60 cm.) in height – in other words, while the shoots are young and tender. They are quite economical to use as some of these shoots can be anything up to 18 inches (45 cm.) in length, even after peeling off the tough outer leaf to reveal the whitish or greenish crisp core which is the part eaten, so you do not need many plants.

The next stage in the growth of the reed mace is the production of the flower spike. While unripe this is sheathed in a green leaf. This can be cut and cooked as a vegetable. Remove the sheathing leaves and boil the unripe flowerhead in lightly salted water for about 15 minutes. Drain and serve hot. It can be eaten like corn on the cob, or it can be sliced and served in a cheese sauce. The unopened buds attached to the central stem of the flower spike form the 'corn' on the 'cob', this latter being discarded.

The buds can be scraped off the central stem and cooked in several different ways. Here is a dish with a Spanish flavour.

Baked Spiced Cattail Buds

½ lb./225 g. cattail buds
2 tablespoons butter
2 chilli peppers
1 root wild garlic (minced)

4 oz./100 g. strong Cheddar
  cheese (grated)
Salt and black pepper to taste

Cook the cattail buds in a large heavy frying-pan with the butter for about 10 minutes over a medium heat. Do not let them burn. Turn from time to time to ensure that they are cooked through. Add the chilli peppers (finely chopped), the minced garlic (use ordinary garlic if you cannot find the wild kind) and the seasonings. Cook for 5 minutes longer. *Remove the chilli peppers.*

Now pour the cooked buds into a shallow ovenproof dish and sprinkle with grated Cheddar cheese. Use a really mature Cheddar, not one of the mild varieties. Bake for 10 minutes in a pre-heated oven at 400°F./200°C. (Regulo 6) and serve hot. This quantity serves 5 to 6.

Here is another dish using cattail buds but this time spiced with sweet aromatic spices instead of the kind which are liable to blow your head off if you are careless.

Cattail Flips

½ lb./225 g. cattail buds
2 tablespoons butter
½ teaspoon ground ginger
¼ teaspoon ground cinnamon
6 oz./175 g. flour (or cattail
  pollen)

2 teaspoons baking powder
2 tablespoons sugar
Pinch of salt
2 eggs
½ pint/275 ml. milk

Sift flour (or pollen) with the baking powder, sugar and salt. Beat the eggs and blend with the milk and melted butter (reserving a little for cooking). Stir the liquid ingredients into the dry ingredients. Lightly cook the cattail buds by boiling for a few minutes and draining, and stir them into the batter together with the cinnamon and ginger. Cook exactly like ordinary pancakes, and serve with honey or maple syrup. This quantity makes about 12 pancakes.

WALNUT (JUGLANS REGIA)

The walnut is not a native tree but was introduced from Southern Europe nearly 500 years ago. Despite this length of time, the species has not become widely established and is probably not well adapted to our precarious climate. It has, however, frequently been used as an ornamental tree and planted in parks, gardens etc. It is a spreading tree which can grow to 100 feet (20 m.) in favourable conditions. The bark is grey, smooth in young specimens. The leaves are pinnate and faintly aromatic. The nuts, which appear in the autumn, are brown and enclosed in a green case. Since one tree can yield up to 150 pounds of nuts, perhaps it does not matter too much, from the wildfood enthusiast's standpoint, that there are not all that many trees around.

If you can manage to get hold of sufficient walnuts, you can, and should, pickle some. The taste bears no resemblance whatsoever to the woody offerings of the commercial producers available at some of the larger supermarkets. Before you start, I must warn you that the walnuts will stain your skin, clothing and any surface on which you prepare them black unless adequately protected, and that their stain is almost impossible to remove. You *must* wear rubber gloves and your oldest clothes plus a plastic apron, and use piles of old newspapers on the preparation table. Put a layer of black plastic dustbin bags under the newspapers, to stop moisture seeping through and ruining the table-top.

Pickled Walnuts

For pickling, the walnuts have to be picked in July while they are still green and fairly soft. Prick them all over with a fork, rather as though they were sausages, and steep them for a week in a bucket of strong brine. By the end of this time they should have all turned black, at which stage remove them from the brine, rinse them in plain cold water, and spread them out to dry on a flat surface in a warm place, but out of hot sunshine and away from direct heat – you do not want them to look like wrinkled old prunes! Leave them for three days, then pack them into sterilized glass jars and fill the jars right to the top with hot spiced vinegar (see page 164). Seal and label in the usual way. Remember that metal lids must not be used for vinegar pickles. And another thing – don't use your white plastic winemaking bucket for walnuts or you'll ruin it!

Pickled walnuts should be kept for at least three months before using, longer if possible.

The walnut is a much commoner tree in America, and all the recipes I am now going to give you come from the States.

Walnut Soup

½ lb./225 g. shelled walnuts
2 oz./50 g. butter
2 heads celery
1 onion

2 pints/1150 ml. stock or water
5 fl. oz./150 ml. single cream
Salt and black pepper to taste

Melt the butter in a large frying-pan, chop the onion and celery as finely as possible and cook gently in the butter until soft. The heat should be low and the onion and celery must not be allowed to burn. Liquidize the chopped walnuts with a little of the stock (or water) in a blender, and mix with the vegetables in the pan. Now transfer to a big soup saucepan and add the rest of the stock or water and the seasoning. Keep stirring while gently cooking until the soup is smooth in texture. Remove from heat, stir in the cream and serve piping hot. This quantity serves 6 to 8.

Walnut Bread

6 oz./175 g. chopped walnuts
1 lb./450 g. wholemeal flour
4 teaspoons baking powder
1 pint/575 ml. milk

2 eggs
6 oz./175 g. Demerara sugar
½ teaspoon salt

Beat the eggs well and stir in the sugar. Sift the flour with the salt and baking powder. Add to the sugar and egg mixture a little at a time together with the milk, until a soft pliable dough forms. Stir in the chopped walnuts. Divide the dough into two and put each portion into a well-greased loaf-tin. Leave to stand in a warm place for about half an hour, and then bake at 350°F./180°C. (Regulo 4) for 45 minutes. This quantity makes two one-pound loaves. If you like, you can sprinkle a few larger chopped walnut pieces, or halved walnuts, on top of the loaves before putting them into the oven, for decoration.

Walnut Cheese

Finely chopped walnuts can be mixed with cottage or cream cheese.
A good sandwich filling may also be made by grating Cheddar cheese
and mixing in finely chopped walnuts and a dash of Worcestershire
sauce or Tabasco, if liked.

Walnut Topless Pie

No point in hiding all the goodness of this filling with a crust!

For the base:

8 oz./225 g. graham crumbs (digestive biscuits)	4 tablespoons Demerara sugar
	4 oz./100 g. butter

For the filling:

8 oz./225 g. chopped walnuts	4 oz./100 g. butter
6fl. oz./175 ml. golden syrup	4 eggs
4 oz./100 g. soft moist brown sugar	2 lemons

To make the graham crust, crush the digestive biscuits to a fine
crumb consistency and mix with the sugar. Melt the butter and blend
well together. Press into a 12-inch (30 cm.) flan-tin (well-buttered),
and chill in the fridge while you are preparing the filling.

Cream the butter and sugar and beat the eggs into the mixture.
Warm the golden syrup slightly and beat into the mixture. Add the
chopped walnuts and the juice and grated rind of the lemons. Spoon
the mixture into the prepared flan-case and bake at 350°F./180°C.
(Regulo 4) for about 45 minutes, or until golden-brown. Serve cold
with cream. This quantity serves 6.

Orange, Lemon and Walnut Marmalade

3 lbs./1350 g. oranges	½ lb./225 g. chopped walnuts
3 lbs./1350 g. lemons	4 tablespoons water
6 lbs./2700 g. white sugar	
2 lbs./900 g. raisins or sultanas, or a mixture of both	

Chop the oranges roughly. Do not remove the peel, but remove the white pith and any pips. Do the same with the lemons. Throw the lot into the preserving pan with the (seedless) raisins and/or sultanas, the chopped walnuts and the water, and the sugar. Cook until boiling-point is reached and then continue with a fast rolling boil until jam-setting temperature (220°F./140°C.) is reached. Pot into hot sterilized jars, seal and label.

Walnut Toffee

½ lb./225 g. chopped walnuts	1 lb./450 g. Demerara sugar
½ lb./225 g. butter	1 lb./450 g. golden syrup

Melt the butter in a heavy pan and stir in all the other ingredients, mixing well. Keep stirring until hard ball stage (250°F./125°C.) is reached. Pour into a well-buttered flat tin and leave to cool. When almost set, mark into squares and leave until quite cold before turning out.

Biscuits using walnuts seem to be among the most popular of American recipes. Here are four which are not too difficult to do.

Walnut Rounds

½ lb./225 g. chopped walnuts	6 oz./175 g. butter
12 oz./350 g. flour	6 oz./175 g. sugar

Cream butter and sugar, then add flour and chopped walnuts. Roll into small balls (about ½ inch in diameter) and place on a greased baking sheet, spaced about an inch apart, in a pre-heated oven (350°F./180°C. or Regulo 4). Flatten each ball with the bottom of a glass, and bake for about 15 minutes or until rich golden-brown. Cool on a wire rack, sprinkling with sugar while still warm. When quite cold, store in an airtight tin. This quantity makes about 30 biscuits.

Walnut Squares

½ lb./225 g. chopped walnuts
6 oz./175 g. flour
½ teaspoon salt
¼ teaspoon baking soda

12 oz./350 g. dark brown
  Muscovado sugar
3 eggs
1 teaspoon vanilla essence

Beat together the eggs, brown sugar and vanilla essence. Into another bowl sift together the flour, salt and baking soda. Gradually beat the dry ingredients into the liquid ingredients, adding the chopped walnuts last. Pour the mixture into a greased flat baking-tin not less than 13 inches by 9 inches (23 cm.) in size – bigger if possible. Pre-heat oven to 350°F./180°C. (Regulo 4), and bake for about 25 minutes, or until light brown and springy when gently pressed with a finger-tip. Remove from oven and cut into squares while still hot, and leave in the tin. Remove only when quite cold. Makes about 24 squares.

Walnut Drops

½ lb./225 g. chopped walnuts
6 oz./175 g. butter
6 oz./175 g. brown sugar (any
  kind)

1 teaspoon vanilla essence
½ teaspoon salt
12 oz./350 g. flour

Cream butter and sugar, then add salt and vanilla essence. Beat in flour, and add the walnuts. Shape into small balls (about ½ inch across) and place one inch apart on a greased baking sheet. Preheat oven to 350°F./180°C. (Regulo 4) and bake for about 15 minutes, or until golden brown. Remove from sheet and roll in sugar while still warm. Cool on a wire rack and store in an airtight tin. Makes 40 to 45 cookies.

Walnut Folds

50 halved walnuts
1 lb./450 g. flour
½ lb./225 g. sugar

½ lb./225 g. butter
2 teaspoons vanilla essence

Cream butter, sugar and vanilla essence. Fold in the flour and mix thoroughly. Wrap the dough in foil and leave to chill in fridge until firm. Then with floured hands pinch off small walnut-sized pieces of dough, and pat each piece until round and flat, and about ¼ inch thick. Place a half-walnut in the middle of each round, folding the dough over it from two sides. Space the biscuits one inch apart on a greased baking-sheet and put into a preheated oven (350°F./180°C. or Regulo 4) and bake for about 15 minutes or until golden-brown.

Remove from oven and place on a wire rack to cool, sprinkling them with sugar while still warm. When quite cold, store in an airtight container. Makes 50 biscuits.

15

THE 20 BEST MUSHROOMS

Nowhere in the field of wildfood gathering is correct identification more vital than when mushroom-hunting. If you are intending to make sorrel soup and you pull dock instead of sorrel you will not be poisoned, although the soup will not taste so good. But drop a destroying angel into your stew instead of St George's mushroom, and it will be St Peter rather than St George you'll be meeting rather sooner than you had hoped.

While there are over a hundred good edible species of mushroom to be found growing wild in the British Isles, there are also four deadly species which are ninety per cent likely to kill you, and another dozen or so species which, although not fatally toxic, would make you so ill that if you ate them the painful and unpleasant symptoms could put you off mushroom-collecting for good. That would be a great pity as you would then be depriving yourself of enjoying the ones which are good eating. Some are so delicious that they are a gourmet experience in themselves and you will wonder why you did not try to find out more about them sooner. So, without more ado, I am going to describe the ones to avoid.

THE DEATH CAP (*Amanita phalloides*)

This is the deadliest of Britain's four most highly poisonous species of fungi. Its name is well deserved, since it is responsible for perhaps ninety per cent of all the fatalities caused by mushroom poisoning. It is the most dangerous fungus known, and the consumption of only a minute quantity will cause intensely painful symptoms, usually followed by a lingering and agonizing death.

To the uninitiated, superficial resemblances between this species and certain edible mushrooms have doubtless been responsible for catastrophic results. However, there are sufficient differences, as opposed to similarities, which can be learned and committed indelibly to memory. This is the *only* safeguard.

1. The gills of the death cap are *always* white at all times, and *never* darken or change colour with age.
2. The gills are *free* from the stem (see diagram).
3. There is a *ring* on the stem, easily visible in young specimens, less apparent in older ones but still discernible.
4. The base of the stem is sheathed in a cup-like volva (see figure) which is usually buried in the soil, though sometimes, in light, friable soils, the loose irregular upper edges may show above the surface. It therefore behoves the mushroom-collector to *dig out* any white mushrooms and unequivocally reject *any* which have this characteristic volva at the base. It is a diagnostic feature of *Amanita phalloides*.

The cap is at first egg-shaped; as it expands, it becomes convex or flattened. It can measure from 2 to 4 inches (5–10 cm.) in diameter. Its colour is typically a light olive or yellowish, with a few darkish streaks, especially near the centre.

A white variety sometimes occurs in which the cap is pure white, but it is rather uncommon. This has been given specific status, as *Amanita verna*, by some authorities, while others consider it to be merely an albino form of *A. phalloides*. Whatever its botanical status, it still possesses all the other distinctive features of *A. phalloides* and is equally deadly.

In young specimens there may remain on top of the cap a few torn fragments of the white membrane or 'veil' that covers the fungus as it emerges above the surface of the earth, but these soon disappear. The cap is smooth when dry, but slightly slimy when moist.

The stem is white, occasionally with a pale yellowish or greenish tinge, and is smooth, with a few closely adhering scales just below the ring. It is rather slender, narrower at the top and usually longer than the diameter of the cap which it supports. The stem becomes hollow in old specimens. To its upper part the ring is attached, white above and pale yellowish below, thin and hanging downwards like a frill. It is easily rubbed off, but one can usually see fairly easily where it was attached.

The gills are white, crowded and free from the stem, and rounded at the ends adjacent to the stem. The spores are white. The flesh is soft and white, and the cap peels off easily. The fungus has a sweetish smell, more noticeable in older specimens.

The death cap is common in deciduous woodlands and is sometimes found in adjoining grasslands. It is mainly a summer species, sometimes continuing to appear until mid-autumn, especially in warm seasons.

Learn to identify this most deadly mushroom of all, which causes many fatal cases of poisoning every year, especially on the Continent, where wild mushroom-gathering for the pot is more often practised than in Britain. Once you have compared a specimen with any edible white agaric of comparable size, you will never again confuse them.

IF IN DOUBT
GO WITHOUT!

THE DESTROYING ANGEL (*Amanita virosa*)

No less poisonous than the death cap is this closely related species, but far fewer deaths have been attributed to it, purely and simply because it is quite rare. It grows, where it occurs, in both deciduous and coniferous woodlands in summer and autumn. It should be noted that this species does not grow in open grassland. Pure white throughout, it does not attain the size of *Amanita phalloides*.

The cap, which is slightly viscid, is at first distinctly conical, often asymmetrical, giving it what John Ramsbottom, the eminent authority on fungi, has succinctly described as 'rather a tipsy look'. The central boss is always retained, even when the cap is fully expanded.

The white stem, which grows from a membranous sheath or volva, is slender and covered with woolly-looking scales, and frequently grows curved rather than straight. The ring, which is entirely white and silky, is usually lower on one side, remaining attached to the edge of the cap at several points.

The gills are pure white with notched, flaky-looking edges. The flesh is white, with a heavy, cloying smell, and the spores are white.

Fatal cases of poisoning have been caused by collectors confusing this species with St George's mushroom, the horse mushroom, the

THE DEADLY FOUR

a, Death cap; b, Destroying angel; c, Red-staining inocybe;
d, Leaden entoloma

1 Gills *white* in all four, but becoming pinkish in (d) with
age
2 Ring round stem in (a) and (b); no ring in (c) or (d)
3 Volva (bulbous sheath) at base in (a) and (b); no volva in
(c) or (d)

field agaric and other white-capped species. Remember that *no edible agaric has white gills*; they may be pale pink or some shade of beige, but *never* white. Nor do edible species ever have any cup-like structure at the base of the stem. You are unlikely to make any fatal errors of identification if you remember these two basic rules.

Avoid gathering *any* wild mushroom in the undeveloped 'egg' or 'button' stage, as the gills cannot be seen until the cap begins to expand and the enveloping veil is torn. There are cases on record where even people with a good knowledge of fungi have been poisoned by gathering the early stages of white-capped poisonous species which looked exactly like young specimens of their edible counterparts. The couplet to remember now is:

**IF NOT GROWN
LEAVE ALONE!**

THE RED-STAINING INOCYBE (*Inocybe patouillardii*)

This is not normally a very common species, but in some years it appears much more abundantly than usual in its grassy habitats in the southern counties, especially after a season of heavy rains. Unlike many other fungi, it is a late spring and summer species, occurring in parkland and deciduous woodland, where it is usually found in clearings, beside paths, at the edges of woods and in similar light and open situations.

The red-staining inocybe, which is one of Britain's four really dangerous species, has been eaten, both in Britain and on the Continent, with fatal results, but it is difficult to imagine with what edible species it could have been confused. Although entirely pure white and silky at first, if touched in any way, even superficially without breaking the skin, it immediately becomes stained with bright sealing-wax red, a character which at once serves to distinguish it from any edible species, all of which can be handled with impunity without developing any coloured streaks or blotches. The mushroom also acquires this bright red staining naturally with age, on both cap and stem.

The cap is fleshy, from one to 3 inches (2.5 to 7.5 cm.) in diameter, conical at first, then flattened with a prominent central boss. The edges of the cap are frequently folded or lobed, even in young specimens, giving it a very irregular shape, and as the cap expands with growth, it may split from the edge inwards.

The stem is fibrous without any ring, fairly stout, firm and solid, and usually narrower at the top, where its surface appears somewhat mealy. The gills are crowded, narrow and almost free from the stem; at first white, they later become olive-brown with white edges. The spores are the exact shade which artists call raw sienna. The red-staining inocybe has a pleasant fruity smell, which may well have been a misleading factor to the unfortunate persons ignorant of its identity.

This very dangerous species must be avoided at all costs. When gathering any white mushrooms, press the cap or stem with a fingernail, or cut the edge; if no red stain appears it is not *Inocybe patouillardii*, but check against the descriptions of other white mushrooms in case it may be another poisonous species.

Remember –

IF IN DOUBT
GO WITHOUT!

THE LEADEN ENTOLOMA (*Entoloma lividum*)

This is a highly toxic mushroom which causes a number of serious cases of poisoning, some fatal, every year. Unlike the death cap and the destroying angel, in which the symptoms do not appear until from 12 to 24 hours after eating, the symptoms of poisoning by the leaden entoloma are rapid in their onset, appearing within from 20 minutes to 2 hours of its consumption. Violent retching and vomiting, accompanied by equally violent purging, are the main symptoms, which, although they lessen in intensity after a time, take a week or more to subside completely; in several cases death has resulted from eating this species. It is frequently mistaken for St George's mushroom (*Tricholoma gambosum*), which it resembles, particularly when young.

The gills of the leaden entoloma, though white at first, soon become flesh-pink as the spores develop; it is this character which has led to confusion with the pink-gilled *Tricholoma gambosum*. Furthermore, the leaden entoloma has a pleasant smell and taste which has lulled many an unwary experimenter into a sense of false security, so that by eating more than originally intended the symptoms were intensified. The cap is also firm and fleshy, like that of *Tricholoma gambosum*. However, *Entoloma lividum* appears much later than St George's mushroom, usually in summer and autumn, and seldom, if ever, before the end of May, whereas St George's mushroom is a spring species, being found mainly from late April (23 April is St George's Day, hence its name) into May. The leaden entoloma grows in open deciduous woods, sometimes in numbers, but is not found everywhere; it is locally very common in parts of the Midlands.

The cap, which can reach a diameter of 5 inches (12.5 cm.), has a shiny, silky look, but is never viscid. It is convex at first, later becoming wavy-edged and irregular. It is smooth and of a greyish-beige or greyish-ochre colour, and the central boss is not very pronounced. The skin cannot be peeled off easily.

The stem is whitish, finely striated, rather short and stout, firm and solid, and often slightly club-shaped at the base. There is no ring or volva. It frequently grows more curved than straight.

The gills, which are white only in the very young stage, soon assume a salmon-pink colouration as the spores, which are a dull pink, mature. Occasionally they exhibit a yellowish tinge at their edges. They are somewhat crowded and, though at first touching the stem, later become almost free. The flesh is white, thick and firm-textured and has a distinct mealy smell.

Avoid the leaden entoloma, despite its attractive appearance, pleasant smell and firm 'mushroomy' texture. You could, at the very least, end up in hospital at the wrong end of a stomach-pump.

The above four species are the four most deadly mushrooms in Britain or, indeed, in Europe, but there are also several others to avoid which cause varying degrees of vomiting, diarrhoea, hallucinations and double vision, to mention a few of the unpleasant symptoms, though these species are not normally fatal. A few do not have popular English names. These species are as follows.

FLY AGARIC (*Amanita muscaria*)

This is the very common and conspicuous 'gnomes' toadstool', bright red with white irregular blotches, which makes such an attractive picture on those greeting cards showing autumn woodland scenes. It is distinctive enough to require no further description. You will note that the gnomes are always shown sitting on it but never eating it for it is very poisonous!

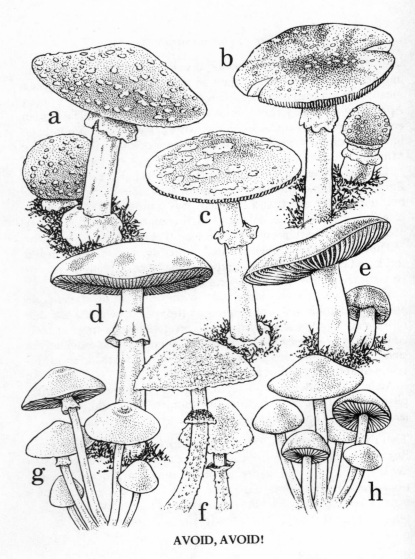

AVOID, AVOID!

a, Fly agaric; b, Panther cap; c, False death cap;
d, Yellow-staining mushroom; e, Sickener; f, Verdigris agaric; g, Crested
lepiota; h, Sulphur-tuft

1 Gills *white* in (a), (b), (c), (d) (darkening with age), (e), (g);
gills purple in (f), yellowish-green in (h)

2 Ring present in (a), (b), (c), (d), (e), (g); no ring in (f) and
(h)

3 Volva present in (a), (b), (c); volva not present in (d), (e),
(f), (g), (h)

THE PANTHER CAP (*Amanita pantherina*)

Another member of the toxic *Amanita* genus to avoid. It is sometimes known as the False Blusher. It grows in deciduous woods and can be found fairly commonly from August to October. The cap is about 4 inches (10 cm.) in diameter and is brownish, dotted with white irregular blotches just like *A. muscaria*, and the edge of the cap is frequently finely striated. The crowded gills are white and free from the stem. The stem is about 4 inches (10 cm.) long, swollen at the base where it emerges from the volva (the sheath-like cup at the base). It is white and has a shining, silky appearance, with a thin, irregular ring. The flesh and the spores are white. Both the white blotches on the cap and the ring are easily washed off by rain, or disintegrate with age, and the mushroom can then be confused with similar-looking ring-less agarics with a smooth brownish cap. The panther cap, however, has *a strong smell of raw potatoes*, which will help to distinguish it, as well as the diagnostic *Amanita* feature of the volva, which is not found in edible agarics.

FALSE DEATH CAP (*Amanita citrina*)

This is the *A. mappa* of the older books, but *citrina* is a more descriptive specific name, referring to the lemon-yellow colour of the cap. This, however, often appears more whitish, owing to the presence of remnants of the veil adhering in patches. The crowded white gills are free from the stem. The stem itself is about 4 inches (10 cm.) tall, white and striated above the ring. The stem is grossly swollen at the base almost like an onion-shape. The spores are white. The ring is white, striated above, downy beneath and drooping. The flesh is white, and this species, too, has a smell of raw potatoes, though less pronounced than that of the preceding species. The false death cap grows in pine and beech woods and is quite common from August to October.

YELLOW-STAINING MUSHROOM (*Psalliota xanthoderma*)

The white cap of this species stains bright yellow when bruised, so this species can be easily eliminated when you apply the thumbnail test (see page 188). Apart from this, the cap is about 3 inches

(7.5 cm.) across, smooth, and easily separates from the stem, frequently falling off as it is picked. The crowded, free gills are white to start with, then turning pink and finally brownish, with the increasing age of the mushroom. The spores are a purplish chocolate-brown. The stem reaches about 3 inches (7.5 cm.) in height and is white, yellowish at the base. The stem, too, stains bright yellow when bruised. The ring is thin, white and membranous, the flesh white. The mushroom has a rather unpleasant smell, rather like carbolic soap. This should be enough to put you off even before you touch it to test it for staining. It is a fairly common species of parks and pastureland, appearing from August to October.

THE SICKENER (*Russula emetica*)

Both the popular name and the scientific name of this one are descriptive enough for anybody, so all you have to do is give it a wide berth. It's easy to spot, being bright red (though the shade of red is different from that of the fly agaric – it's a more 'rosy' red), and although most books give the diameter of the cap as 3 inches (7.5 cm.), I have found them considerably bigger. One I found was 5 inches (12.5 cm.), though this is, perhaps, unusual. It is shiny and slimy-looking, and the colour fades in older specimens to a sort of muddy pink. The skin peels easily.

The gills are white and free from the stem, and the spores are white. The stem is about 3 inches (7.5 cm.) high, solid and rather brittle, and pure white without any ring. This mushroom is very common and grows in woods and wooded scrub from August to November.

VERDIGRIS AGARIC (*Stropharia aeruginosa*)

This is a very pretty verdigris-green species, easily recognizable. It is usually very small, seldom more than 2 inches (5 cm.) across the cap, which is slimy. The gills are adnate (see diagram) and violet at first, becoming dark brown. The spores are purple. The stem grows up to 3 inches (7.5 cm.) tall, whitish green and slimy, with a whitish ring. The mushroom smells strongly of radishes. The flesh is pale green. The species is not particularly common but grows in beechwoods from July to November, and occasionally in pinewoods.

CRESTED LEPIOTA (*Lepiota cristata*)

This is a strong and unpleasant-smelling relative of the edible and delicious parasol mushroom (*Lepiota procera*). Unlike this latter species, the crested lepiota does not grow to any great size, 1½ inches (3.5 cm.) in diameter being about average. The white cap has a reddish-brown central disc of granulose scales. The white gills are thin and crowded, free from the stem. The stem itself is pinkish-white, very fragile, and grows to about 5 inches (12.5 cm.); it is slender, smooth and silky and usually reddish-brown at the base. The ring is white, thin and membranous, rather inconspicuous, and frequently disappears altogether with age.

The flesh is pinkish-white. The mushroom grows in parks, gardens and pastureland, frequently on lawns and compost-heaps. It is fairly common and occurs from August to November.

SULPHUR-TUFT (*Hypholoma fasciculare*)

This, as its name implies, grows in tufts (the specific name *fasciculare* means 'in bundles') mainly on beech trees, appearing at any time from April to October, and is exceedingly common. It should not be confused with the edible honey-tuft (*Armillaria mellea*) which will grow on the trunks of practically any tree and is, if anything, even more common, but which appears much later in the year, rarely before September. The cap of the sulphur-tuft is about 2 inches (5 cm.) across, sulphur-yellow with adnate (see diagram) gills, crowded and yellowish-green, darkening with age. The spores are purple, the flesh yellow. The stem is about 4 inches (10 cm.) tall, hollow, yellow and often curved. There is no distinct ring, but occasionally a faint scar. The fungus has an unpleasant odour.

BOLETUS LURIDUS

The *Boletus* mushrooms belong to an entirely different family from the agarics. The cap is spongy rather than fleshy, and instead of gills they have spores contained in a network of tiny holes, the *pores*. Their stems are thick and stockily built, never slender, and usually bulging out at the base. They have no ring or volva – these are strictly agaric features. The skin of the cap is usually a different colour from the underside, though not invariably.

The genus contains a number of very good edible species, such as the cep (*Boletus edulis*) which plays such an important part in French and German cookery. The one presently to be described, however, is highly toxic. However, fortunately it is easy to identify; its specific name, *luridus*, gives some indication of its appearance. It is the stem which is a garish mixture of brilliant purple and yellowish ochre, not the cap, which is a plain beige colour. The hues of the stem are combined in a coarse network of veins, not unlike some of the lurid pictures in some medical books showing the veins of the human body. Combined with this appearance, the fungus has a sour smell. The pores (underside of the cap) are a rust-red.

Boletus luridus is found in beech and oak woods, especially on chalk soils. It is also partial to parkland where lime trees grow. It may be found from June to September. The cap can be 6 inches/15 cm. across, but is usually rather smaller.

BOLETUS SATANUS

In an attempt to translate the specific name of this fungus into 'popular' English, some writers have called it the 'Devil's Boletus'. It can cause very violent symptoms of enteric poisoning, so the name is apt.

This is another large species; a 6-inch (15 cm.) cap is quite common. The stem has a coarse network of veins, as in the preceding species, but these are darker in colour, lighter beneath the cap. The cap itself is pale whitish green, the pores bright red. The fungus does not have much odour. The flesh is white, becoming blue when broken. This species is confined mainly to the south of England and affects chalk soils only.

BOLETUS PIPERATUS

This boletus is not 'poisonous' in the usually understood sense of the word but its taste is unacceptably pungent, hot and peppery – a tiny portion touched to the tip of the tongue tastes like a mouthful of raw chillies! The species is easily recognized by having a much more slender stem than most other *Boletus* species, the chrome-yellow patch at the base of the stem, the rust-coloured spores and the cinnamon-coloured cap and stem (it is unusual in this group to have a species with 'matching' cap and stem). The cap is shiny when dry and is much smaller than the other two species just described, seldom more than 3 inches (7.5 cm.) and usually smaller. It has very little scent. This little boletus is widely distributed and is found in both deciduous and coniferous woods.

We come now to the edible mushrooms. There are more than a hundred edible species in Britain. Some are, perhaps, more edible than others, so I have chosen the twenty best ones to look for.

Most recipes recommend a specific species, but in a good many cases you may substitute other species as and when available, if they are a similar type of fungus. One thing you MUST do, however, whichever kinds you use, is to check them before use with a *good* illustrated botany book giving the identification of the species in the form of colour plates (photographs are usually a more accurate guide than coloured drawings). Some good reliable books for identification are listed in Appendix II. You can either take a pocket-sized book with you when going out on a fungus foray (as mushroom-gathering is called), or, if the book you use is a large and heavy one, check them when you return home before you start cooking! In this case it is advisable to keep each species gathered in a separate bag, box or basket. If you find you have inadvertently gathered a harmful species, be sure to wash your hands thoroughly after destroying them, before starting to cook with the ones that are good.

BLEWIT (*Tricholoma personatum*) AND WOOD BLEWIT (*T. nudum*)

These two are, to my mind, just about the most delicious of all our native wild mushrooms. They also share with some of the other good edible kinds a most welcome feature: owing to their distinctive coloration it is very unlikely that they could be confused with any other species.

A hundred years ago – regrettably, no longer – blewits were sold in London's Covent Garden market. Nowadays 'bluelegs' (as they are called in the Midlands) are still occasionally sold on market stalls in that region, though far less frequently than formerly. During the last 12 years I have seen them offered for sale in greengrocers' shops in Northampton, Rugeley, Cannock, Poynton and Crewe. However, since they are quite common and fairly well distributed, you should be able to find them without much difficulty, from early October

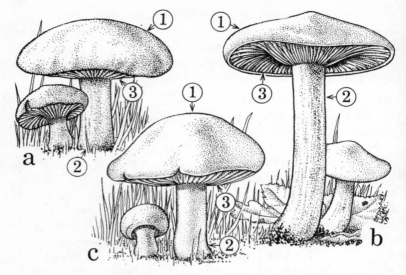

a, Blewit (*Tricholoma personatum*); b, Wood blewit (*T. nudum*); c, St George's Mushroom (*T. gambosum*)

1 (a) and (c) Cap rounded
2 (a) and (c) Stem thick
3 (a) Gills separate from stem
3 (c) Gills sinuate

1 (b) Cap flattened
2 (b) Stem more slender
3 (b) Gills decurrent

onwards, on pastures and downlands, often growing in large rings.

The cap of *T. personatum* is smooth, rounded and fleshy, from 2½ to 5 inches (6.5 to 12.5 cm.) in diameter, its edge characteristically overhanging the gills. With growth the cap tends to flatten out somewhat but, unlike the next species, it never loses its original rounded look – a feature which helps to distinguish the two species. The colour of the cap is pale beige.

The stem is very stout, short (usually not more than 3 inches (7.5 cm.) high), solid and cylindrical, often swollen at the base. There is no ring. Its characteristic blue colouration is the diagnostic feature which will enable you to identify this very tasty mushroom without fear of confusion (except, possibly, with the next species, the wood blewit (*T. nudum*) which tastes just as good!).

The gills are whitish at first, darkening with age. They are broad and crowded and can easily be separated from the cap. The spores are pale pink. The flesh is white when dry, greyish when moist and has a very pleasant odour.

As the taste and texture of blewits and wood blewits are similar, I have given the recipes at the end of the description of the next species.

WOOD BLEWIT (*Tricholoma nudum*)

The wood blewit appears later than *T. personatum*, seldom being found before mid-October and continuing well into late November. I have often found it even when there was a sharp frost. It can also frequently be found growing on old compost-heaps, especially those which have dead leaves as their main constituent.

In colour it is much like the preceding species, but the blue tint is more of a delicate lilac and also tinges the cap, which usually grows larger than that of *T. personatum*; the cap of *T. nudum* can reach 5 or 6 inches (12.5 to 15 cm.) across. I once found a beautiful 7-inch (18-cm.) specimen on Wimbledon Common; it weighed a pound and made a meal for four! Its shape is different from that of the preceding species; at first convex, it soon becomes flattened, or even concave. Its margin is incurved and wavy. The colour of the cap darkens with age, as in *T. personatum*, but it never loses the characteristic lilac tinge.

The ringless stem is rather more slender than in *T. personatum* and the gills narrower, giving a more crowded appearance. As the cap expands with growth, the gills sometimes run down the stem slightly. They are bluish, never developing a brownish coloration; this is another point which will help you to distinguish between these two closely allied species. Yet another diagnostic feature of the present species is that the flesh, too, is bluish, unlike that of *T. personatum*. The spores are pinkish. The odour is less pronounced than that of the preceding species and can best be described as a faint but pleasant 'mushroomy' smell.

Blewits and Wild Celery Casserole

Either blewits or wood blewits can be used in any of these recipes. If wild celery (*Apium graveolens*) cannot be found, ordinary celery may be used.

6 oz./175 g. blewits
1 head wild celery
½ pint/275 ml. milk
1 oz./25 g. plain flour
2 oz./50 g. butter
2 oz./50 g. grated Cheddar
 cheese

1½ oz./37½ g. breadcrumbs
1 onion (chopped)
Dash of paprika
Salt and white pepper to taste

Slice the mushrooms and cook gently in the milk until tender but do not overcook or they will become mushy, which ruins them. Remove from milk with slotted spoon, and reserve milk. Place mushrooms in casserole dish.

Fry onion and celery (chopped, including the green leafy parts) gently in butter for 5 minutes. Blend in the flour, then add the milk in which the mushrooms were cooked. Season with salt, pepper and paprika, and pour the mixture over the mushrooms in the casserole. Sprinkle a mixture of breadcrumbs and grated Cheddar cheese over the top, and cook in the oven, without a lid, until the crumble topping is golden-brown. A moderate oven (350°F./180°C. or Regulo 4) should have them ready in about 20 minutes.

Stewed Blewits

Just stew the blewits in milk, adding salt and white pepper to taste, adding an Oxo if you want to transform the milk into 'gravy'. Cook on a moderate heat until just tender, and eat with a bread dip (fingers of bread dipped into the 'gravy'). It's very frustrating to have to go without this superb dish until the late autumn – blewits will not freeze, nor can you dry them.

Blewits in Parsley Sauce

For the parsley sauce:
½ pint/275 ml. milk
¼ pint/150 ml. single cream
1½ oz./37½ g. butter
1 oz./25 g. plain flour

4 tablespoons chopped fresh
 parsley
Salt and white pepper to taste

Blewits or wood blewits – enough for 4

Cook the blewits, chopped into pieces (but not too small) in the milk over a low heat for about 7 minutes; then remove to a dish. Now lower the heat as far as possible and add the cream, butter and flour, parsley and seasoning. Whisk all together with a wire whisk (not a rotary beater) gently while cooking until the mixture is absolutely smooth and thickened. Then drop the blewits back into the mixture and keep over the heat just long enough for them to be reheated through. Stir all the time. Whatever you do, the mixture must not be allowed to boil. Serve hot with toast wedges or croûtons. If you have enough blewits this makes a satisfying main dish in itself.

Blewits cooked like tripe

This Midlands recipe is slightly adapted from John Ramsbottom's book on edible fungi (see Bibliography at the end of this book).

'The stems are chopped up finely with an equal amount of onions and packed round the caps in a shallow dish with a little butter and sage. After cooking slowly for half an hour, the liquid is poured off, thickened with flour and butter, boiled and seasoned, and poured back. The whole is then stewed under cover for a further half hour and served with mashed potatoes together with apple sauce.'

Creamed Blewits

Slice the blewits and cook them very gently in a pan with enough double cream to cover them completely. Add a little salt and pepper to taste but do not overdo the seasoning. Be sure not to let the contents of the pan boil. When tender (about 7 minutes) serve piping hot.

PARASOL MUSHROOM (*Lepiota procera*)

Specimens have been found measuring a foot (30 cm.) across. I've never found any that size but have frequently gathered 7-inch (18 cm.) specimens and occasionally 8-inch (20 cm.) examples. Thus, to make a meal for four you do not need more than one or two, as they are quite heavy when they reach that size. The species also grows quite tall, anything from 10 inches (25 cm.) to 14 inches (35 cm.)

Parasol mushroom (*Lepiota procera*)

being quite usual. The mushroom is also very distinctive in appearance. The only other species with which it can possibly be confused is the much rarer and much smaller *Lepiota rhacodes*, or shaggy parasol mushroom, which is also edible but less tasty, or, possibly, the poisonous crested lepiota (*L. cristata*) described on page 193. However, this latter species never grows to any great size and has a strong unpleasant smell. All in all, it's unlikely that you will confuse the good and tasty *L. procera* with any others in the genus.

It is quite common throughout Britain, occurring in deciduous woodland, especially on the edges of clearings and on the outskirts of copses, and sometimes on pastureland. I found it once growing very commonly on the golf course on Hayling Island. Where you find one you find several – it is very gregarious. The cap has a typical pointed boss in the centre, brownish in colour, and the rest of the cap is covered with brownish scales, giving it a rather roof-like or 'shingled' appearance. The background colour of the skin of the cap is greyish or very pale whitish-beige. The stem is also scaly and somewhat similar in colouration, sometimes darker. There is a whitish ring, and the base of the stem is thicker than its upper portions. It is found from July to October. The mushroom has a very pleasant scent and a nutty taste if a portion is sampled raw.

This mushroom is best fried with bacon just like ordinary mushrooms, but the stem below the ring should be cut off as it is tough and stringy.

Lepiotas are not very moist-fleshed and so they are slow to decay and therefore can be dried for winter and spring use. Thread a fine string or cotton through the centres of the caps (having removed the stems completely) and hang up in a warm place. Knot the string or cotton between each cap so that they do not touch, thus facilitating the circulation of air around them so as to avoid mould developing. Don't hang any mushrooms for drying in any part of the kitchen where steam from kettles or cooking-pots will dampen them.

The young caps, while they are still cup-shaped and unopened, are ideal for stuffing. They can be stuffed with sage and onion stuffing, minced meat and herbs, sausagemeat etc and then arranged on a greased baking-dish alternately with rolled-up rashers of bacon. Cook in a medium-slow oven (300°F./150°C. or Regulo 2) for about half an hour, basting occasionally with the bacon fat. Allow four caps and four rashers for each person, for a main meal dish. Parboil some potatoes, slice them across into thinnish rounds, and hash-brown them or fry them in bacon fat to go with this dish.

Dorothy Hartley, in her book *Food in England* (see Bibliography) says of this species: 'Put it between two buttered saucer or soup plates, according to size, and steam over a pan, season lightly and eat with bread and butter. Do not overcook this mushroom, as its flavour is very delicate and the texture as light as a good omelet.' I would only point out that your specimens may be far too big to fit between two soup plates, never mind saucers.

She also goes on to suggest cutting it into strips, tossing in butter until cooked and piling on to hot buttered toast.

Like the blewits, this species is another of our wild mushrooms that I prefer to eat cooked without any other ingredients apart from the butter or fat used to cook them and a little light seasoning. However, lepiotas lend themselves to a number of 'prepared' dishes, i.e. dishes including other ingredients besides the mushrooms *per se*. Here are some recipes.

Mushroom Dumplings

4 oz./100 g. self-raising flour
2 oz./50 g. shredded suet
1 medium onion

4 oz./100 g. mushrooms
Salt and black pepper to taste
Cold water to mix

Sift the flour, salt and pepper into a mixing-bowl, and stir in the suet. Grate or mince the onion, chop the mushrooms (caps only) finely, and add to the mixture. Add the water a little at a time to make the dough, using the flat blade of a knife to mix, until finally kneading with floured hands to make a fairly stiff dough which leaves the sides of the bowl without sticking. Divide the dough into 8 portions and roll each portion into a dumpling shape. Drop into a soup or stew about 20 minutes before the end of cooking time. Allow two dumplings per person.

Spaghetti with Bacon and Mushrooms

4 oz./100 g. spaghetti
Water to cook
2 teaspoons salt

Two 5-inch lepiotas (caps only)
1 oz./25 g. butter
4 rashers back bacon
  (unsmoked)

Cook the spaghetti in salted boiling water until tender but not mushy – about 8 minutes. Fry the bacon, chopped into small pieces, in the butter until crisp, and at the same time fry the mushrooms, similarly chopped, in the bacon fat. Take care that the mushrooms are not frizzled by being overcooked. When the spaghetti is ready, drain through a colander and place in the serving-dish. The fried bacon and mushrooms should be sprinkled over the spaghetti, together with any remaining butter. Serves 4 to 6.

Wild Mushroom Stuffed Cabbage

Species suitable for this dish include the parasol mushroom (*Lepiota procera*), the tawny grisette (*Amanitopsis fulva*), the fairy ring champignon (*Marasmius oreades*) etc. A lidded frying-pan is required for this dish.

4 large cabbage leaves (savoy is best)
2 oz./50 g. butter
½ lb./225 g. mushrooms (minced)
2 tablespoons double cream
2 tablespoons chopped chives (or green spring onion tops)
1 tablespoon shredded fresh parsley
1 tablespoon minced capers (or pickled nasturtium seeds)
½ lb./225 g. potatoes
Pinch coriander
Pinch lovage (optional)
Salt and water for cooking potatoes and cabbage leaves

Boil cabbage leaves briefly in lightly salted water. Remove from water with slotted spoon and leave to cool. Boil potatoes (peeled) in lightly salted water, cutting into smaller pieces if very large. When cooked, remove from water and mash with the cream and 1 oz. of the butter. Add the mushrooms, chives, coriander, parsley, lovage (if used) and capers (or nasturtium seeds).

Divide the filling into 4 portions and fill the middle of each cabbage leaf. Wrap outer parts of leaf securely round filling, fixing with a *wooden* (*not* plastic!) cocktail stick, or tying with cotton (*not* nylon) thread.

Heat the remaining butter in the frying-pan and put in the cabbage 'parcels'. Cook over a high heat until the leaves begin to redden on all sides. Cook for a further minute after reaching this point and then reduce the heat to very low and continue cooking, covered, until all the liquid has been absorbed.

ST GEORGE'S MUSHROOM (*Tricholoma gambosum*)

Make a good note of the distinguishing characteristics of this species, in order to avoid confusing it with the leaden entoloma (see page 188) with which it can be, and unfortunately has been, confused. St George's mushroom is found from the latter part of April until June, and it is very partial to calcareous soils, though it also occurs in other habitats. The cap is very rounded-looking, up to 3 inches (7.5 cm.) across, and is a pale creamy-white inclining to light yellowish in the centre, especially when moist. The skin is soft to the touch, like a kid glove. The stem is thick, short and cream-coloured, often curved or irregular in shape and slightly larger at the base. The gills are sinuate (see diagram) and are whitish or pale cream, narrow and crowded. The spores are white. The flesh is solid, firm and white and may be up to an inch (2.5 cm.) thick in the middle of the cap. When cut it has a strong odour of meal.

This mushrooms grows in pastures or on open downland, and its stocky appearance is reminiscent of blewits, to which, of course, it is closely related.

The full-bodied flavour of St George's mushroom is particularly suited to soups. The species is also very tasty fried or grilled. For the following three different German recipes for this mushroom I am indebted to Lotte Heidemann of Düsseldorf.

Mushroom soup (first recipe)

12 oz./350 g. mushrooms (minced)
2 tablespoons flour
1 medium onion or leek
2 pints/1150 ml. vegetable stock

2 tablespoons chopped fresh parsley
Butter for cooking
Salt and black pepper to taste

Heat the butter in a heavy frying-pan and cook the finely chopped or minced onion (or leek) until golden. Add the minced mushrooms and cook until tender. Stir in the flour and the seasoning. When thoroughly blended, pour into the soup saucepan and add the vegetable stock, stirring continuously over a medium heat until boiling-point is reached. Then reduce heat and simmer for 30 minutes. Add the fresh chopped parsley just before serving. Serves 6 to 8.

Mushroom Soup (second recipe)

1 lb./450 g. mushrooms
2 tablespoons butter
2 tablespoons flour
2 pints/1150 ml. stock (any kind)

2 eggs (yolks only)
½ pint/275 ml. single cream
Salt and black pepper to taste

Mince the mushrooms, or chop very finely, and fry in the butter in a heavy frying-pan. Sprinkle in the flour, and when blended turn out into the soup pan. Add the stock and seasoning, bring to the boil, then simmer, with a lid, for half an hour. Remove from heat and put through a sieve. Beat the egg yolks with the cream, add to the soup and re-heat, stirring continuously and taking care not to boil or you will get scrambled eggs and curdled cream. Just heat through, no more. Serve immediately. This quantity gives 7 to 8 portions.

Barley and Mushroom Soup

6 oz./175 g. pearl barley
2 pints/1150 ml. vegetable stock
½ lb./225 g. mushrooms
2 tablespoons fresh chopped
  parsley

Butter to cook mushrooms
Salt and white pepper to taste
Dash of nutmeg

Boil the barley in the stock until tender. Fry the mushrooms in the butter until cooked. When the barley is tender, add the mushrooms to the stock, season with salt and pepper and cook for a further 5 minutes over a very low heat. Serve sprinkled with chopped fresh parsley and a dash of nutmeg. Serves 6 to 8.

HORSE MUSHROOM (*Psalliota arvensis*)

The horse mushroom is very closely related to the common field mushroom (*P. campestris*) but grows much larger; the cap can grow up to 8 inches (20 cm.) across quite commonly, sometimes even larger. My experience is that the larger the cap the tastier the meat! (This applies to the ordinary field mushroom too, including the cultivated kind.) The 'button' stage is, in any case, best avoided, as these mushrooms in this stage look little different to the uninitiated from certain poisonous agarics, but when they expand they are very different indeed and much less liable to be confused.

The horse mushroom is essentially a field species, never occurring in woodland. It is particularly common in cultivated fields. Its cap is rounded and ball-like in the early stages, creamy-white in colour, hence its French name of *boule de neige* (snowball), and has a smooth texture like a kid glove. It grows from June to October. The gills are dark brown when mature, and the spores purplish-brown. The stem is thick and white, becoming more distended at the base. The flesh is

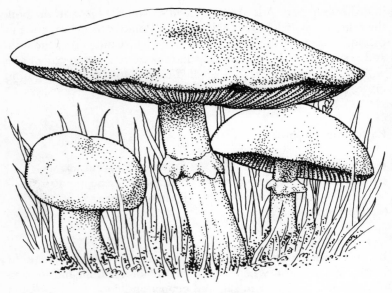

Horse mushroom (*Psalliota arvensis*)

firm and white and has a strong 'mushroomy' smell. The taste is stronger than that of the common field mushroom, and it is thus particularly suited to the making of mushroom ketchup.

Mushroom Ketchup

4 lbs./1800 g. mushrooms
Mixed spice
4 onions

Dash of black pepper
Cooking salt used in
    preparation
Flour for thickening

Chop the mushrooms roughly and lay them in an earthenware dish, and cover with cooking salt. Leave for three days in a cool place. From time to time, turn them over with a wooden spoon.

Turn out into an enamel pan and boil the mushrooms in their own liquid, after first removing any loose salt that may remain on top. (Do not overdo the salting in the first place.) Add the pepper and the mixed spice, and chop the onions very finely before adding to the boiling mixture. Stir in flour, a little at a time, until the desired thickness is obtained. Do not overdo the flour either, or you will end up with a solid gooey mess! Boil for about 20 minutes or so, and when cooked remove from heat and leave to cool. Strain through a sieve to remove the chillies, blades of mace etc and bottle. This ketchup will keep for 6 months or longer in a cool place, but the lid must fit tightly. Old sauce bottles with plastic screw-top lids, when washed and sterilized with boiling water, are ideal. Label with the date.

How do you get the ketchup into the bottle? With a plastic funnel, of course – how else? And, while on this subject, jam can be put easily into jars straight from the cooking-pot by using a plastic funnel with the bottom cut off, leaving only about half an inch of the narrow part protruding. And you avoid any sticky jammy splodges on the outside of the jars.

Try horse mushrooms in the following recipe, which is very well suited to a strong-tasting mushroom, and as they grow so big, you do not need more than one or two.

Mushroom Rissoles

1 lb./450 g. mushrooms	2 oz./50 g. breadcrumbs (crisp
2 onions	type for coating)
4 slices white bread	Salt and white pepper to taste
2 oz./50 g. butter	Dash of tomato purée
2 eggs	Pinch of sage

Chop the mushrooms fairly small. Soak the bread in a little water and squeeze it out like a sponge. Fry the mushrooms in the butter together with the onions, finely chopped. Place in a basin together with the squeezed-out bread, beat the eggs well and add to the mixture. Add the salt, pepper, sage and tomato purée and mix well. Shape the mixture into rissoles and coat them with the breadcrumbs. Fry them in the mushroom-flavoured butter left over from frying the mushrooms, until golden-brown on both sides (you can add a little more butter if there is not enough). Makes 8 rissoles.

Like field mushrooms, horse mushrooms can also be eaten raw in salads, cut into strips. The younger specimens will be best for this use as they are more tender, but it is better to be on the safe side and avoid the 'button' stage, at least until you are thoroughly experienced in fungus-hunting.

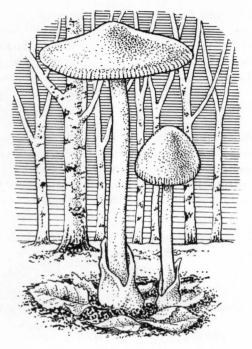

Tawny grisette (*Amanitopsis fulva*)

TAWNY GRISETTE (*Amanitopsis fulva*)

This fungus has a good taste but, since it is rather small, you need to gather quite a lot of them to make them worth while cooking. As against this, they are as common as mud – or perhaps I should say common *in* mud, because damp, boggy woods are where you are most likely to find them. Deciduous woods, where there is a lot of leaf-mould humus, are the best places to look. They also grow in mixed woodland, and occasionally in coniferous woodland. They are found throughout Britain. Usually where there is one there will be a dozen, so if you have found a good habitat, you will most likely find them to be locally very common and thus be able to gather enough for the pot without having to walk miles.

The tan-coloured cap is small – seldom more than 1½ inches (4 cm.) in diameter – and has a distinctive *striated edge* and a *prominent boss* in the centre. The cap is very thin and insubstantial-looking and is easily knocked off the stem. The stem is fairly tall – up to four inches (10 cm.) high – and rather slender, and is easily broken. Such fragile little fungi tend to 'cook down' quite a bit, and you will therefore need to gather about twice as many as you *think* you need. However, the taste is very rewarding and quite distinctive, as it is very delicate and unlike most other mushrooms.

The gills are white and free from the stem. The spores are whitish. The flesh is white, and there is little odour. It grows in summer and autumn.

The mushroom has a pleasant taste for eating raw in salads, and being so small there is no need to slice it. The caps may be dried for winter and spring use (see page 201). As mentioned above, this fungus is so small and insubstantial that it is best perhaps cooked together with other larger species. Not for nothing is it called by the Germans 'the Dwindling'.

FAIRY RING CHAMPIGNON (*Marasmius oreades*)

This is another small fungus but it is firmer and tougher than the preceding species. It is very common and you are likely to find it on

Fairy ring champignon (*Marasmius oreades*)

your first fungus foray, in summer or autumn, especially after a spell
of rain. This is the species that is known by the popular name of the
'fairy ring' fungus owing to its habit of growing in rings, so often seen
on lawns, parks and downlands. It is found throughout Britain.

The cap is smooth, one to two inches (2.5 to 5 cm.) across, and can
be rounded or flattened according to age but always has a rounded
protuberance or boss in the middle. This is less conical than that of
the preceding species, and the present species also does not have the
striated edge to the cap. Apart from these two main differences, the
two species are not dissimilar in appearance. The colour is about the
same, slightly darker if anything (it is described as 'reddish buff' in
one book). The stem is about the same colour, very straight and
slender. Unlike that of the preceding species, the stem does not snap
easily when handled.

The gills are pale buff-coloured, thick, broad and set rather far
apart. They are alternately long and short, the long ones not being
fastened to the stem. This alternation of length in the gills is another
diagnostic feature, but apparent only on close examination. The flesh
is whitish, and the odour very pleasant, especially when the fungus is
dried. One author has likened the scent to that of clover.

Drying is, in fact, the best way to use this fungus. It has a very
useful quality from the culinary point of view, and that is, of
shrivelling to a small volume when dried and swelling up to full size
and smoothness again when reconstituted with any kind of moisture,
such as being dropped into soup. The stems are too tough to be used
and should be discarded.

Owing to its small size this is another fungus which is best used
with other species in cooked dishes, either fresh or dried. If omelets
are being made where only a small quantity of a mushroom is needed
for flavouring, this species (fresh) may be used. It also has a delicate
taste raw, so that it may be used in salads.

GIANT PUFFBALL (*Lycoperdon giganteum*)

We go now from one extreme to the other – from tiny, delicate-
looking fungi to one the size of a football. The puffballs belong to a
different family from the agarics (the gilled fungi we have been
talking about so far) and make a welcome change. Usually, only the
largest member of the family, the giant puffball, is used in cookery.
This is not because the other members of the family are dangerous

Giant puffball (*Lycoperdon giganteum*)

but because they are edible only in their early stages and, at that stage, can easily be confused with certain other members of a related group which can cause serious gastric disturbances, even if not exactly deadly. It is therefore prudent to stick to the distinctive *L. giganteum*.

The giant puffball is quite common in summer and early autumn in meadows and the grassy parts of woods, even in gardens where the right conditions obtain – grassed areas with plenty of compost and humus. The young specimens are spherical, but with approaching maturity the mushroom becomes more pumpkin-shaped, wider than it is high, or a flattened oval. The outer skin is a creamy-white, and smooth as kid. At first the interior is also firm and white, with the consistency of a firm but soft white cheese. Only in this condition is the fungus fit for food – and delectable it is, too. Later, as the spores ripen, the interior becomes a powdery mass, first yellowish and then a brownish olive. The skin then bursts open in several places, releasing the spores. Therefore the giant puffball should be sought early, up to about the end of August, as by September the spores will be fast developing.

The skin should be peeled off and the flesh cut into strips for frying; if desired, the strips, about half an inch thick, can be coated with egg and breadcrumbs, like cutlets. When very young the flesh can be eaten raw in salads, cut into thin slices. Thicker slabs may also be coated in batter and fried in deep fat. Little ones may be eaten whole cooked in this manner. Do not allow them to become darker than a light golden-yellow. Sprinkle with a light dusting of salt and white pepper. They make a super dish piled in the middle of an oval plate surrounded by lightly cooked chopped spinach.

Dorothy Hartley, in her book *Food in England*,[1] has quite a lot to say about the giant puffball. She says that the texture and flavour are exactly like sweetbreads, and that one can sometimes be a feast in itself: 'I remember' (she says) 'a huge one found by a shepherd of the wolds near Loughborough. It was about 24 inches in diameter. We cut it in slices, egg-and-breadcrumbed them and fried them, and one giant puff-ball served six people.'

Here is one of Dorothy Hartley's recipes for small, young specimens of the giant puffball.

Stewed Puffballs in White Sauce

Says Dorothy: 'Puff-balls, to my mind, are the most delicious fungi. The little round ones should be gently stewed in milk, till you can pierce them easily with a skewer. Then pour off the milk, and use it to make a white sauce with butter and a dust of mace, some white pepper and salt. Return the puff-balls to [heat] through and serve hot, with brown bread and butter.'

She goes on to give another recipe, this time for medium-sized puffballs. I have very slightly adapted it from her book.

Puffballs in Onion Sauce

'Take one dozen puffballs, about the size of hens' eggs. Wipe them carefully, and see that all are firm and white. Roll them in flour seasoned with white pepper and salt, and drop them into a deep earthenware pan with barely enough milk to cover them. Add a small bay leaf and two medium-sized onions thinly-sliced, and simmer gently until soft. Lift them out carefully on to a dish. Thicken the milk in which they were cooked with butter and cornflour, season delicately, and cook thoroughly. Pour back over the puffs, and garnish the dish with parsley. The smooth white puffs in their own creamy sauce, white against the vivid green parsley, look good and taste delicious.

1. Macdonald, 1954.

Richard Mabey says that a large giant puffball could be baked whole in the oven, hollowing it out first from the bottom where it grows out of the ground, and stuffing it with a mixture of what he calls the 'chopped hollowings' and some minced fat meat, preferably bacon, with some parsley and seasoning. He says the whole should then be wrapped in foil and cooked fairly slowly in a slow oven, though he does not say *how* slow. He admits that he has never tried it this way, and neither have I. So perhaps one of you might be lucky enough to find a puffball big enough to cook in this way. I suggest 40 minutes at 300°F./150°C. (Regulo 2) and see what happens.

MOREL (*Morchella esculenta*)

This fungus, which is not very common, is widely distributed and sometimes locally frequent in a particular area. However, it does

Morel (*Morchellus esculentus*)

take a bit of finding. It occurs in spring in the clearings in woods, especially on calcareous soils, though it is not confined to these habitats. The morel is not an agaric but belongs to an entirely different group, in which the spores are contained in little sacs which give the fungus its characteristic 'honeycombed' appearance. The cap is usually dark brownish or blackish but in some specimens can be lighter. The fungus is quite small, usually about 2 to 3 inches (5 to 7.5 cm.) high, on a short and stocky white stem, which is grooved at the base. The cap itself is usually about 3 inches (7.5 cm.) in width when mature. Its shape is rounded, sometimes more or less pointed at the apex. Both cap and stem are hollow.

Morels have been known and appreciated by gourmets for hundreds of years. They can be used both fresh and dried. Before cooking they should be carefully cleansed of any grit or other 'foreign bodies' (some with six legs!) that may be lurking in the pits. They have a delicious aromatic flavour and make a most welcome addition to soups, stews, sauces, stuffings, pies and other savoury dishes. They are very good used in Italian risotto dishes. They can also be cut in slices and fried, either as they are or coated with batter or breadcrumbs, or they can be used as fillings for omelets and pancakes. They are very good stuffed — being hollow they lend themselves to this treatment better than the flat-topped type of mushroom. With all these versatile and delicious uses they could, conceivably, make your reputation as a wildfoods cook. There is one problem, though: they do take a lot of finding! If you do succeed, here are some recipes.

Morels in Yoghourt

½ lb./225 g. morels
1 oz./25 g. butter
4 tablespoons plain yoghourt
2 tablespoons minced chives
  (or green spring onion tops)

½ teaspoon paprika
Pinch cardamom

Wash and dry the morels. Cut in half if large specimens. Grill sufficiently to cook through. Heat the butter in a saucepan and add the chives (or spring onion tops), paprika and cardamom. Add the morels and the yoghourt and mix well. Cover the pan and leave to simmer on a very low heat for 10 to 15 minutes, stirring from time to time.

Stuffed Baked Morels

8 large morels (if you're lucky)
½ lb./225 g. minced meat
2 tablespoons parsley (fresh
 chopped)
2 cloves crushed garlic

2 slices white bread
Salt and white pepper to taste
2 medium onions
Oil for cooking

Wash and dry the morels. Mix the minced meat with the parsley, garlic and seasoning. Chop the onions finely and add to the mixture. Squeeze the bread out in water to moisten it and mix with the other ingredients. Stuff the morels with this mixture, brush with oil and place in an oiled baking-tin or dish at 300°F./150°C. (Regulo 2) for 10 minutes. Allow two stuffed morels per person.

Morels in Wine

½ lb./225 g. morels
2 tomatoes
2 tablespoons butter
2 teaspoons fresh chopped
 parsley

5 fl. oz./150 ml. white wine
Salt and white pepper to taste

Slice the washed and dried morels and slice the tomatoes. Fry these gently in the butter over a low heat. Add the chopped parsley and cook for a further 5 minutes, stirring all the time. Season to taste and add the wine, re-heating through (about 3 minutes) and serve as an accompaniment to a main dish.

Creamed Morels

½ lb./225 g. morels
5 fl. oz./150 ml. double cream

Salt and pepper to taste
Dash of paprika

Slice the washed and dried morels. Heat the cream in a heavy pan. On no account allow it to boil. Cook the morels in the cream, seasoned, until soft and cooked through – about 10 minutes. The heat must be kept low all the time and the morels turned with a spoon from time to time. Serve piping hot with brown bread and butter.

CHANTERELLE (*Cantharellus cibarius*) AND HORN OF
PLENTY (*Craterellus cornucopioides*)

These two mushrooms are closely related and can be cooked in
exactly the same recipes. For the sake of simplicity I shall refer in the
recipes to the chanterelle, but it is interchangeable with the horn of
plenty.

The chanterelle is unmistakable from its colour alone – a brilliant
yellow like the yolk of an egg. The species affects beech and oak
woods, birch plantations and pinewoods alike; it is fairly catholic in
habitat. It is frequently found beside well-trodden paths and roads
through such wooded country. It occurs from July to November, but
only after a damp season, when it can be quite common in its
favoured localities.

The gills and the cap appear continuous, and the overall shape is
funnel-like, with wavy edges and lobes. It has a pleasant apricot-like
smell. It is about 2 to 3 inches (5–7.5 cm.) across, and about 3 inches
(7.5 cm.) high. The stem is the same bright yellow colour as the cap.
Gills that run down the cap in this way are known as *decurrent* (see
diagram). Despite the overall yellow colour, the spores are white.
The flesh is white, thick in the middle, becoming thinner towards the
edges, sometimes becoming also yellowish near the margin.

The horn of plenty is exactly the same shape as the chanterelle, but
its colour is brownish or bluish-black. It grows in both deciduous
and coniferous woods. It is especially common in beechwoods and in
hazel coppices, and it has a predilection for shady places where it is
often hidden among leaves and undergrowth, but if you look for it
assiduously, you usually manage to find it – at least I do. What makes
it much more difficult to find than the chanterelle is its dark colour
blending into the background; it is certainly not rarer than the
chanterelle, rather the reverse.

In size the horn of plenty is about the same as the preceding species,
but it appears much later in the year, in August and September.

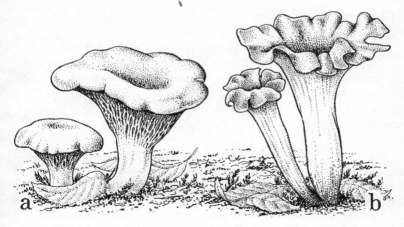

a, Chanterelle (*Cantharellus cibarius*); b, Horn of plenty
(*Craterellus cornucopioides*)

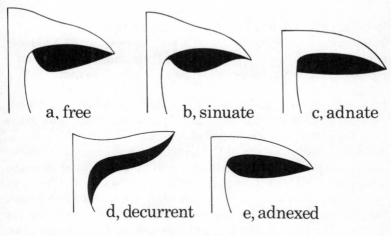

Arrangement of gills in agarics

Chanterelles with Tomatoes

1 lb./450 g. chanterelles
4 large tomatoes
2 medium onions
Salt and pepper to taste
Dash paprika
Small quantity flour

1 tablespoon lemon juice
3 tablespoons single cream
1 tablespoon chopped fresh
  parsley
Oil for cooking

Chop the onions and fry in the oil. Slice the tomatoes and cut the chanterelles into 4 quarters, add to the onions and cook over a gentle heat for about 10 minutes. Season with salt, pepper and paprika, and sprinkle with flour, a little at a time. Add the lemon juice and cook a little longer until the chanterelles are tender. The heat must be kept low. When ready, remove from heat and stir in the cream, blending well, and serve sprinkled with parsley.

Chanterelle and Rice Patties

½ lb./225 g. chanterelles
½ lb./225 g. brown rice
Oil for cooking
1 pint/575 ml. vegetable stock

2 oz./50 g. butter
6 tablespoons grated Cheddar
  (or Parmesan) cheese
Salt and pepper to taste

Fry the chanterelles, chopped, in the oil until cooked through (about 10 minutes, over low-medium heat). Rinse the rice and cook in the vegetable stock until tender and increased in bulk, by which time it will have absorbed some of the liquid. Cream the butter with the grated cheese, in a mixing-bowl, then add the rice and seasonings, mixing well. Add the chanterelles, draining them so as to remove as much of the oil as possible. When the whole mixture is well blended, the best way to bake them to make the patties is to put a spoonful of the mixture into each recess on a shallow bun-tin (you will need two 12-hole tins). The recesses must be well greased (butter, margarine or cooking-fat is better than oil as it does not all run down to the bottom before you put in the patty mixture). Neaten the top of each patty to flatten it by pressing lightly with the back of a wooden spoon or a spatula. Bake for about 15 minutes at 325°F./160°C. (Regulo 3) and serve hot with a white sauce and new potatoes, glazed carrots and spinach. This quantity makes 24 patties.

Horn of Plenty Sautée

½ lb./225 g. horn of plenty
mushrooms
Juice of half a lemon
2 tablespoons water
½ teaspoon onion salt

1 teaspoon garlic salt
1 teaspoon ground black pepper
¼ teaspoon basil
1 oz./25 g. butter
Pinch cardamom

Wash and dry the mushrooms. Spread out on a dish and dust with onion salt, black pepper and basil, and sprinkle with lemon juice. Leave to marinate for about 15 minutes.

A lidded frying-pan is required to cook this dish. Heat butter gently in the pan, and when a slight haze rises put in the mushrooms together with any liquor in the dish. Sauté each side for one minute over a medium heat if the mushrooms are young specimens, longer if they are older specimens. Then reduce heat and add the water, salt, garlic salt and cardamom. Mix well, cover the pan and cook for a further 5 minutes. Serve hot as an accompaniment to a main dish.

SAFFRON MILK CAP (*Lactarius deliciosus*)

This mushroom is rather *Tricholoma*-like in its stocky appearance, thick stem and low stature and, in some specimens, the shape of the cap. However, it has a number of differences. When the cap is cut, it exudes a saffron (reddish-orange) coloured milky juice. The cap itself can be up to 4 or 5 inches (10–12.5 cm.) across, at first slightly convex with an inrolled margin, but later with maturity the central part reverses inwards into a fairly well-defined concavity. The colour is orange, or brick-coloured in some specimens, sometimes a combination of the two, with concentric markings (not in clear rings but irregular) in the darker shade. Older specimens sometimes have greenish tinges which look like stains or blotches. These are not harmful in cooking, but younger specimens which do not show these green blotches are always preferable to the more mature examples.

The stem is more or less the same shade as the cap but paler. It stains verdigris-green when bruised (at any age). Soon after the mushroom has attained a reasonable size the stem, which averages about 2½ inches (6.5 cm.) in length, becomes hollow. The gills, which are narrow and crowded and the same saffron colour as the other parts, are decurrent (see diagram). The spores are pinkish, and

Saffron milk-cap (*Lactarius deliciosus*)

the flesh off-white, becoming orange when cut or broken, and green if the cut surface is exposed to the air for any length of time. The mushroom has a slight but pleasant 'fruity' odour. It is an early autumn species.

The saffron milk cap is not uncommon and occurs in coniferous woods, by roadsides near or passing through pinewoods, and on open land in the vicinity of pines.

If saffron milk caps have to be chopped prior to cooking, do this immediately before they go into the pot. You will thus avoid their assuming the green coloration mentioned above. While not toxic in any way, it may be found off-putting by some.

Saffron milk caps should not be eaten raw. If required for use in a salad, they should be boiled for a short time first and then cooled. The stems should not be used in cooking. Don't panic – nothing untoward will happen if you do – but when cooked they become rather hard and woody, and it is unlikely that you will eat them anyway!

Saffron Milk Cap Casserole

½ lb./225 g. saffron milk caps
2 medium onions
Oil for cooking
2 tablespoons fresh soft white
  breadcrumbs

5 fl. oz./150 ml. sour cream
Salt and black pepper to taste
Dash of paprika
1 tablespoon lemon juice
Dab of butter for each
  mushroom

Place mushrooms (caps only) in an ovenproof dish, gills uppermost, and season with salt, pepper, paprika and a sprinkling of lemon juice. Cover with a lid and cook at 350°F./180°C. (Regulo 4) for about 30 minutes. Meanwhile fry the onions, sliced, in a little oil over gentle heat until golden and soft. Drain off excess oil and blend with soft white breadcrumbs (crusts removed). Remove from heat and stir in the soured cream. Pour the mixture into the casserole dish over the mushrooms and continue cooking for a further 10 minutes. Serve with spinach and creamed potatoes. A dab of butter is placed in the centre of each mushroom when serving.

Potato Nests with Saffron Milk Caps

½ lb./225 g. saffron milk caps
2 oz./50 g. butter
1 medium onion
2 cloves garlic
4 tablespoons sour cream
1 lb./450 g. boiled potatoes
  (cooked weight)

Salt for cooking potatoes
White pepper to taste
2 tablespoons fresh chopped
  parsley

Heat the butter in a heavy frying-pan and cook the sliced onion over gentle heat with the crushed garlic until just soft and golden. Add the chopped mushrooms, pepper and continue slow cooking until the mushrooms are soft. Remove from heat and stir in the soured cream. Meanwhile mash the boiled potatoes while still hot and cream with a little of the butter (previously reserved for this purpose). A dash of milk may be added to advantage, but not too much or the potatoes will become sloppy. Make a 'nest' of potato mixture in a large serving-dish, with a space in the centre for the mushroom mixture. Decorate the potato mixture by making ridges with a fork lengthways on the surface. Pour the mushroom mixture into the dish, and sprinkle with chopped fresh parsley. If liked, the dish can be placed under the grill for a short time until the potato 'nest' has browned. (If you wish to do this, the dish should be made of ovenproof glass – china and earthenware ones are likely to crack, and plastic ones will melt!)

SHAGGY CAP OR LAWYER'S WIG (*Coprinus comatus*) AND INK-CAP (*Coprinus atramentarius*)

WARNING

These two mushrooms are excellent edible species but **must not be consumed at the same time as alcohol**. Not only must you not drink wine, beer, cider or spirits with the meal but you must not eat either of these mushrooms within 24 hours of having partaken of, or intending to partake of, any alcoholic substance. These mushrooms have been found to contain a chemical substance identical to the active ingredient of the drug Antabuse which is used in the aversion-therapy treatment of alcoholism. It causes violent vomiting and nausea. The couplet to remember is therefore:

> *Wigs and inkcaps do not choose*
> *If you want a glass of booze.*

The shaggy cap or lawyer's wig is unmistakable: it looks for all the world like a huge white busby. It is a very common species and too large to escape notice even by the non-dedicated fungus-hunter. It can grow up to 9 inches (23 cm.) high, and even young undeveloped specimens just coming up out of the earth are the size of a large hen's egg. The cylindrical white cap has a shaggy look owing to the loose scales with which it is covered. The top of the cap is usually covered with light brownish scales.

The shaggy cap grows very quickly – literally overnight – and in summer and autumn great quantities of them appear, especially after rain, in parks, gardens and commons and by the wayside, along the edges of woods and on agricultural land. It likes a lot of humus in the soil and is therefore particularly prevalent on compost heaps, manure heaps and rubbish dumps. Avoid taking specimens which

a, Shaggy cap or Lawyer's wig (*Coprinus comatus*);
b, Ink-cap (*C. atramentarius*)

(a) Cap shaggy	(b) Cap smooth, not shaggy
Much larger than (b)	Much smaller than (a)
Mushrooms grow separately	Mushrooms grow in clusters

may have been in contact with manure or sewage, rotting refuse and the like. You will find plenty of this common species growing in grass, where it cannot be contaminated with harmful bacteria.

The gills are white at first, soon turning rose-pink and finally black. Gather the fungus only when the gills are white or pink. As soon as the gills have turned black, they dissolve into an inky black fluid (called 'deliquescence') and are then useless for food. Young specimens, however, are very tasty, and Nilsson and Persson, in 'Fungi of Northern Europe', Vol. 2[1] have written that they 'can compete with any other mushrooms as delicacies for the table'.

The stem is white, silky in appearance, and at first bears a flimsy ring which is soon rubbed off and disappears. The stem is hollow. The spores are black. The black inky fluid produced on deliquescence can be used for writing.

1. Penguin Books, 1978.

The ink-cap (*Coprinus atramentarius*) is the close relative of the shaggy cap and is almost as common as its congener, but smaller, with bell-shaped caps without the shaggy appearance as it does not have the scaly covering. The mushrooms grow in clusters, the overall colour being greyish-white, with occasional touches of light brown, not evident on all specimens. The stem is shorter in proportion to the cap than in the previous species. The gills are light grey until they blacken and then become inedible though good to write with! The 'Antabuse' effect of this species in combination with alcohol is even more severe than in the case of the shaggy cap. The ink-cap is more slender than the shaggy cap and has no ring. The ink-cap appears at the same seasons of the year and affects lawns, old tree stumps and craters where old tree roots have not been completely dug out. Wooded parkland where felling has been taking place is a good place to look for it. This species also, of course, has black spores.

Both species are interchangeable so far as their culinary properties are concerned. Owing to their rapidly deliquescing tendency, these species are particularly well suited to making mushroom ketchup, but you must be very careful to remember to label the bottle with the name of the species, so as to avoid its use with a meal in which wine is used in cooking one of the dishes or with which wine, beer, cider or spirits are served. The recipe to make the ketchup is the same as the one on page 205, given for the horse mushroom.

Lawyers' Wigs in Cream

8 large lawyer's wigs   Salt and black pepper to taste
10 fl. oz./275 ml. double cream

The mushrooms should be firm young specimens. Strip off the shaggy scales, cut in half lengthways and lay in a casserole dish. Sprinkle with seasoning and cover with the cream. Bake (covered with a lid) for two hours at 300°F./150°C (Regulo 2), by which time the cream will have clotted to form a rich, thick sauce. Serve immediately.

Stuffed Shaggy Caps

8 large shaggy caps
¼ lb./100 g. minced meat
2 cloves garlic
1 medium onion
1 tablespoon fresh soft white
  breadcrumbs

Yolk of 1 egg
Dripping for cooking
Salt and pepper to taste

Mix the minced meat, crushed garlic, finely chopped or minced onion, breadcrumbs and seasoning, and bind with beaten yolk of egg. Detach the stalks from the mushrooms and carefully stuff the caps, having first removed the scales. Lay the stuffed caps in a baking-tin with enough dripping to ensure that the tin is well greased to prevent burning, and roast at 325°F./160°C. (Regulo 3) for about an hour and a quarter, or until cooked through. These are good with chips – but the calorie-conscious may prefer boiled new potatoes sprinkled with parsley.

EDIBLE BOLETUS (*Boletus edulis*), ROUGH-STALKED BOLETUS (*B. scaber*) AND ORANGE-CAPPED BOLETUS (*B. versipellis*)

These three will be taken together, since a recipe which will suit one boletus will usually suit another. The edible boletus is the famous *cèpe* of France, *Steinpilz* of Germany and 'Penny Bun Mushroom' of the old English cookery books, written in the days when a bun really did cost only a penny; whatever you have to pay for a bun these days, this boletus looks almost exactly like it, sitting atop a short stalk. It has a superb flavour and is eminently suitable for transforming a mediocre soup or stew into an aromatic feast. It is one of the very best mushrooms for drying, and the commercially produced dried mushrooms imported from France and Germany and sold in delicatessens here are usually this species.

You need not purchase supplies, however, as this boletus is a common denizen of both deciduous and coniferous woods, but I have found it most often in the latter. A warm and moist season will encourage the species to multiply profusely in its favoured habitats. From May to September the mushroom can be found, more commonly in the latter part of its season.

a, Edible boletus (*Boletus edulis*); b, Rough-stalked boletus
(*B. scaber*); c, Orange-capped boletus (*B. versipellis*)

1 (a) stem bulbous and swollen
1 (c) stem thicker than (b)
    but much less so than (a)
       2 (a) and (c) large-capped

1 (b) stem much more slender
    than (a)
2 (b) much smaller cap

The boletus group of mushrooms do not have gills like the agarics
but a system of pores, giving the underside of the cap the appearance
of a sponge. In the edible boletus this is whitish or pale yellowish and
when cut reveals white flesh. The cap, as we have seen, is bun-shaped
and chestnut-brown of the exact shade of a well-baked bun. It can,
however, grow up to 8 inches (20 cm.) across, in which case it looks
more like a loaf!

The stem is very stout, cylindrical basically but frequently swollen
and bulbous-looking. Towards the top it is covered with a fine
network of raised white lines, tapering off and merging into the
general whitish-fawn ground colour of the remainder of the stem. No
boletus has a ring. The stems of boletus mushrooms may be used in

cooking, if sound and undamaged by insects or mice. The tubular pores may be removed from the flesh before cooking; they can be detached very easily.

The rough-stalked boletus (*B. scaber*) has, as its name implies, a rough stem. It is a smaller species than *B. edulis* and appears in early autumn, principally in birch woods, though they sometimes can be found growing in pinewoods. The stem is much more slender than that of the edible boletus and is usually striated with brownish, greyish or blackish interrupted lines, which are raised from the background surface, thus producing the 'rough' feel. The colour of the cap is a soft greyish fawn or light brown. The shape is similar to that of the preceding species, and the surface has a 'moist' feel, absent in *edulis*.

The flesh is white, and the pores also, becoming a dingy olive in old specimens. It is always best to choose firm, young specimens when gathering mushrooms of this group.

The orange-capped boletus (*B. versipellis*) can be distinguished, as its name implies, by a bright orange cap. It, too, has a rough stem which is also thicker and more solid-looking than that of *B. scaber*. Crowded tufts of black scales on the stem, however, are responsible for the 'rough' characteristic of the stem in *versipellis*. This is another big species, growing up to 8 inches (20 cm.) tall and the same size across the cap. The pores are grey at first, fading to ochreous in time. The white flesh soon changes colour on cutting, but this does not affect the taste, which is excellent. The stem can be eaten if scraped first, before cooking. The orange-capped boletus occurs between August and October and prefers birchwoods, usually growing actually under the trees, in some years profusely. All in all, these three species are common enough to ensure that, if your fungus foray takes place during a month when all three occur, you are pretty sure to find at least one of them. I know of at least three woods in which birch grows as well as conifers, and in these woods all three species have turned up. A mixed coniferous and deciduous wood is one of the best places to hunt fungi.

As mentioned earlier, any kind of boletus mushroom can be used in the following recipes. They are frequently called 'ceps', which is merely an anglicized version of the French '*cèpe*' which, *sensu strictu*, refers to *B. edulis*, but for convenience the word 'ceps' will be used to mean any species of this group.

Cream of Ceps

½ lb./225 g. ceps
4 tablespoons plain yoghourt
4 tablespoons double cream
4 oz./100 g. butter
1 teaspoon salt

2 cloves garlic
Black pepper to taste
Pinch cayenne pepper
Pinch cumin
Water to cook

Prior to cooking, the ceps should be steeped for 24 hours in lightly salted water. Change the water two or three times; finally remove the mushrooms and rinse in plain water.

Heat half a pint or so of water, add the ceps and crushed garlic and bring to the boil. Simmer until the ceps are tender over a medium heat. Remove ceps with a slotted spoon, cool and pat dry with a kitchen paper towel, and slice into strips about 2 inches long and ½ inch thick. Heat the butter in a heavy frying-pan and sauté the ceps for two minutes, turning frequently so that both sides are covered. Blend the cream with the yoghourt. Now turn the heat to its lowest setting and add the cream and yoghourt mixture to the ceps, sprinkling in the cumin, cayenne, salt and black pepper. Stir well to blend all the ingredients, then cover the pan with a lid and turn off the heat, leaving for 5 minutes before serving.

Boletus Stew

This is a good recipe in which to use all three of the edible boletus species I have described together. You can also vary the vegetables if you wish – parsnips, turnips, swedes, beans etc. can be substituted for, or added to, the ones I have mentioned. Don't vary the quantities, though – you don't want to mask the delicious mushroom flavour and aroma with masses of vegetables. The boletus is the thing.

1 lb./450 g. ceps
3 medium onions
4 medium carrots
3 tomatoes
2 cloves garlic
2 tablespoons fresh chopped
  parsley

3 medium potatoes
2 tablespoons flour
Salt and black pepper to taste
Pinch of paprika
1 pint/575 ml. vegetable stock
  (or water)

Chop the mushrooms (but not too small) and chop the onions roughly. Slice the carrots into rings (not too thin). Cube the potatoes into dice about an inch each way. Throw the whole lot into a pan of stock (or water) and bring to the boil, then season with crushed garlic, salt, pepper and paprika, and simmer on a reduced heat until the ceps are tender and the vegetables cooked but not mushy. Try to avoid the kind of overcooking that results in the disintegration of shapes. Now add the tomatoes, skinned and chopped (if added at the start they disintegrate). Stir in the flour, a little at a time, to thicken. Finally stir in the chopped parsley, cook for a further couple of minutes, and the stew is ready.

This can be stretched to feed 6 by the addition of dumplings, which usually enhance any stew. In the case of this recipe, what I do is to omit the chopped parsley from the stew proper and mix it in with the suet dough for the dumplings instead. Drop the dumplings in about 20 minutes before the time you have calculated that the stew should be ready.

Ceps au Gratin

1 lb./450 g. ceps
2 medium onions
1 clove garlic
2 tomatoes
2 tablespoons flour
Salt and black pepper to taste
Pinch of paprika
2 tablespoons breadcrumbs

4 tablespoons grated Cheddar (or Parmesan) cheese
Butter for cooking
4 fl. oz./100 ml. sour cream
2 fl. oz./50 ml. single cream
2 tablespoons chopped fresh parsley

In a heavy frying-pan heat the butter and put in the ceps, chopped but not too small, the onions ditto, the tomatoes, skinned and cut into slices, the crushed garlic and all the seasonings. Cook over a low-medium heat, turning frequently, until the whole lot is golden-brown, soft and well blended. Sprinkle with the flour and stir thoroughly to blend and thicken. Now transfer to an ovenproof dish (no lid is needed) and cover with a mixture of sour cream and single cream, then over this sprinkle a mixture of breadcrumbs and grated cheese. A few dabs of butter can be put on top if you like. Pop into a pre-heated oven (300°F./150°C. or Regulo 2), or under the grill if preferred, and cook for about 20 minutes (in the oven – less if under the grill) until the topping is golden-brown.

Honeytuft (*Armillaria mellea*)
Compare with the Sulphur-tuft (*Hypholoma fasciculare*) on
page 190, which is inedible

HONEYTUFT (*Armillaria mellea*)

You can hardly fail to find this species, which is one of the commonest of all our woodland fungi. In one woodland glade you can
find literally thousands of these mushrooms. The one thing you have
to do is to ensure that you can tell the difference between this species
and the sulphur-tuft (see page 193).

The sulphur-tuft is bright yellow and has no ring; the honeytuft
has a ring, and its colour is a brownish honey shade, with darker
brown central area. The cap is much flatter-looking than the much
more rounded sulphur-tuft. It is frequently spotted with darker

brown, looking rather like freckles. The yellow species does not have these markings.

The gills of the present species are off-white in young specimens, becoming brownish as the mushroom matures. The gills of the inedible species are greenish or yellowish and free from the stem, whereas the gills of the honeytuft are decurrent (see diagram). The colour of the spores, too, differs: in the honeytuft they are white, in the sulphur-tuft violet. Spore colour is one of the main bases for group division in fungi: *Melanosporae* (black-spored fungi), *Leucosporae* (white-spored fungi) and so on. The honeytuft is a late autumn species.

The stem can be from 4 to 6 inches (10–15 cm.) tall and is frequently curved, swelling very slightly towards the base. It is the same colour as the cap, paler above (sometimes whitish) and becoming darker towards the base. The flesh is white, off-white in older specimens. There is a barely discernible 'mushroomy' odour.

Since the honeytuft does not have a very strong or pronounced flavour, far less a distinctive one, it is more suitable as a pickle.

Honeytuft Pickle

1½ lbs./675 g. young honeytuft mushrooms	1 tablespoon salt
2 pints/1150 ml. water	2 tablespoons paprika
6 oz./175 g. Demerara sugar	2 tablespoons ground coriander
5 cloves garlic, minced	1 tablespoon onion salt
Juice of 2 lemons	1 teaspoon basil
2 medium beets, grated raw	1 teaspoon ground black pepper
4 tomatoes, sieved pulp only	Pinch cayenne pepper
2 small dried chillies	1 large bay leaf
	2 tablespoons tomato purée

Wash and dry the mushrooms. Mix garlic, lemon juice, paprika, cayenne, coriander, onion salt, basil, black pepper, bay leaf and salt. Place in pan with grated beet, tomato pulp, tomato purée and sugar. Add the water, bring to the boil and drop in the chillies. Simmer until the liquid is reduced by half, then remove the bay leaf and fish out the chillies. Add the mushrooms and continue simmering for about 10 minutes or until the liquid is reduced to a 'pickle' consistency. Pour while hot into sterilized glass jars, seal, cover and label.

Honeytuft Stuffed Potatoes

4 very large potatoes
4 tablespoons chopped
  honeytuft mushrooms
2 oz./50 g. butter, oil or cooking
  fat
2 tablespoons chopped onions
2 tablespoons chopped fresh
  parsley

1 tablespoon grated fresh bread
  crust
2 eggs
Salt and white pepper to taste
Dash of nutmeg

Wash and peel potatoes. Slice off one end and scoop out the centre of each. Stand the potatoes, cut side uppermost, in an ovenproof casserole dish, which must be *very well greased*. (I recommend dripping.) Fry the onions, breadcrumbs and mushrooms in the butter, oil or fat. When tender and well mixed, add the salt, pepper and nutmeg. Beat the eggs and blend into the mushroom mixture. Spoon this into the hollows in the potatoes, and replace their 'lids'. Sprinkle with chopped parsley, put the lid on the casserole and bake at 325°F./170°C. (Regulo 3) for about an hour, or until the potatoes are cooked through and nicely browned. Serve with a dab of butter on top of each.

You can baste the potatoes from time to time if you like, but if you put enough fat in the casserole dish to start with there should not be any need. I've cooked this dish a good many times, using various other kinds of mushrooms as well as honeytuft, and have never encountered any difficulty.

Honeytuft Kebabs

About 24 medium-sized
  honeytuft mushrooms (caps
  only)
4 very small new potatoes
4 small tomatoes

4 very small onions
Salt and pepper to taste
Pinch of nutmeg
Dripping to cook

Four skewers will be needed. Push these through the mushroom caps, potatoes, tomatoes and onions, alternately. You should be able to get 6 mushroom caps on one skewer interspersed with one potato, one tomato and one onion per skewer. When all are firmly skewered, dust with salt and pepper and sprinkle sparingly with nutmeg. Heat dripping in a heavy, large flat frying-pan (if you pan is not big enough you can use a wok, but you will need more fat). Hold the skewers with a cloth and turn them slowly round in the fat so that all the ingredients are cooked equally on all sides. When tender, serve with buttered steamed spinach or broccoli. Cooked in this way, the kebabs do not take long to do. Don't try this recipe using large, tough mushrooms, or you'll have frizzled the other ingredients to death long before the mushrooms are ready. Small, not very fleshy agarics are the only kinds suitable.

SPINDLE-SHANK (*Collybia fusipes*) AND VELVET-SHANK (*C. velutipes*)

These are two very closely related agarics with, like the preceding species, a propensity for growing in clumps on old tree stumps and at the roots of living trees. From June until the autumn the spindle-shank can be found abundantly in deciduous woods, particularly in association with oak and beech trees, while the velvet-shank takes over from where its relative leaves off, appearing in late autumn and carrying on through winter right up to spring. Indeed, this species is a very characteristic winter mushroom in a season when agarics are usually few and far between. Fortunately it is less particular about which trees to attach itself to, and can be found on most tree species of deciduous woods. If anything it is even commoner than the spindle-shank, which is a good thing too, as it is much the tastier of the two.

The spindle-shank's cap is between 1½ and 4 inches (4–10 cm.) in diameter, usually smaller rather than larger. It is rounded at first, soon assuming a somewhat flattened bell shape, ochraceous, red-dish-brown or rust-coloured, often spotted with red or reddish, especially in older specimens. The gills are pale pinkish or whitish, becoming darker, even reddish, in mature specimens, often with red spots like the cap. The stem is a distinctive spindle shape, tapering almost to a point at the base; this feature should help to distinguish it from any other species of comparable size growing on a rotting log or tree stump. The stem has coarse longitudinal furrows and is reddish-brown, paler at the top, and is tough and firm, and from 2½ to 4 inches (6.5–10 cm.) in length. The flesh is whitish, with spores of the same colour, and has no discernible odour.

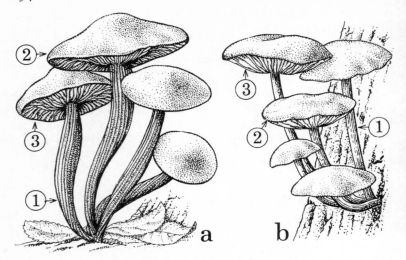

a, Spindle-shank (*Collybia fusipes*); b, Velvet-shank
(*C. velutipes*)

1 (a) Stem spindle-shaped	1 (b) Stem not spindle-shaped
2 (a) Cap much larger than (b)	2 (b) Cap much smaller than (a)
3 (a) Gills fairly crowded	3 (b) Gills distant (uncrowded)

This mushroom is best used in conjunction with other species in stews, soups etc. as its flavour is too mild to be particularly distinctive. The stem is too tough to be used. Young caps can be pickled in the same way as those of the honey-tuft.

The velvet-shank is smaller, the cap being from ¾ inch to 2½ inches (2–6.5 cm.) in diameter. It is a smooth honey colour, darker in the centre and slightly slimy when moist. It has a thin, transparent membrane at the edge through which the gills are discernible from above. These are known as *distant* (not set close together or crowded) and are a pale yellowish or beige with rounded lobe-like ends free from the stem. This latter is normally longer than the diameter of the cap, thus giving the mushroom a tall and slender appearance. It is quite thin, whitish just beneath the cap and then deepening to yellowish on the way down and finally reddish, shading to chestnut brown at the very bottom. The whole surface of the stem has a velvety look and texture; this is a diagnostic feature. The flesh is pale yellowish and has no discernible odour, and the spores are pale whitish.

This mushroom is described in 'A Handbook of Mushrooms' by Pilat and Ušák[1] as 'a good edible mushroom which is suitable for soups and other dishes and is highly valued as it grows when other mushrooms are not to be found'. I can hardly improve on this description, beyond saying that stews as well as soups can be improved by the addition of this species, either alone or with other kinds. I frequently use it in winter for omelets. These very small and thin-capped species are not really the best choice for making into the more substantial dishes described in the recipes given for large agarics, but they are ideal for adding taste to an otherwise indifferent soup or stew, and as a filling for pancakes, omelets and the like, or as an addition to bacon and eggs. They are also good dropped into a steak and kidney pie.

1. Spring Books, 1961.

16

SEAWEEDS FROM THE SHORE

Those of us who for medical reasons have to keep to a very strict low-sodium diet will find the use of foods made from seaweeds unacceptable, since these obviously have a very high salt content. Since I am in this low-sodium diet category, I have never used any of these plants for food, so I am unable to give you any recipes. Instead, I will describe the various seaweeds and their habitats, with an indication of the kinds of food they may be used for in cooking. Recipes for all the dishes I shall mention will be found in several of the books given in the Bibliography (Appendix III).

If, however, you have no such dietary limitations and you live near enough to the sea to make foraging for seaweeds worth while, you may like to try some of the following.

CARRAGEEN (*Chondrus crispus*)

On any of the shores fringing the Atlantic this purplish-brown seaweed may be found spreading its fan-shaped fronds. It grows abundantly on rocks and stones. In this country, it is commonest on the coasts of the south and west. It is best gathered young, in April or May. It can be used fresh or dried for later use. It is gelatinous and is often used commercially as the basis for jellies, blancmanges and aspics.

To dry the weed, wash thoroughly to remove any sand, grit, shells or small marine creatures that may be clinging to it. Never use any seaweeds found on oil-polluted beaches. Lay the washed weed out to dry on a flat surface, preferably out of doors. Throw a bowl of cold water over it from time to time. After a while it will become bleached to a creamy-white colour. Trim off any tough stalks and complete the drying process by bringing it indoors. Store in bags.

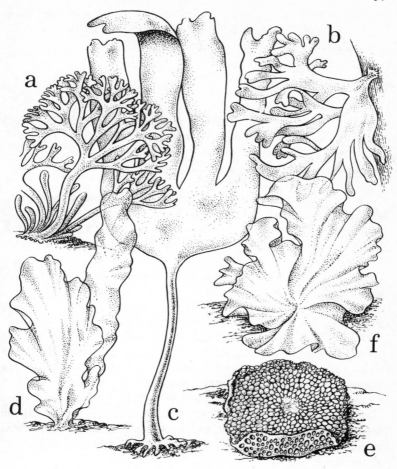

Seaweeds: a, Carrageen (*Chondrus crispus*); b, Dulse
(*Rhodymenia palmata*); c, Kelp (*Laminaria digitata*); d,
Laver (*Porphyra umbilicalis*); e, Rock tripe (*Umbilicaria
pustulata*); f, Sea lettuce (*Ulva lactuca*)

DULSE (Rhodymenia palmata)

This is a red seaweed abundant on stones, rocks and even attached
to other seaweeds, on most British coasts from the middle shore to
low-water mark. The fronds, which are wide and flat-lobed, grow to
about 15 inches (40 cm.) in length. Only the young fronds are used,

and the stalks are discarded owing to their toughness — they are known as 'leather bootlaces' in some parts of the country! Dulse can be used as a vegetable and as a condiment.

KELP (*Laminaria digitata*)

The specific name *digitata* refers to the finger-like fronds. The weed grows at low-water mark on rocky shores all around the British coast. It is chiefly used in salads, either raw or cooked. To cook, simply wash well and boil in water until tender. Use only young fronds, and discard the stalks.

This weed is said to be very rich in minerals and is now being increasingly processed by health food manufacturers as powder and tablets to provide mineral supplements. I imagine swallowing a tablet would be far easier and more palatable than eating the stuff.

LAVER (*Porphyra umbilicalis*)

This is the best-known and most widely-used of the British seaweeds for food. There is a long-standing tradition of its use in Wales and the West Country, where it is gathered by the armful and sold in the shops and markets to those who prefer to save themselves the toil and trouble of prising it off the slippery rocks where it grows. It looks like laminated sheets of brown silk, and is at its best in April and May. The wavy-edged fronds are unmistakable and it is unlikely to be confused with any other species. Although it occurs on all coasts, Welsh and West Country shores are the areas of particular abundance.

Laver has a versatile repertoire of uses. It is used to make laver bread, as a sauce for beef, mutton or lamb, as a savory to serve on toast, as a soup, and as a purée eaten in Wales with potatoes.

ROCK TRIPE (*Umbilicaria pustulata*)

This is not strictly a seaweed but a lichen which grows on rocks and walls in western areas of Britain, and has a somewhat seaweed-like appearance. It may be recognized easily by its rather garish orange colour and 'pebbly' appearance. Some of the explorers in Polar regions have managed to survive for weeks on end eating this stuff and boiling snow for water.

SAMPHIRE

There are two species, marsh samphire or glasswort (*Salicornia europaea*) and rock samphire (*Crithmum maritimum*). Although somewhat seaweed-like in appearance, with fleshy leaves, and affecting maritime habitats, neither of these two plants is a seaweed but both are flowering plants. However, I feel that they are best dealt with in this chapter.

Believe it or not, the marsh samphire or glasswort is a member of the Chenopodiaceae, the same family as fat hen and Good King Henry. No plants could be more dissimilar, but the botanists must have had good reasons for classifying them together. The marsh samphire has succulent fleshy leaves, and grows all around our coasts

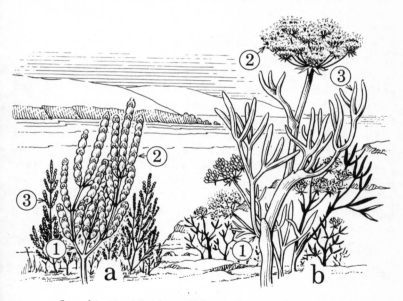

Samphires: a, Marsh samphire or glasswort (*Salicornia europaea*); b, Rock samphire (*Crithmum maritimum*)

1 (a) Stem usually unbranched	1 (b) Stem much branched
2 (a) Flowers inconspicuous	2 (b) Flowers conspicuous
3 (a) Leaves opposite in pairs	3 (b) Leaves 1-2-pinnate

on mud-flats and estuaries. It is quite small, only about 10 inches (25 cm.) high, and bears orange flowers in August and September.

Samphire is a traditional foodplant and steeped in folklore, especially in East Anglia, where it has been gathered and used for centuries. It is said to be tasty, delicious pickled or cooked, and a 'food experience' (which I don't doubt) and popular enough to be sold commercially in the areas where great quantities of it occur and can be gathered for sale.

When setting out on a samphire-gathering expedition, wear your oldest clothes and your wellies, and expect to be covered with mud from head to foot by the time you have finished. As you return to the bus stop, or car park, you may well be what the Reverend J. G. Wood would have described as 'grinn'd and stared at by the vulgar'. More important is to beware that the tide does not come in and catch you unawares, as it is frequently apt to do on treacherous mudflats on, for example, the Essex coast. Go with a companion, don't take children with you and don't take non-swimmers. Tide tables are obtainable from all coastguard offices.

The rock samphire (*Crithmum maritimum*) is not related to the marsh samphire but is a member of the *carrot* family, of all things! Despite this seeming anomaly, it is said to taste very similar to the previously-described plant, and to taste so much like true asparagus that it is frequently dubbed 'sea asparagus'. It is eaten and cooked in the same way as marsh samphire.

This plant is found throughout Britain but is more frequent on rocky coasts in the south and west. It flowers from July to September, producing umbelliferous clusters of yellow blossoms. The leaves are fleshy, faintly aromatic and cut into narrow untoothed leaflets. The plant grows up to a foot (30 cm.) or so high, but is more bushy-looking than the marsh samphire. Cliff-bordered shingly beaches are the best places to find it.

SEA BEET (*Beta vulgaris*)

The sea beet is the wild ancestor of the cultivated beet of our gardens and allotments. The leaves only are used (the root of the cultivated beetroot was developed only in the horticultural varieties), and are used, and taste, exactly like spinach, just as cultivated beet tops do. One can sometimes find the wild plants bearing red-veined leaves just like the cultivated kind.

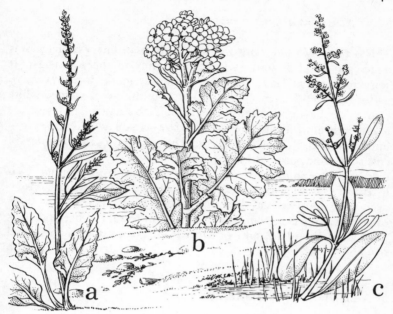

Seashore vegetables: a, Sea beet (*Beta vulgaris*); b, Sea kale
(*Crambe maritima*); c, Sea purslane (*Halimione
portulacoides*)

The plant is very common on banks and shingle by the sea, except
in Scotland. It flowers from June to September, bearing tiny green
blossoms borne on long leafy spikes, just like the flower-spikes of fat
hen – the sea beet belongs to the same family, the Chenopodiaceae.
The leaves at the bottom of the plant can be really huge, and taste just
as good as the younger, smaller ones at the top. These latter are good
raw in salads, while the larger ones should be cooked, in only a very
little water, just like 'ordinary' spinach. They can then be eaten 'plain
boiled' or tossed in butter, as you prefer. Don't throw out the water
they have been cooked in – it is full of nutrients and minerals. Use it
as a basis for vegetable stock, or add it to soups made with other
vegetables.

SEAKALE (*Crambe maritima*)

This is a cabbage-like plant and is used just as ordinary cabbage. It is a denizen of cliffs and rocky shores, only in the south-east. It sometimes grows right down to low-water mark. It grows up to about two feet (60 cm.) high, and in May the sweet-scented white flowers can be found, often lasting through to August. The leaves are a rather beautiful blue-grey shade. Use as you would cabbage – boiled, stuffed, chopped or shredded into soups, tossed in butter, in cole slaw – the permutations are endless.

I had better point out that this plant is not nearly so common as it used to be, and restraint should be exercised in gathering it. However, since the lower leaves usually grow to a tremendous size – some can reach two feet (60 cm.) long – a few only should suffice. If there is more than one plant, take one leaf from each, rather than several from one plant.

SEA LETTUCE (*Ulva lactuca*)

A seaweed proper this time – reasonably common on most types of shore. It is very like laver in appearance but green instead of brown, and smaller. It has the same kind of crinkly or wavy edges, and is to be found attached to rocks and stones. Use in exactly the same way as laver.

SEA PURSLANE (*Halimione portulacoides*)

Here we are again back with the Chenopodiaceae. This member of the family is common on salt marshes in southern and eastern England, also on parts of the Welsh coast. The dull yellowish flowers bloom from July to September, and the plant grows up to 2 feet 6 inches (75 cm.) tall. The succulent oval leaves are said to be good raw in salads, and can also be boiled in water for a short time and served with butter or cream like French beans. The leaves can also be pickled.

17

TEA AND COFFEE SUBSTITUTES

If you would like a change from the ubiquitous tea and coffee, a number of wild plants can be used to make beverages of varying degrees of attraction. Some are delicious, some fair to middling, and some I would rather avoid; experiment for yourself and decide which you will continue to use. After all, tastes vary and what one person may find very palatable another may not. The page numbers refer to the descriptions of plants already referred to in this book; others will be described in passing.

ANGELICA (*Angelica sylvestris*, page 38)

The leaves of angelica can be used to make a tea, or *tisane*. The leaves may be used fresh or dried; when using the latter use only half the amount stated in the recipe (this applies to other leaf teas and also to flower teas). Use three teaspoons of chopped fresh leaves to the pint of boiling water, which should be poured over them. Leave the infusion to stand for about 7 minutes, then strain through muslin and sweeten with honey.

To dry leaves, strip them from their stalks and lay them out on a clean flat surface in a warm dry place but away from direct heat. Leave for two or three days, or until brittle enough to crumble at a touch. They are then ready for storing in airtight jars. Label with the name so that you know which is which!

Flowers can be dried in similar fashion. Many of them retain a characteristic scent, and a few become even more aromatic in the process, such as woodruff and melilot.

BILBERRY (*Vaccinium myrtillus*, page 131)

Bilberry leaf tea is made in the same way as most other leaf teas but the proportions to use are one tablespoon of the fresh chopped leaves to one pint of boiling water. Only the young leaves should be used. The tea needs sweetening with honey.

BLACKBERRY (*Rubus fruticosus*, page 140)

This is the nearest wild equivalent to the raspberry leaf tea recommended by herbalists for pregnant women. Even if you're not pregnant (or you're not a woman!) blackberry leaf tea is a pleasant beverage and, drunk hot with lemon juice and honey, is said to be helpful if you have a cold or a cough.

The proportions recommended for raspberry leaf tea are 2 teaspoons per pint, so you can use the same proportions when using blackberry leaf tea, whether you are pregnant or just in the throes of the common cold. If you're in both these conditions at the same time, you don't have to double the proportions.

BORAGE (*Borago officinalis*, page 40)

Three teaspoons of the chopped fresh leaves are used to the pint of water. The method is the same – infuse, strain and sweeten with honey to taste.

BURDOCK (*Arctium lappa*, page 95)

Peel the burdock root, cut into short lengths and roast in a slow oven (250°F./130°C. or Regulo ½) until browned and brittle. Boil in water for 10 minutes, then filter off the liquid through a sieve. It has quite a snappy flavour of its own, but you can sweeten it if you wish, or add a dash of nutmeg, cinnamon or ginger. It is said to be a good blood purifier and general tonic. In the North it is combined with dandelion and put up commercially as a sparkling drink known as 'dandelion and burdock' and tastes quite pleasant and refreshing. This tastes not unlike the drink known as 'Tizer' but is a dark reddish colour.

CHICORY (*Cichorium intybus*, page 42)

The method for preparing chicory for use as 'coffee' is given with the description of the plant on page 98, but I give here an American recipe for what they call 'half and half'. Fill a percolator up to the 8-cup mark, and put into the percolating basket 4 tablespoons of ordinary ground coffee and four tablespoons of the ground chicory root (previously dried and roasted as already described). Brew in the same way as you would normally brew coffee. Serve hot with sugar and cream. Makes 8 cups.

CLOVERS (*Trifolium repens and T. pratense*)

The common red and white clovers make a delicious honey-flavoured and scented tea which requires no sweetening as these flowers are rich in honey. Too familiar to need description, they can be found in almost any meadow or hedgebank, flowering from May to October. They are also widely cultivated for fodder.

All you have to do is to pour a pint of boiling water over an ounce of the flowerheads from which all green parts have been removed. Let it steep long enough for the honey to flavour the water and disseminate the clover scent. Then strain out the flowerheads, reheating the liquid if necessary. No sweetening is required.

COMFREY (*Symphytum officinale*)

The leaves of this plant have been mentioned by some authors for use as vegetable greens, but studiously omitted by others. This is because they are far too glutinous for most people's tastes. However, the leaves when dried and crumbled can be used to make a good tonic tea, using the proportions of two teaspoons to the pint.

DANDELION (*Taraxacum officinale*, Chapter 8, page 75)

The method for making dandelion 'coffee' is given on page 99, to which I would add that in a personal communication the writer says that the best way to make it is in a percolator. To the amount of water needed to fill this to the 8-cup mark, use 6 tablespoons of the ground roasted roots. She also adds a pinch of salt, though she omits to mention her reason for this. It is then brewed in the usual way.

Dandelion tea is less well-known but worth experimenting with. The flowers make delicious wine and the leaves are good in salads as well as cooked, so the tea, whether made from the leaves or the flowers, cannot taste too bad.

To make the tea from the flowers, use 4 tablespoons of fresh (2 if dried) flowers, from which all green parts have been removed, to the pint of boiling water. Steep for 5 minutes only before straining and add a sprig of fresh mint and a slice of lemon. Sweeten to taste if desired with honey.

Dandelion leaf tea is made by infusing a few leaves, fresh or dried, in boiling water for 3 minutes (3 or 4 leaves to the pint is enough). Remove the leaves if fresh, or filter out if dried, and sweeten as desired.

ELDER (*Sambucus nigra*, Chapter 11, page 112)

Both the berries and the flowers make really delicious non-alcoholic drinks as well as wines.

Elderflower Froth

Put a large bunch of elderflower blossom, carefully looked over and any creepies removed, into a large jug. On no account wash the blossom or you will remove the fragrance which imparts such a heady delight to the beverage. Pour boiling water on to the blossom and fill up the jug. Leave to cool.

When cool, strain off the liquid, sweeten with honey and pour into a large glass jug nearly to the top. Drop in a few ice cubes and top up with soda-water. Don't overdo the honey – elder blossom has quite a lot of natural sweetness. Try it first before sweetening and adjust accordingly.

Elderflower Ice Cream Soda

Make the drink in the same way as the preceding recipe, but at the final stage fill the glass jug only three-quarters full. Instead of ice cubes, put in one scoop of vanilla ice cream (preferably dairy ice cream, not synthetic) and then fill up the jug with soda-water. Less honey will be required for sweetening – you may even find that you do not need it at all, since the ice cream will be sweet enough.

Elderberry Joy

Make a juice base by boiling elderberries in water, in the proportion of a pound (450 g.) of berries to 4 pints (2300 ml.) water. After about 15 minutes' boiling, remove from heat and allow to cool. Then place a large pan under the point where you will suspend a jelly-bag containing the boiled berries. The liquid will run straight through, and the remainder will drip through gradually and thicken and augment the liquid as long as the bag is suspended. I find overnight is just the right length of time to extract all the juice, as well as its not being in the way in the daytime when I want to wash up – I always suspend jelly-bags over the kitchen sink, which is the safest place.

Boil the juice with a little sugar to sweeten (adjust the quantity to taste). Boil only long enough to dissolve the sugar – if you keep on boiling it will become jam! Then leave to cool.

To make up the drink, mix the juice with cold water in the proportion of ½ pint (275 ml.) of juice to every 2 pints (1150 ml.) of water. Serve with a sprig of mint or a slice of lemon. If you wish, you may fizz it up with soda-water. The addition of ice cubes is optional.

HEATHER (various *Erica* and *Calluna* species)

Heather teas (often called moorland teas) have been known for centuries and are particularly popular in Scotland, where the heather flowers and leaves are sometimes admixed with blackberry or bilberry leaves, wild thyme, wild strawberry and other moorland leaves.

The commonest species to look for are the common heath or ling (*Calluna vulgaris*), abundant throughout Britain on moors, heaths, bogs and duneslacks, often dominating extensive acreages. The leaves are in opposite rows, and the flowers are pale purple, in leafy stalked spikes, blooming from July to September.

The bell heather (*Erica cinerea*) is found throughout Britain but more commonly in the western parts of the country. The leaves are in

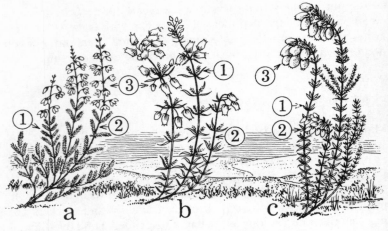

Heather species: a, Common heath or ling (*Calluna vulgaris*); b, Bell heather (*Erica cinerea*); c, Cross-leaved heath (*E. tetralix*)

1 (a) Leaves in opposite rows
1 (c) Leaves in whorls of 4
2 (a) and (c) Stem downy
3 (a) and (b) Flowers in stalked spikes

1 (b) Leaves in whorls of 3
2 (c) Stem hairless
3 (c) Flowers in compact heads

whorls of three and dark green, often bronze-tinged. The flowers, in stalked spikes, are reddish-purple and bloom from May to September. This species prefers a drier habitat than the previous one and, subject to this, can be found in similar situations, also in the open parts of woodlands in dry heathy areas.

The cross-leaved heath (*Erica tetralix*) has leaves in whorls of four. The flowers are pink and borne in compact heads, appearing from June to October. In contrast to the preceding species, the cross-leaved heath prefers moist localities and will be found throughout Britain, especially in eastern parts, on wet heaths and boggy moorlands.

The above three species are the only heathers common in Britain. All other species found in this country are rarities and should never be picked.

The tea is made from the dried flowerheads, with or without the leaves, the leaves not usually being employed alone. A few sprigs are boiled in water (three or four sprigs to the pint) for about five minutes, then removed. Heather is abundantly supplied with natural honey so should not really need any further sweetening.

JUNIPER (*Juniperus communis*, page 153)

A herb tea can be made from juniper berries. From 12 to 18 of the berries are used per pint of water. Bring to the boil and simmer for 15 minutes, then remove.

WILD HOP (*Humulus lupulus*)

While the flowerheads are used for beermaking, as is well known, it is much less generally known that the leaves can be used to make a herbal tea. The plant is not uncommon as a climber twining in hedgerows, and I have sometimes found it growing on waste land in inner-city habitats, climbing up trees and bushes. The leaves are toothed and palmately-lobed, and the square stems twine clockwise. The plant is dioecious, i.e. it bears male and female flowers on separate plants; the familiar cone-shaped flowers used in brewing are

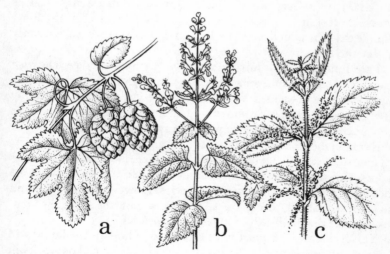

Some astringent teas: a, Wild hop (*Humulus lupulus*);
b, Wood sage (*Teucrium scorodonia*); c, Stinging nettle
(*Urtica dioica*)

the female flowers. The male flowers, too, are green, but are much smaller and more insignificant-looking, in branched clusters. The flowers appear from July to September.

The leaves are dried in the usual way and crumbled when brittle, and 2 teaspoons per pint (575 ml.) of water are boiled for 2 or 3 minutes. The liquid is then strained and sweetened to taste. This tea is said to be soporific and soothing to the nerves.

LADY'S MANTLE (*Alchemilla vulgaris*, page 65)

Here we have another soporific herbal tea made from the leaves only, in which the flowers are not used. The dried leaves are infused for 7 minutes in boiling water (2 teaspoons to the pint/575 ml.), strained and sweetened. All the sweetening in the world won't disguise the vile taste of this stuff.

LIME (*Tilia vulgaris*)

Lime blossom is well-known for the making of linden tea, which is imported from Germany and sold in most delicatessens, but it is much more fun to make your own, and does not cost anything. Unlike the last-named plant, this one makes a delicious tea, naturally sweet and fragrant.

Late June and early July will see the drooping creamy-yellowish clusters of scented blossoms appearing among the characteristically light-green heart-shaped leaves of the lime. A really sound healthy tree can reach 130 feet in a favoured habitat – the lime does not like too much bright sunlight but appreciates a fairly shady situation. For this reason they make ideal trees for planting in city streets – and this, of course, is where you will find most of them, along with city parks and squares. It is less of a woodland tree, because there the shade becomes a little *too* much for this species. However, it can be found in open woodland, though here, as often as not, the species is more likely to be the small-leaved lime (*Tilia cordata*).

This is a tea which *must not* be allowed to boil, or the liquid will turn an unappetizing red. Gather the flowers and spread out to dry in the usual way. One teaspoon of the flowers will suffice per pint of water which has been heated to just below boiling-point and left a few moments before pouring on to the flowers. Steep them for not longer than 3 minutes. Very little, if any, honey will be required to sweeten, as the lime flower is abundantly supplied with natural honey. Neither is it necessary to remove the flowers from the bottom of the glass, provided that the tea is drunk immediately it is ready. If it is to be left for a longer time, or chilled, the flowers should first be removed by filtering in the usual way.

Lime blossom tea may be drunk hot or cold.

MARJORAM (*Origanum vulgare*, page 46)

Wild marjoram makes an aromatic tea. The leaves are used, dried, one teaspoon per pint of boiling water being infused for 5 minutes. A sprig of mint may be put in the glass. Little sweetening is required, the addition of too much honey tending to mask the distinctive aroma.

NETTLE (*Urtica dioica*, Chapter 7, page 68)

Make nettle tea by infusing the fresh young leaves in boiling water for 20 minutes, then remove the leaves and reheat. Sweeten to taste with honey. Nettle tea is well known as a blood purifier and tonic, and the plant is one of the richest sources of iron and other minerals to be found in these islands. Don't use the larger lower leaves – they can be unacceptably bitter. The four topmost leaves are only mildly astringent in spring, but later in the year even these can be unpleasantly so. It is best, therefore, to make the tea *before* the plant comes into flower.

ROSE (*Rosa canina*, Chapter 12, page 125)

The tea is made from the hips, the red berries which are the autumn fruits of the dog rose or wild rose. The important thing to remember is to be sure to eliminate entirely the seeds which bear sharp-pointed hairs.

Two large heaped tablespoons of rose hips are soaked in 3 pints/1725 ml. of water overnight. Then, the next day, bring them to the boil (in the same water) and simmer for an hour. Strain through a piece of muslin folded four times placed inside either a jelly-bag or a fine-meshed nylon sieve. Sweeten with honey if desired – though most people find rose-hip tea sweet enough without any addition. This tea is full of Vitamin C. The hips keep a long time in a cool dry place, so you can gather more than you need and keep them to supply you through the winter and through into the spring.

SALAD BURNET (*Poterium sanguisorba*)

This attractive little herb, with its serrated pinnate leaves and unusual spherical flowers, is abundant on chalk and limestone soils in grassy areas. There are no petals; the upper female flowers have numerous red styles, the lower male flowers bearing clusters of yellow stamens. The flowers appear from May to September. It is the leaves that are used to make a herbal tea with the refreshing flavour of cucumber. Three teaspoons of the fresh chopped leaves per pint of water are used (1½ teaspoons if dried), and the water is first boiled in the usual manner when making these teas. Steep for 7 to 10 minutes, filter out the leaves and reheat. This is one of the better herbal teas: I recommend it. I think sweetening spoils the delicate flavour, but it is up to you.

YARROW (*Achillea millefolium*)

This plant, sometimes called milfoil, is a native perennial of the daisy family or Compositae, and one of Britain's commonest roadside wild plants, occurring also in gardens and cultivated areas as a 'weed', on grass verges and hedge banks and in meadow and pasture. It grows up to 18 inches (45 cm.) or so in height and has pinkish, whitish or purplish flowers, often all three in close proximity (though not on the same plants) which bloom from June to November. The leaves are very dark green and feathery-looking, and the whole plant is aromatic. The flat-topped flowerheads are strongly reminiscent of the flowerheads of the plants of the Umbelliferae or carrot family, and the novice may well think the plant is a member of that family.

The leaves are used to make a tea. They can be used either fresh or dried. Do not use too many, and do not steep them in boiling water for more than 2 minutes, as the flavour is quite strong. It is not an unpleasant taste, but it does take a little getting used to.

In Chapter 6, about the uses of wild herbs, I have covered the teas to be made from lemon balm, chamomile, various mint species, wild thyme, wild sage, ground ivy, meadowsweet, lady's bedstraw, melilot and woodruff.

The British are renowned for their tea-drinking – but it's always puzzled me why we have to import it from India, Ceylon and China when we have literally dozens of different kinds growing all around us – sometimes even in our own back gardens!

A CALENDAR OF WILDFOODS

FLOWERING PLANTS

Name of Plant	Flowering season	Habitat (Found throughout Great Britain except where otherwise stated)
Allgood *see Good King Henry*		
Angelica, wild	July–September	Moist grasslands, fens, woods and cliffs
Applemint	July–September	Roadsides, ditches, waste places; commoner in S. W. England
Arum lily	April–May	Woods, shady hedge banks
Ash	April–May	Woods, hedges; also commonly planted in parks and city gardens
Balm	July–September	S.E. and S.W. England (garden escape)
Basil, wild	July–September	Dry grasslands and scrub, on lime
Bee balm *see Balm* Beech	April–May	Woods, commoner in Midlands and south
Bilberry	April–July	Heaths, moors, open woods, not on lime; commoner in north

Bitter vetch	April–July	Woods, heaths, scrub
Bistort	June–October	Meadows, woods; often near water
Blackberry	May–August	Woods, hedges, scrub, commons, open and waste places, even in inner cities
Blackthorn	March–May	Hedges, woods, scrub
Blaeberry *see Bilberry*		
Blueberry *see Bilberry*		
Bog myrtle *see Gale, sweet*		
Borage	May–September	Roadsides, waste land
Bramble *see Blackberry*		
Broom	April–June	Heaths, commons, open wooded scrub
Bullace	April–May	Hedges, borders of woods; commoner in the Midlands
Burdock	July–September	Shady situations, waste ground, hedge banks
Calamint	July–September	Dry grasslands, open woods, scrub; on lime
Catmint	July–September	Hedge banks, roadsides on chalk; S. and E.
Cattail *see Reed-mace*		
Celery, wild	June–August	Moist grasslands near sea
Chamomile, wild	June–July	Roadsides, waste land, S. England and S.W. Ireland
Chervil, wild	April–June	Ubiquitous everywhere: hedge banks, shady situations, commons and scrub
Chestnut, sweet	July	Planted in parks and gardens; occasionally naturalized escape

Chickweed	All year	Ubiquitous everywhere on waste and cultivated ground, even in inner cities
Chicory, wild	June–September	Grasslands, waste places
Cicely, sweet	April–June	Roadsides, hedges, woods, grassy places; N. England, W. Scotland
Clover, red	May–October	Abundant everywhere; widely cultivated
Clover, white	May–October	Abundant everywhere; widely cultivated
Cobnut *see Hazel*		
Comfrey	May–June	Roadsides, grassy places, hedgebanks, neglected gardens
Coriander, wild	June–August	Bare and waste ground
Corn salad *see Lambs' lettuce*		
Couch grass	June–August	Ubiquitous everywhere: weed of cultivated and waste land
Cow parsley *see Chervil, wild*		
Crab apple	May	Hedges, woods, open scrub, commons
Crow garlic	June–August	Grasslands, cultivated land
Cuckoo-pint *see Arum lily*		
Dandelion	All year, but especially April–June	Ubiquitous everywhere: grassy and waste land even in inner cities
Dewberry	May–August	Damp heaths, scrub, especially on lime; S.

Dock, broad-leaved	June–October	Abundant everywhere; bare and waste ground, weed of cultivated land even in inner cities
Dock, curled	June–October	Weed of cultivated land even in inner cities; ubiquitous everywhere
Dock, northern	June–July	Damp grassy places, river banks; northern Britain only
Dog Rose *see Rose, wild*		
Elder	May–July	Woods, hedges, scrub, commons
Fat hen	June–October	Abundant everywhere: waste ground, even in inner cities
Fennel, wild	July–September	Bare and waste ground, commoner by the sea
Fenugreek, wild	June–July	Dry bare and waste land; commoner in south
Flowering rush	July–September	In and beside shallow fresh water, not on lime; commoner in S. and Midlands
Gale, sweet	April–May	Bogs, wet heathland: W.
Garlic, field	June–August	Grassland, cultivated land
Garlic mustard	April–August	Hedge banks, open woods
Garlic, wild *see Garlic, field*		
Goatsbeard	May–August	Grassy places
Good King Henry	June–October	Waste ground, commoner in S.
Ground ivy	March–June	Abundant everywhere: bare and waste ground, woods,

		hedge banks, grasslands; common garden weed
Hawthorn	May–June	Hedges, woods, commons, scrub
Hazel	January–March	Hedges, woods, scrub
Heath, common	July–September	Heaths, moors, bogs, open woodland, dunes
Heath, cross-leaved	June–October	Wet heaths, moors, bogs
Heather, bell	May–September	Dry heaths, moors, open woodland; W. only
Herb bennet	May–September	Woods, shady situations
Honeysuckle	June–October	Woods, hedges, scrub
Hop, wild	July–September	Hedges, escape of cultivation; not on uplands
Horsemint	July–September	Damp roadsides, waste places
Horseradish	May–August	Moist places, roadsides in S.

Jack-by-the-Hedge *see
  Garlic mustard*
Jack-in-the-Pulpit *see
  Arum lily*
John-go-to-bed-at-noon
  see Goatsbeard

Juniper	May–June	Coniferous woods, moors, heaths, scrub, uplands

Keck *see Chervil, wild*

Lady's bedstraw	June–September	Dry grasslands
Lady's mantle	May–September	Grasslands
Lamb's lettuce	April–August	Waste and arable land, dunes, by walls

Lamb's quarters *see Fat Hen*
Lemon Balm *see Balm*

Lime, common	June–July	Widely planted and common except in Ireland
Lime, small-leaved	June–July	Fairly common especially on limestone soils
Ling *see Heath, common*		
Lords and Ladies *see Arum lily*		
Lovage	June–August	Grassy uplands and mountains
Mallow, common	June–October	Roadsides, waste land, garden weed
Marjoram, wild	July–September	Dry grasslands, scrub, on lime
Marshmallow	August–September	Moist places, especially near sea
May *see Hawthorn*		
Meadowsweet	June–September	Marshes, fens, bogs, wet meadows, moist woodland, river banks
Melilot	June–September	Bare and waste ground
Milfoil *see Yarrow*		
Mint, corn	July–September	Moist waste land, weed of cultivated ground
Mint, water	July–September	Wet places
Mint, whorled	July–September	Damp places, weed of cultivated ground
Mountain ash *see Rowan*		
Nettle, stinging	June–September	Ubiquitous everywhere: woods, hedge banks, waste and cultivated land, gardens; abundant even in inner cities
Oak	April–May	Deciduous woods, parks widely planted

Parsnip, wild	June–September	Grasslands, bare and waste places
Peppermint	July–September	Wet places
Pignut	May–July	Open woods, shady situations, grasslands
Rampion	July–August	Dry grassland, on lime
Ramsons	April–June	Woods, shady situations
Reed-mace	June–July	By fresh water, except N. Scotland
Rest harrow	July–September	Dry grassy places, hedge banks
Rose, wild	June–July	Hedges, woods, scrub; commoner in south
Rowan	May–June	Woods, heaths, moors, uplands; not on lime
Rush, flowering *see* Flowering rush		
Sage, wild	June–August	Bare and waste land (rare)
Sage, wood *see* Wood sage		
Salad burnet	May–September	Dry grassy places, mainly on lime; S.
Salsify	April–June	Grassy places; escape of cultivation
Samphire, marsh	July–October	Saltmarshes, cliffs and shingle; commoner in E.
Samphire, rock	July–October	Cliffs, rocks by sea; commoner in E. and S.
Sea beet	June–September	Coastal areas, commoner in S.
Sea holly	June–September	Coastal sand and shingle

Sea kale	June–August	Coastal sand and shingle
Sea purslane	July–October	Saltmarshes, commoner in S.
Silverweed	May–August	Damp grasslands
Sloe *see Blackthorn*		
Sorrel, common	May–August	Grassland, woods, heaths, commons, roadsides, hedgebanks
Sow thistle	May–November	Hedgebanks, bare and waste ground; weed of cultivation
Spearmint	July–October	Moist waste land, S.
Spignel-meu	June–August	Upland grasslands
Star of Bethlehem	May–June	Grassy places; escape of cultivation. S.
Stinging nettle *see Nettle*		
Stitchwort, greater	April–June	Woods, hedges, especially on clay soils
Tansy	July–October	Grasslands, waste land
Thyme, wild	June–September	Dry grasslands, heaths, dunes, on lime
Turnip, wild	April–August	Waste land, especially near streams and near cultivated ground
Twitch *see Couch grass*		
Violet, wild	March–May and June–September	Woods, grasslands, uplands, mountains
Wall lettuce	June–September	Shady situations beside walls and rocks
Walnut	April–May	Planted in parks and gardens; occasional naturalized escape
Woodruff	April–June	Woods

Wood sage	July–September	Dunes, cliffs, screes, open woods, scrub; on chalk, W.
Wood sorrel	April–May	Woods, shady situations, uplands, mountains
Yarrow	June–November	Grasslands

FUNGI

Name of mushroom	Fruiting season	Habitat
Blewit	Early October to early November	Open deciduous woods, commons, grasslands
Blewit, wood *see Wood Blewit*		
Blueleg *see Blewit*		
Boletus, edible	August–September	Deciduous and coniferous woods
Boletus, orange-capped	August–October	Birch woods, occasionally mixed woodland
Boletus, rough-stalked	September	Birch woods, sometimes coniferous woods
Cep *see Boletus, edible*		
Chanterelle	July–November	Coniferous woods, beside paths and roads across moors in association with pines
Fairy ring champignon	June–November	Meadows, pastures
Giant puffball	July–August	Pastures, meadows, heaths
Honey-tuft	May–November	Deciduous and coniferous woods
Horn of plenty	August–September	Coniferous and deciduous woods, especially hazel and beech

Horse mushroom	June–October	Arable land, open grassy parts of woods
Ink-cap	July–September	Wooded parkland, especially after tree felling
Lawyer's wig *see Shaggy cap*		
Morel	May–June	Grassland, especially cultivated land; more often on lime. Commoner in S. and E.
Parasol mushroom	July–October	Deciduous woods, occasionally pastureland
Saffron milk cap	August–September	Coniferous woods; roadsides or paths traversing pinewoods
Shaggy cap	July–September	Parks, gardens, cultivated ground; common on tree roots, stumps and root craters
Shaggy parasol mushroom	August–October	Deciduous woods, occasionally pastureland
Spindle-shank	June–October	Deciduous woods, especially oak and beech
St George's mushroom	Late April to June	Pastures, downland on calcareous soils
Tawny grisette	August–October	Damp deciduous or mixed woods, occasionally coniferous woods
Velvet-shank	November–March	Deciduous woods
Wood blewit	Late October to late November	Coniferous woods

APPENDIX II

BIBLIOGRAPHY

BOOKS FOR THE IDENTIFICATION OF WILD PLANTS

Barrett, J. and Yonge, C. M., *A Pocket Guide to the Seashore* (for seaweeds) (Collins, 1958)

Fitter, R. S. R. and Fitter, A., *The Wild Flowers of Britain and Northern Europe* (Collins, 1974)

Fitter, R. S. R., *Finding Wild Flowers* (Collins, 1971)

Ministry of Agriculture & Fisheries, *Edible and Poisonous Fungi* (HMSO, 1945)

Mitchell, A., *A Field Guide to the Trees of Britain and Northern Europe* (Collins, 1974)

Nilsson, S. and Persson, O., *The Fungi of Northern Europe* 2 volumes, (Penguin, 1978)

Phillips, R., *The Wild Flowers of Britain* (Pan Books, 1977)

Phillips, R., *Mushrooms* (Pan, 1981)

Ramsbottom, J., *Mushrooms and Toadstools* (Collins, 1953)

BOOKS FOR FURTHER READING

Bay Laurel, A., *Living on the Earth* (Random House, New York, 1971)

Beedell, S., *Pick, Cook and Brew* (Pelham, 1973)

Deadman, P. and Betteridge, K. *Nature's Foods* (Unicorn Books, 1973)

Hartley, D., *Food in England* (Macdonald, 1964)

Hatfield, A. W., *How to Enjoy your Weeds* (Müller, 1969)

Mabey, R., *Food for Free* (Collins, 1972)

Richardson, R., *Hedgerow Cookery* (Penguin, 1980)

Urquhart, J., *Food from the Wild* (David & Charles, 1978)

INDEX

Page numbers in italic refer to illustrations